WORLD RECORD WHITE·TAILS

A complete history of the number one bucks of all time

By Gordon Whittington

Edited by Ken Dunwoody
and David Morris

WORLD RECORD WHITE· TAILS

By Gordon Whittington

Long Beach, California

Bigfork, Montana

The trademark Safari Press ® is registered with the U.S. Patent and Trademark Office and in other countries.

Whittington, G.

Special edition

Safari Press Inc.

2002 Long Beach, California

ISBN 1-57157-216-9

Library of Congress Catalog Card Number: 98-60865

10 9 8 7 6 5 4 3 2 1

Readers wishing to receive the Safari Press catalog, featuring many fine books on big-game hunting, wingshooting, and sporting firearms, should write to Safari Press Inc., P.O. Box 3095, Long Beach, CA 90803, USA. Tel: (714) 894-9080 or visit our Web site at www.safaripress.com.

Dedication

*To my parents, who still wonder
what I'm going to be when I grow up.*

ACKNOWLEDGMENTS

No one could write a book on world-record whitetails without help, and plenty of it. There simply are too many of these deer scattered across too much real estate and too many years for such a volume to be a solo project. Fortunately, I realized early on that trying to go it alone would be a serious mistake. And so, not long after this idea hatched in my mind it left the nest, nurtured along by a number of key individuals.

First were David Morris of Venture Press and Ludo Wurfbain of Safari Press, who listened to the concept, liked it and committed their resources to making it happen. Next, we solicited the help of Steve Vaughn, president and publisher of Game & Fish Publications, whose *North American WHITETAIL* magazine I've edited since 1984. Steve liked the idea as well and graciously allowed us to dip into the company's files for many of the unique photos sprinkled throughout the following pages.

At this point, it was time to turn to professionals whose hands-on efforts could transform the raw materials into a finished product. Fortunately, we found some of the best in the business. For editors, I sought out David Morris and Game & Fish Publications' editorial director Ken Dunwoody, both guys with a real knack for turning mangled prose into something worth reading. They did much to bring clarity and continuity to each chapter. Once editing was done, Tom Bulloch arranged the text,

photos and graphics into a far more appealing form than I ever could have. The results of this team effort are in the pages that follow.

Even as I was writing the chapters, valuable assistance came from all corners. One of the major contributors was my wife, Catherine, who patiently kept stepping over my stacks of research materials for more than a year as the book was taking shape. I can't thank her enough for putting up with it all, and for letting me postpone all of those home-improvement projects for months on end.

Also, I can't adequately express my appreciation for the staffs of the three leading organizations that keep tabs on record whitetails. From the start of this process, the Boone and Crockett Club's Director of Big Game Records, Jack Reneau, patiently answered innumerable questions for me, as did his able assistant, Chris Tonkinson.

Meanwhile, over at the Pope and Young Club, Executive Secretary Glenn Hisey and his son, Kevin, were doing the same. And Jim Salmon, one of the founding fathers of the Longhunter Society, helped me straighten out several questions involving that group's record listings. It might be possible to write a book on world-record whitetails without the assistance of these folks, but I am glad I didn't have to try.

Also proving to be lifesavers were Larry Huffman and his sons, Troy and Greg. Larry owns the "Legendary Whitetails" collection, an assemblage of many of the world's all-time best trophy bucks, including several profiled in the following chapters. In 1996, David Morris, Dick Idol and I collaborated with Larry to produce *Legendary Whitetails*, a lavishly illustrated volume featuring 40 of the biggest deer in that collection. When I told Larry about my project, rather than view it as competition for that book, he immediately offered me whatever photos and information he had. The Huffmans even allowed me the special privilege of using Troy's beautiful computer-generated image of the famed Jim Jordan buck on the cover. Their generosity hasn't been lost on me.

And, thanks to Ron Van Gilder and Wild Wings, Inc., Lake City, MN 55041 (1-800-445-4833) for the use of Ron's beautiful paintings of several of the world records.

A number of other persons also made important contributions to the project—especially John Stein of Big Rack Publications and Duncan Dobie of Bucksnort Publishing, each of whom loaned me a number of photos that appear in these pages. They and many other members of the "whitetail community" are folks I know not just as business contacts, but as friends. Time after time, they bailed me out, despite no real promise of tangible reward for doing so. That's about as good a working definition of a "friend" as I can come up with. I thank them all.

Ellen Amrhein	Duncan Dobie	Barry Leach	Jim Rathert
Mary Andrews	Jack Ehresman	Bill Lilienthal	Dale Ream, Jr.
Forrest Armke	Bob Estes	Beverly & Gary Luckey	Don Roper
Dr. Chuck Arnold	Tom Evans	Stephen Lyons	Jim Samis
James H. Arnwine	Jack Felton	Ivan, Peggy & Jerry Mascher	Don Schaufler
Joe Arterburn	Gloria Ferber	Mike Matthews	Frank Scott
Steve Ashley	Chantal Fortier	Gene McCammack	Don Schwab
Del Austin	Tom Foss	Daniel McDonnell	Roger Selner
Don Boucher	Dave Foote	Greg Miller	Don Stemler
Ron Boucher	Nick Gilmore	Eva Milstead	Jim Stoltz
Joe & Janet Brewster	Gilbert Guttormson	Frank Moldovan	Leigh Ann Smith
Jack Brittingham	Milo & Olive Hanson	Joe Moore	Jim Smith
Bob Bromm, Sr.	Randal Harris	Tom Mosher	Lawrence Sowieja
Terry Burns	Vic Heincker	Kenneth Mullins	Paul Thomas
Rick Busse	Glenn Helgeland	Marc Murrell	Ross Triplett
Joe Byers	Randy Herberg	Lionel & Rodney Newman	Amy Verone
George Chase	Jack Hoffarth	Shirley Nore	Ron Van Gilder
Sam & Judi Collora	Jim Holdenreid	Aaron Pass	Don Vraspir
Bill Cooper	Dick Idol	Jimye & Lloyd Pipes	Rick Williams
Tim Condict	Tony Kalna	Jerry Polesky	Dave Wilson
Rod Connelly	Myles Keller	Jennifer Post	George & Millie
Craig Cousins	Ed Koberstein	Kent Price, Jr.	Winters
Lionel Crissman	Mary Reed Krauss	John Pritzl	David Wissehr
Wallace Dailey	Dr. James C. Kroll	Tad Proudlove	Kenn Young
Larry Deaton	Larry Lawson	Kathy Rainbolt	Dean Ziegler

TABLE OF CONTENTS

"The next No.1 deer could be taken by a prince or a pauper, a veteran of 50 autumns in the woods or a wide-eyed kid sitting in his first deer stand. It could happen just about anywhere, from the snowy crests of the Rocky Mountains to a weed field just beyond the city limits of your own hometown. The way I see it, that does a lot to explain why no other trophy in the world means so much to so many."

From the "Introduction" by Gordon Whittington.

POPE & YOUNG TYPICALS

POPE & YOUNG NON-TYPICALS

BLACKPOWDER TYPICALS

BLACKPOWDER NON-TYPICALS

CONTENDERS AND PRETENDERS

CONCLUSION

FOREWORD

By Ken Dunwoody
and David Morris

"He has uncovered and compiled the stories of every whitetail that has ever been recognized as a world record in any category. Nowhere else in the world—including the records books themselves—can you find these detailed accounts of all the No.1 deer."

Can anything grip the heart of a hunter like the dream of a world-record whitetail? If you've been a deer hunter for more than a day or two, chances are you have wondered what it would be like to come face to face with the biggest buck ever. In those dreams, maybe it's the great antlers you spot first, moving almost imperceptibly through the tall grass.

Or perhaps, you're startled by the sound of the giant buck crashing through the woods, then suddenly bursting into the clearing in front of your stand, eyes glistening, neck bulging. More likely,

though, the deer of your dreams simply materializes in the shadowy morning light, hovering on the edge of a clearing like a mirage, his antlers a tangle of impossibly long tines and massive beams.

These visions, of course, are nothing new. Ever since the record books came into existence, hunters across the continent have dreamed of world-record whitetails. For a fortunate few, however, those dreams have been transformed into reality, resulting in some of the most legendary hunts in whitetail history. Some of those record-breaking tales are known to the hunting public, but many others have been lost, overlooked, misunderstood or inaccurately reported...at least until now.

Through years of research and interviews, Gordon Whittington has accomplished what the author of no other book, magazine or video has even attempted. He has uncovered and compiled the stories of every whitetail that has ever been recognized as a world record in any category. Nowhere else in the world—including the record books themselves—can you find these detailed accounts of all the No.1 deer.

What you'll discover in these pages, though, is much more than just dates, names and scores. You'll learn about the hunters, their lives and the strange twists of fate that have shaped deer-hunting lore. These remarkable tales—many of them told here for the first time—offer fascinating glimpses into more than a century of deer hunting in North America. Together, they combine all the drama, irony, humor, emotion, perseverance, skill and just plain luck that characterize deer hunting and make the sport hopelessly addictive to more than 12 million sportsmen.

———◆———

We believe World Record Whitetails *is a book of historic significance and is destined to become a landmark in the field.*

———◆———

Only Gordon Whittington could have written this book. As the long-time editor of *North American WHITETAIL* magazine, Gordon has been reporting on trophy whitetails most of his professional career. He is, in our opinion, simply the best there is at what he does. Without his passion, exper-

ience and skill, a book of this magnitude would not have been possible. But, we have to confess that this project started with a certain amount of trepidation.

When Gordon first started talking to us about the book idea, our initial thought was that the project was near-impossible to carry out. After all, there was no single source to even identify the possible players. Many of the hunters were virtually unknown or had long since passed away. Where would he get the information, the photos or any reliable accounts, firsthand or otherwise, of the events? How would he find out about people and deer heads now lost in history? But, impossible though it may have seemed, we knew that if it could be done, Gordon was the man for the job. And, dozens of interviews, countless phone calls, several long road trips and many months of research later, Gordon accomplished the monumental task of ferreting out the untold stories of our greatest deer.

We believe *World Record Whitetails* is a book of historic significance and is destined to become a landmark in the field. But, this volume is more than just the definitive book on world-record whitetails—it is also an immensely entertaining collection of remarkable hunting stories, researched and reported with a dedication to detail and accuracy that is Gordon's trademark. We hope and believe you will enjoy it as much as we have.

And if you read closely, you may even learn a few things that will make you a better deer hunter. Perhaps that knowledge will come in handy some day. After all, as Gordon notes, there are whitetails haunting the woods and fields today that could shatter many of the records listed in this book. So, the next time you see a fresh track or glimpse a patch of brown through the trees, be ready. You never know, the next chapter in whitetail history may belong to you!

INTRODUCTION

By Gordon Whittington

"Being a great hunter is no guarantee you'll ever get a crack at a world-record buck, just as being an average hunter is no guarantee you won't. The next No. 1 deer could be taken by a prince or a pauper, a veteran of 50 autumns in the woods or a wide-eyed kid sitting in his first deer stand."

The white-tailed deer today occupies more land, and more dreams, than any other native big-game animal in North America. Although several million are harvested annually, their numbers continue to rise. Most estimates now put the continent's whitetail population at more than 25 million. That doesn't even count whitetails living in Central or South America or herds that have been the introduced into such far-flung places as Finland, Hungary or New Zealand.

Closer to home, this highly adaptable species is such a familiar part of the environment that virtually everyone who lives east of the Continental Divide has seen at least one whitetail standing alongside a roadway or feeding in a field. Even urban children know a whitetail when they see one. But for all its abundance and its often-cavalier attitude toward man, this animal is considered by most expert hunters to be the most challenging game species on the face of the earth. Forget the nonchalance shown by a doe in a petting zoo—in the wild these deer are no pushover for any predator, even one armed with superior intelligence and sophisticated weapons!

More than 12 million North American hunters pursue whitetails each fall, both for recreation and to put meat on the table. Many of these sportsmen take their deer hunting very seriously. Any animal that can not only survive but actually thrive in the face of such intense hunting pressure clearly has big-time survival skills. And, no other whitetail displays those skills as often or as well as the mature buck. He is the most reclusive of all deer. He has no other choice. After all, he's born with a price on his head.

Traditionally, hunting pressure has been focused far more on bucks than on does. In many parts of North America, the majority of males in a herd are taken by hunters before they pass the age of 1 1/2 years. Any buck seeing his fourth, fifth or sixth birthday has almost assuredly run a gauntlet of potentially fatal encoun-

Many shed antlers from potential No.1 bucks have been found over the years, but in remarkably few cases have hunters ever bagged those deer. The mounted sheds of this Nebraska buck, found in 1959, are a great case in point. Although the deer's rack was plenty big enough to make him a world record, he eventually disappeared without a trace. Photo by Tom Evans.

ters, not only with legal hunters but also with poachers, speeding vehicles, natural predators, fences, bad weather, disease and the sharp antlers of his rivals. A buck that has reached his prime is a true survivor, bearing no more resemblance to a naive yearling than a World Series MVP does to a Little League benchwarmer.

It is to these old warrior whitetails that this book pays tribute. There are no youngsters among the dozens of great bucks in these pages. Here, you will only find animals that successfully endured the many trials and blossomed into magnificent specimens. Granted, age alone has not produced these phenomenal antlers. These giants also were blessed with the right genetics to become world-class trophies, and they consumed enough of the right food to grow outlandish headgear. To call the biggest bucks in history true miracles of nature would hardly be overstating the case.

During the past 100 years, which might be broadly termed the "modern" era of whitetail hunting, literally tens of millions of bucks have been shot by hunters or found dead under various circumstances. Yet, of that staggering total, only a relative handful have ever been proclaimed official world records. In other words, each world-record buck is the product of many millions of days of cumulative hunter effort. Those are tough odds indeed for a would-be record-holder. But, there is a good side to the story. Many of these historic deer were alive at some point during the past two decades. And, there's no doubt in my mind that as I write these words, even more potential No.1 bucks are walking the earth. There have been too many reliable sightings and too many huge shed antlers discovered to think otherwise. It has been said and written a thousand times, but these really are the "good old days" of deer hunting. That's not something you can say for many other species of big game.

◆

Each world-record buck is the product of many millions of days of cumulative hunter effort…and rarely the culmination of a carefully-orchestrated game plan.

◆

It's my guess that you are reading this book not only to admire monster bucks and relive the thrill of the hunt, but also to pick up some tidbits of knowledge that will further your own quest for a trophy. If you read these accounts with care, you should be rewarded. Many of the hunters in the chapters that follow were serious sportsmen who used out-of-

the-ordinary tactics to achieve spectacular results. Even those hunters whose kills must honestly be attributed more to good fortune than skill did something right on their way to the record book. To a large extent, it is up to you to figure out what that something was and to see if it might be adapted to your own hunting situation. Certainly, these hunters have provided us with many clues.

◆

There is no doubt that even more potential No.1 bucks are walking the earth.

◆

As you read this book, you will see that whitetail hunting's most historic hunts have rarely been the culmination of a carefully orchestrated game plan. While many of the record-holders have indeed been hardcore trophy hunters, even their most momentous hunts didn't unfold exactly as planned. While we all might dream of methodically locating, hunting and finally outwitting a huge whitetail, successful encounters most often result from unexpected snippets of serendipity. And usually, the encounter lasts only a few seconds, with almost no chance to count the rack's points or even guess at its score. Indeed, in many instances, the true magnitude of the kill isn't fully known, or appreciated, until some time later.

For the sportsman who prefers his hunt to follow an orderly and systematic plan, such a realization may be disheartening. But in the real world, hunting trophy-caliber whitetails seldom lends itself to predictability. When you are in pursuit of monster bucks, you must seize the moment, or it will surely seize you.

Even in those rare instances in which a hunter knows of the existence of a potential world-record whitetail and formulates a good strategy for hunting that deer, the smart money is still on the buck. I've known some excellent hunters over the years who have told me that they had targeted specific deer they knew were potential world records in one category or another. In each instance, some unexpected problem prevented history from being rewritten. When a super buck does material- ize, the usual routine is for him simply to fade away, usually without even offering a shot. The stunned hunter may be left with little trace of the deer's existence, perhaps only a massive dropped antler, a track or an unforgettable Technicolor image burned into his brain.

What can we make of these facts? Perhaps only this: Being a great hunter is no guarantee you'll ever get a crack at a world-record buck, just as being an average hunter is no guar- antee you won't. The next No.1 deer could be taken by a prince or a pauper, a veteran of 50 autumns in the woods or a wide-eyed kid sitting in his first deer stand. It could happen just about any- where, from the snowy crests of the Rocky Mountains to a weed field just beyond the city lim- its of your own hometown. For this reason, the playing field is more level for those who hunt white- tails than for those who pursue any other species of big game. The way I see it, that does a lot to explain why no other trophy in the world means so much to so many.

When a super buck does materialize, the usual routine is for him simply to fade away, usually without ever offering a shot.

THE HISTORY OF WHITETAIL RECORDS

Only a few decades ago, there were no hunting record books and no world-record whitetails. Here's how the records came to be and a look at the scoring system that made it all possible.

Not that long ago, when everything in the world seemed simpler than it does today, it was easy to describe a whitetail buck. At first, you could drop him into a basic category, such as "little," "decent," "big" or maybe even "huge." Of course, the longtime favorite is counting antler points—a "nice 8-pointer," for instance. Gradually, the hunting community developed more descriptive terms, including "spike" and "forkhorn." On occasion, you might have heard something as colorful as "old mossyhorn with a rocking-chair rack." While hunters continued to invent and refine their specialized lingo, most terminology remained pretty simple to comprehend…until recently, when a change began.

Though many of these older terms and phrases are still favored by today's casual hunter, more and more serious whitetail hunters have begun to speak in a different tongue, one largely based on numbers. A buck that a half-century ago would have been described simply as a "huge 12-pointer" might today be referred to as a "22-inch 6x6 with 12-inch G-2s and 38 inches of mass, grossing 179 and netting 172."

If such a description leaves you scratching your head, you're probably not familiar with the copyrighted scoring system devised by the Boone and Crockett Club (B&C), a system that relies on specific antler measurements to determine an overall antler score. Once a score has been determined, that score can then be compared to those of other bucks. If the score meets or exceeds a certain minimum standard, that buck is eligible to be listed in the appropriate record book. All of the major non-profit organizations that maintain lists of whitetail "world records"—B&C, the Pope and Young Club (P&Y) and the National Muzzle Loading Rifle Association (NMLRA)—use the B&C measuring system.

If we are to fully appreciate the size and significance of the world-record whitetails profiled in this book, we must understand how the B&C scoring system works. That will be covered later in this chapter. First, however, it's important to understand *why* the system was developed and how it came to be so widely accepted. To do so, let's go back in time more than a century, to when North America's conservation movement was just getting off the ground.

THE BOONE AND CROCKETT CLUB

In 1887, Theodore Roosevelt, George Bird Grinnell and a handful of other visionary sportsmen founded the Boone and Crockett Club (named after legendary outdoorsmen Daniel Boone and Davy Crockett). The club was formed to help preserve an American environment that was being raped by all manner of market hunters, timber thieves and plunderers. The country's great game populations and virgin forests had been reduced significantly, and there was every reason to believe the situation would only become worse. Fearful that nothing wild would be left unless swift action was taken, B&C's founding fathers exerted their considerable influence in a variety of ways, starting with the creation of Yellowstone National Park. B&C's list of accomplishments has continued to grow for over a centu-

Clad in his deerskin suit, young Theodore Roosevelt posed for this memorable portrait in 1885. Two years later, the avid hunter and several fellow conservationists met in New York to form the Boone and Crockett Club, which became a leader in measuring and scoring North American big-game trophies. Photo by George Grantham Bain, courtesy of the Theodore Roosevelt Collection, Harvard College Library.

ry, and to this day, the club holds a special place among the world's conservation organizations. (For information, contact Boone and Crockett Club, 250 Station Dr., Missoula, MT 59801.)

An overwhelming majority of B&C members have always been avid hunters, beginning with Roosevelt himself, who when on to become president in 1901. In fact, he, Grinnell and Archibald Rogers were judges for the club's first big-game competition in 1891, held in New York just four years after the club was founded. To my knowledge, there's no record of the criteria these men used to judge the trophies. But, we can be sure it was not the modern scoring system since that would not come along for another six decades.

The first steps toward the B&C system we know today were taken by member James Clark, a well-known taxidermist with the American Museum of Natural History in New York. Those original trophy rankings debuted in 1932, when the club published the 1st edition of *Records of North American Big Game.* To describe this ranking procedure as a "system" would be generous. The sole means of comparing one whitetail rack to another was by the length of the main beams, and only the longer beam counted! Similarly simplistic measurements also were used to compare trophies of other species. When shouts of dissatisfaction arose, efforts were made to devise a better way of comparing trophy animals. Through the 1930s, Clark kept tinkering with ways to make the rankings more equitable. His efforts ultimately formed the framework of what would become the modern scoring system.

Unfortunately, Prentiss Gray, then head of the club's Heads and Horns Committee, died before that new system could be finalized. Consequently, the 2nd edition of the club's record book, published in 1939, used the same scoring system as the earlier

◆

Trophies taken by any legal weapon—rifle, handgun, muzzleloader, bow or crossbow—are eligible for listing in B&C.

◆

edition (and met with the same howls of protest). The outbreak of World War II interrupted efforts to settle the matter. After the war ended, B&C conducted annual big-game "competitions" in 1947, 1948 and 1949, still ranking trophies on the basis of single antler, horn or skull measurements. But, change was in the air. In 1949, Clark, Samuel Webb, Grancel Fitz and several other knowledgeable trophy enthusiasts began holding regular meetings, hoping once and for all to devise a system that would prove workable, equitable and popular.

They accomplished their goal. In 1950, the team's new system was approved for use in measuring and recording all types of North American big-game trophies. The plan was unveiled to the public in 1952, and that year's 3rd edition of *Records of North American Big Game* contained the first-ever

"official world-record" whitetails with which we'll be concerned in this book. In the years since, there have been only minor changes in the measuring and scoring procedures.

Many hunters mistakenly believe the B&C record book is designed only for big game taken by modern firearms or found dead ("pick-ups"). In truth, trophies taken by other legal weapons—including bows, crossbows, handguns and muzzleloaders—also are eligible for listing. The only restrictions? An animal must be listed under the name of a hunter (as opposed to merely an owner); it must have been taken in accordance with all hunting regulations; and the hunt must have been conducted under conditions commonly referred to as "fair chase."

January 1, 1998, marked the beginning of B&C's 24th Awards Period. Today, these periods last for three years, but from 1947 through 1951, they were conducted annually and from 1952 through 1967 biennially. At the conclusion of each awards period, B&C re-measures all of the top trophies entered during that span. A hand-picked team of official measurers, called a "judges' panel," is brought together to verify the scores. If the panel determines that a trophy's final score is equal to or higher than the current No.1 animal in its category, B&C proclaims the new trophy a "world record."

In this book, listed in chronological order, you will find every whitetail (excluding the Coues subspecies of the Southwestern U.S. and Mexico) that has been officially recognized as a B&C world record. The typicals are profiled in chapters 2–7, followed by the non-typicals in chapters 8-10.

THE POPE AND YOUNG CLUB

While P&Y's structure resembles that of B&C, its history is much shorter and its purpose more narrowly defined. P&Y deals strictly with issues related to archery hunting (excluding crossbows) for North American big game. The club's name honors Saxton

A number of legendary bowhunters attended a 1960 organizational meeting of the Pope and Young Club, among them P&Y founder Glenn St. Charles (middle row, fifth from left) and Fred Bear (middle row, seventh from left). Also present were two men whose world-record whitetails are featured in this book: Bobby Triplett (middle row, second from left) and Don Vraspir (middle row, fourth from left). Don's buck is visible just below the word "BOWHUNTER" on the banner. Photo by Jack H. Williams, courtesy of the Pope and Young Club.

Pope and Art Young, a pair of avid American outdoorsmen who helped revive interest in bowhunting during the early days of the 20th century.

In the 1930s, the National Archery Association was a broad-based group whose membership included persons with a wide variety of archery interests. In 1940, the fledgling National Field Archery Association (NFAA) split off from this main group, taking with it many archers who were more interested in bowhunting than tournaments. In that same year, NFAA also began scoring bowhunting trophies, using the Art Young Big Game Award System.

Around this time, an eager Washington archer named Glenn St. Charles, recognizing that many states still did not allow bowhunting, began to campaign for the expansion of such seasons. In 1948, he become NFAA vice-president. Eight years later, he

was appointed chairman of the new Hunting Activities Committee. Glenn and the rest of his committee immediately surveyed game departments, state archery groups and other concerned parties to discover how they could increase bowhunting opportunities. The result was a bowhunting-only club set up along the lines of B&C, building the framework of what eventually would become the Pope and Young Club.

By the mid-1950s, the modern B&C scoring system had been around for several years and the NFAA asked B&C for permission to use its system for compiling archery-only records of North American big game. (For some time, the NFAA had been holding Prize Buck Contests, in which winners were determined by measurements taken from only one side of a deer's rack.) In 1958, NFAA's 1st Awards Program for big-game trophies was held in

Grayling, Michigan, and the 2nd Awards Period was held there a year later. By that time, support for a bowhunting-only organization had expanded. In 1961, the Pope and Young Club was chartered as a separate entity.

The organization has remained independent ever since, steering North American bowhunting through a long period of sustained growth that mir-

The Pope & Young record book now contains more than 15,000 whitetails.

rors, interestingly, the rapid growth in whitetail hunting. The P&Y record book now contains more than 15,000 whitetails, a clear testament to just how far the sport has come from the days in which bowhunting was viewed as little more than an impractical stunt. Acceptance into this record book has always been based not only on trophy size but also on the hunter's adherence to the principles of "fair chase." (For information, contact Pope and Young Club, P.O. Box 548, Chatfield, MN 55923.)

P&Y's procedure for proclaiming "world records" is similar to that of B&C, with hand-picked measurers meeting after each awards period to verify potential No.1 trophies. Each P&Y awards period lasts for two years. In this book, every world-record whitetail by bow is included chronologically. The typicals are profiled in chapters 11–17; non-typicals in chapters 18–19.

THE LONGHUNTER SOCIETY

Of the various weapons that today enjoy widespread acceptance for deer hunting, only the bow and arrow has a longer history than the muzzleloading rifle. Consequently, it's ironic that it took so long to develop a separate record book for trophies taken with these "old-fashioned" weapons. The

National Muzzle Loading Rifle Association was founded in 1933 by a group eager to keep alive the great tradition of muzzleloading firearms, which had already begun to fade from the scene with the advent of smokeless powders and preloaded cartridges. The NMLRA brought together thousands of recreational shooters who were interested not only in tournaments and "mountain-man rendezvous" events but also in using their smokepoles for hunting. (For information, contact National Muzzle Loading Rifle Association, P.O. Box 67, Friendship, IN 47021.)

As the years passed, muzzleloader hunters periodically tried to produce a big-game record book of their own. In the early 1980s, there was an attempt to compile such trophies into what was to be called a "Carson and Glass" record book. A number of animals (including some impressive whitetails) were measured for entry. However, this record book never reached the printing press, and as late as 1987, it appeared muzzleloader trophies might well remain unrecognized.

In 1988, the NMLRA decided to step in and fill the void with its own records program, the Longhunter (often referred to as the "Longhunter Society"). The first record book was published in 1992, incorporating the old Carson and Glass entries with those of the Longhunter. Since then, the organization has continued to grow. As with B&C and P&Y, any Longhunter entry must be taken legally in fair-chase fashion.

The Longhunter Society has no awards periods and holds no banquets to announce new records, so there's no definitive chronological list of the No.1 whitetails by muzzleloader. Because the first record book incorporated all entries submitted for Carson and Glass in the mid-1980s, I've simply begun my list of muzzleloader "world records" with the biggest bucks entered back then and worked my way to the present. The top Longhunter Society typicals are profiled in chapters 20–22; the top non-typical bucks are in chapters 23–27.

HOW WHITETAILS ARE SCORED

You certainly don't need to be an official measurer to appreciate the deer you will find in this book. However, if you're not conversant in scoring terminology, it will be more difficult to grasp the true magnitude of these racks. With that in mind, let's run through a basic primer on how to measure and score bucks the B&C way.

The various measurements are listed on what is commonly called a "score sheet" or "score chart." The exact number of measurements depends on how many points (tines) the rack possesses. In simplest terms, a "point" is defined as any antler projection of at least one inch in length, though it can be a bit more complex than that. All points fall into one of two categories—"typical" or "non-typical" (also called "abnormal"). Essentially, for a point to be considered typical, it must arise from the top of the main beam and appear to be part of a normal sequence of such points. A point growing off the side or bottom of the main beam, from another point or out of normal sequence are classified as non-typical. (The significance of these categories will be addressed momentarily.)

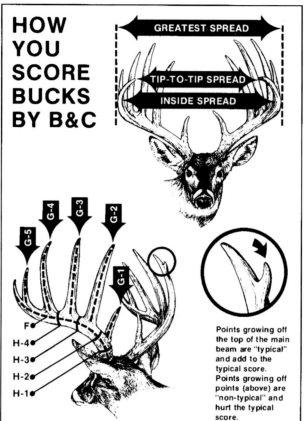

Measuring whitetails by the modern Boone and Crockett system is fairly straightforward, especially for typical bucks. However, not all measurements taken are included in the actual score. For instance, the greatest spread and tip-to-tip spread serve only as supplementary information on the score sheet. Illustration by Allen Hansen.

Using some sort of flexible measuring tape, you can get a rough score of a rack by taking the following measurements to the nearest 1/8 inch—the inside spread of the main beams; the length of each main beam; the length of each point (not counting the end of the main beam); and the four beam circumference measurements (no more, no less) of each antler, starting at the base and sequentially moving up to the next gap between scorable typical points. Then, measure all non-typical points and total their length. Beams and tines are measured along their outside curves, while circumferences are measured at the smallest place between the tines.

Once the various measurements are made, a bit of simple addition and subtraction will quickly get you to both the gross and net score. The *gross* score is reached by adding the total measurements from the right antler to those of the left and then adding in the inside spread. The *net* score, the one by which a trophy is officially ranked in the record book, requires another step or two.

Regardless of whether the rack is considered typical or non-typical, you must subtract from the gross score all the side-to-side differences in the typical portion of the rack (the total of all numbers showing up in the "Difference" column on the score sheet). This number represents the lack of balance between corresponding typical measurements on one antler versus the other. If the buck is being scored as a typical and has no non-typical points, the resulting tally is the net typical score. But if any non-typical points are present, their total length also must be *deducted* to reach the typical net score. This is in contrast to the scoring of non-typicals, where the abnormal points are *added* to the buck's typical score (reached after deducting side-to-side differences) to yield a net non-typical score. This explains why the minimum entry scores in every record book are higher for non-typicals than for typicals.

You'll notice on the score sheet that each of the tines is designated by the letter "G," such as G-1 (brow tine), G-2 (first primary), etc., and that each of the circumferences is an "H" measurement (H-l, H-2, H-3 and H-4). These measurement designations (particularly those of the points) have become so ingrained in the culture of trophy whitetail hunting that they are regularly used as labels for the various parts of the rack. Among those who understand scoring, making a reference to a buck's G-4s is considered clearer and more expedient than saying "the fourth point from the base" or "the third point on the main part of the beam not counting the brow tine."

Confusing? If you're unfamiliar with the scoring system, it certainly can be. But once you understand the terminology and see how it's used to describe trophy bucks, you realize that this verbal shorthand makes perfect sense.

BETTER WAYS TO SCORE?

There are, of course, other means of comparing trophy bucks, and some do have merit. However, in my experience, all of them have fundamental flaws that make them less useful than the B&C system.

For instance, some hunters, especially in New England and eastern Canada, would argue that body size is more significant than antler size. While weight may be a feasible way to measure fish size, it isn't too practical in deer hunting. To start with, certified scales can be hard to find, even at check stations. But more importantly, it is antlers, not body size, that intrigues hunters the most and antler size doesn't necessarily equate to body size.

---◆---

Safari Club International has begun to rank whitetails by gross B&C score, since it reflects true size without subjective judgement about "desirable" trophy traits.

---◆---

What about other antler-scoring systems? Well, there's no shortage of them. The Burkett system, for example, has been around for a number of years. Some experts consider it an equitable method because it greatly rewards mass, but its complexity has limited the system's acceptance. Virginia has its own scoring system, which predates the B&C version. While it shares several similarities with the B&C method, measurements are taken to the nearest 1/16-inch and final scores are consistently far higher than those with the B&C system. To my knowledge, there has never been any interest in or attempt to extend this system beyond Virginia's borders.

One of the groups that has made a big push in the scoring arena in recent years is Buckmasters, whose system purports to give "full credit" for antler growth. There are no scoring deductions for lack of symmetry, which some observers believe is an improvement over B&C's insistence that balance is an important trophy quality. Moreover, the

Buckmasters system gives no credit for antler spread, the rationale being that the distance between the main beams is really just "thin air" and has no bearing on size. True, width doesn't have anything to do with the actual amount of antler grown, but width does figure into the visual impression of size. Thin air or not, spread is an important aspect of trophy quality to nearly all hunters and antler enthusiasts and is impossible to ignore when evaluating a buck.

It is worth noting that Safari Club International has begun to rank whitetails in its record book by gross B&C score, the score favored by many trophy hunters since it reflects true size without subjective judgments about "desirable" trophy traits. It remains to be seen just how well this concept will be received.

One alternate means of antler comparison often proposed involves measuring racks by means of water displacement: that is, dunking them in a container of water then measuring the overflow to determine the volume of the antlers. Again, there are major problems. For starters, such a method doesn't allow for the important visual element of antler spread. Then, there's the practicality of it. I have trouble picturing a guy with a new $350 shoulder mount turning his prized buck upside down over a barrel of water and making the deer practically bob for apples. I have even greater trouble seeing a guy pull into camp with a monster buck on his ATV and then, instead of

All it takes to score a whitetail by the B&C system is a 1/4-inch steel measuring tape, a writing instrument and a sheet of paper on which to jot down the numbers. Learning how the scoring system works not only helps a hunter field-judge antlers more accurately, but also leads to greater appreciation of just how big the world-record racks really are. The heavy Manitoba rack the author is measuring scores in the high 150s. Photo by Catherine Whittington.

scrambling to find a measuring tape, asking the guys to round up a washtub and garden hose! Even if the system were accepted, who would tackle the monumental— make that impossible—job of rounding up decades' worth of whitetails to get them measured by this new system?

Ultimately, the problem of acceptance is the greatest hurdle facing any new scoring system. For all the talk about how to revamp this or that system to make it the best, no other plan is likely to be perceived by the public as more workable or understandable than the one B&C came up with nearly a half-century ago. If it has taken this long to get the hunting public up to speed on that system, I can't imagine this same public would want to start over with an entirely different concept. So, the B&C scoring system is the standard I've chosen for this book.

No, it's not perfect. Many serious trophy enthusiasts fume over B&C's deductions for asymmetry and, in the case of typical racks, for abnormal points. Many of us wish there was a practical way to include tine mass in scores so that massive antlers could get credit for bone that is now being ignored. Still, B&C's way of comparing one trophy to another has become a vital part of today's whitetail culture and has far more pluses than minuses. Overall, it remains the most widely accepted and, arguably, the best system around.

2

NEW BRUNSWICK'S ANONYMOUS RECORD

The identity of the hunter who bagged Boone & Crockett's first world-record typical has been lost to time. Fortunately, the rack hasn't been.

TITLE: FIRST B&C TYPICAL
WORLD RECORD

SCORE: 180 6/8

HUNTER: UNKNOWN

LOCATION: NEW BRUNSWICK

YEAR: 1937

Part of man's fascination with big antlers lies in their ability to endure. Like headstones in a cemetery, they can tell stories literally from beyond the grave. To the devoted antler enthusiast, a well-preserved rack is far more than a mere souvenir of someone's hunting prowess —it is first and foremost an enduring shrine to the animal that wore those antlers. As such, the rack is something to be celebrated, even after the hunter and perhaps his story have faded from memory. After all, the antlers, even if the story behind them isn't known, are capable of conjuring up images in the imagination of the admiring onlooker of the fateful day when the mighty animal came to his end.

This respect for awe-inspiring antlers can be seen in trophy collections all over North America, where the antlers of great whitetails are displayed for everyone to appreciate. But perhaps, no buck is a better example of their ability to reach across time than the one that became the first world-record typical in modern history, a deer from the damp, evergreen forests of eastern Canada.

We know disappointingly little about the history of this buck, only that he is said to have hailed from the maritime province of New Brunswick and that he died in the fall of 1937 at the hands of a "French-Canadian farmer." Within a short time, the deer's tall, massive rack had found its way into the posses-

This great buck, shot by an unknown hunter in New Brunswick in 1937, was certified as B&C's first world-record typical. When the rack was entered, the donor wondered if it might have belonged to a mule deer because of the large fork on the right G-2 tine and the common base shared by the G-2 and G-3. However, the rack is clearly that of a whitetail and was immediately accepted as one. Photo by Peter Buongiovanni, courtesy of the National Taxidermists Hall of Fame.

sion of an American collector named George Dolan. Then in 1947, the rack, unmounted and still on the buck's bleached skull, found its way to the Boone and Crockett Club for measuring. Since this was several years prior to the advent of the modern scoring system, no true score as we know it today was assigned to the trophy. However, the huge rack did come out on top in B&C's 1st Awards Period competition for 1947 on the basis of a main beam length of 31 6/8 inches. (That was the only measurement taken on whitetail racks in those days.)

Brook Dolan, who sent the rack to B&C, openly wondered if perhaps the animal wearing these antlers had been a mule deer. The question was based on the right antler's long, bifurcated G-2 tine, which did somewhat resemble the forked G-2 of a mulie. This alone suggests Brook hadn't actually seen the animal in full body, or even an original photo, for he presumably would have known a whitetail's head from that of a mulie. Regardless, there apparently was no doubt the buck had come from New Brunswick so all such questions were quickly dismissed.

In 1950, B&C's modern scoring system was introduced and the men responsible for putting it into practice were eager to see how the biggest known trophies of various species would stack up. Two of those men were Grancel Fitz and Samuel Webb, and one of those trophies was the whitetail from New Brunswick. So on March 7, 1951, with Samuel as a witness, Grancel put his steel tape to the rack.

When the measurements all had been made and the numbers tallied, there remained a final question. The deer obviously could be listed as a non-typical, for he had 15 6/8 inches of abnormal points. That would put him at 212 2/8 net non-typical, a very respectable score. However, if entered as a typical, with abnormals deducted from his typical frame instead of added, he would net 180 6/8 and be the frontrunner in that category. Because of this, the decision was made to list the buck as a typical.

As it turned out, no other typical scores to match his were recorded in the coming months. So when B&C's 3rd edition of *Records of North American Big Game* came out in 1952, the mystery buck from New Brunswick was listed as No.1. The whitetail that looked like a mulie turned out to be the typical world-record whitetail!

Paul Hartwick poses with the beautifully preserved skull of the New Brunswick giant to provide a perspective on rack size. This impressive 14-pointer, which now belongs to the Academy of Natural Sciences of Philadelphia, is one of three Canadian whitetails B&C has recognized as world records over the years. Photo by Peter Buongiovanni, courtesy of the National Taxidermists Hall of Fame.

Honesty compels me to note that, for all his acclaim, this buck was at no time the largest typical in existence. At the time he was taken, a handful of bucks that would outscore him already were hanging in homes around North America, though none had yet been officially measured. Fortunately, in the years that followed, two of those incredible bucks (profiled in chapters 5 and 6) would go on to become official B&C world records anyway, getting their turns atop the throne.

Let's not allow any of this to detract from the size or stature of the New Brunswick buck. He was enormous by any standard. Without those 15 6/8 inches of abnormal points, he would have netted a stunning 196 4/8 typical, a particularly remarkable score for a 5x5. Even now, decades later, his main beams remain among the longest of any whitetail in the record book. Plus, with the rugged appeal his mass and overall character give him, he simply has everything you could want in a trophy buck.

Everything, that is, except a hunter's name to go with this great rack.

ANONYMOUS, NEW BRUNSWICK, 1937

Measurements	Right	Left	Difference
No. of points	6	8	
Main beam	31 6/8	31 2/8	4/8
1st point (G-1)	7 2/8	6 2/8	1 0/8
2nd point (G-2)	14 0/8	13 5/8	3/8
3rd point (G-3)	12 3/8	9 4/8	2 7/8
4th point (G-4)	7 4/8	6 2/8	1 2/8
5th point (G-5)	–	–	–
1st circ. (H-1)	6 0/8	5 5/8	3/8
2nd circ. (H-2)	5 0/8	5 2/8	2/8
3rd circ. (H-3)	9 0/8	5 7/8	3 1/8
4th circ. (H-4)	5 1/8	6 0/8	7/8
Total	98 0/8	89 5/8	10 5/8
Greatest spread		n/a	
Inside spread		19 4/8	
Gross typical score		207 1/8	
Assymetry deductions		-10 5/8	
Non-typical deductions		-15 6/8	
Net typical score		180 6/8	

A rear view shows off the rack's 31 6/8 and 31 2/8-inch main beams especially well. These remarkable measurements helped push the tall, massive antlers to a world-record score of 180 6/8 despite 15 6/8 inches of deductions for abnormal points. Photo by Peter Buongiovanni, courtesy of the National Taxidermists Hall of Fame.

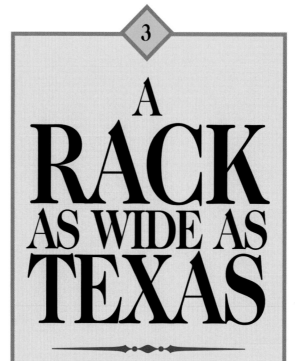

3

A RACK AS WIDE AS TEXAS

Henderson Coquat was a trophy hunter, but he never dreamed he would shoot a buck—a world-record buck, at that—with a spread that looked more like a Texas longhorn than a whiteail!

TITLE: SECOND B&C TYPICAL WORLD RECORD
SCORE: 185 1/8
HUNTER: HENDERSON COQUAT
LOCATION: WEBB COUNTY, TEXAS
YEAR: 1949

Overhead, a scorching desert sun beats down on you; underfoot, rattlesnakes slither. But, don't get too distracted by either of those menaces or you're liable to run smack into a fearsome-looking bush studded with huge thorns, each of them intent on burying itself somewhere in your anatomy.

Why on earth would anyone want to go to South Texas?

If you're a serious trophy hunter, you already know the answer. This huge area, situated between San Antonio and the Rio Grande, just might be the world's best place to match wits with big deer. Here, vast ranches lure sportsmen with such fantastic hunting that the triple threat of sunburn, snakes and thorns seems a minor inconvenience. Cattle and oil may be the lifeblood of this legendary land for most of the year, but when the December rut rolls around, southbound convoys of camo-painted pickup trucks make it clear that the whitetail is king.

It wasn't always that way. In fact, South Texas once was far from ideal deer country. Historical accounts speak romantically of vast plains of grass that were a paradise for cattle and the gritty men who owned them, but those open plains lacked the brushy cover whitetails prefer. While deer certainly could be found across the region, they were usually concentrated along the scattered waterways where they could find thicker vegetation than existed on the plains.

Gradually, the land changed. Overgrazing by vast herds of cattle and horses began to take its toll, reducing the grasses and giving native brush a chance to take root and spread. This wasn't just any brush. It was what Spanish-speaking residents call *chaparral*, a diverse community of drought-tolerant, woody shrubs armed with enough spines to repel a

Sherman tank. The timing of this transition is hard to pinpoint, but it appears to have been well under way in the late 1800s. By early in the 20th century, much of what once had been grassland was blanketed by thornbrush.

It was somewhere back then that the appropriate name "Brush Country" was born, and not coincidentally, so was the region's deer boom. Whitetails began to flourish in their new fortress of impenetrable brush, which provided both security and surprisingly nutritious forage. Not even the abundant predators—eagles, coyotes, bobcats, mountain lions and the occasional jaguar—could prevent the deer from prospering on those big, lightly hunted ranches. Thanks to the efforts of thousands of landowners and hunters, they still do.

Today, South Texas is easily the most intensively managed deer region on the continent. Whitetail hunting is big business there. Sportsmen not only pay top dollar for hunting privileges on the better ranches, but they also patronize motels, restaurants, gas stations and other establishments, bringing a welcome economic boost to this part of the state.

Many companies have sprung up exclusively to provide South Texas hunters with an array of specialty products, including automatic deer feeders, elaborate tower blinds and even management advice, complete with helicopter censusing.

It would be interesting to know just what the late Henderson Coquat would think of this trend. By all accounts, he was one fellow who favored a distinctly low-tech approach to Brush Country hunting, needing only a rifle, rattling antlers and knife for a day afield. Today's sportsmen might shake their heads at his simple ways, but if Henderson were still around to hear their wisecracks, he would have the last laugh. You see, in 1949, he did what no other Texas hunter has ever done—he shot a world-record typical whitetail!

Sadly, there are no field photos showing the hunter with his trophy. Even official B&C measurer John Stein, whose passion for tracking down information on Texas' biggest deer has led to his reputation as "the deer detective," has been unable to find one. For that matter, some of the details of the hunt

Henderson Coquat's awesome 13-pointer from Webb County, Texas, has an outside spread of 30 2/8 inches, making it the widest world-record typical ever recognized by B&C. The buck stood as the No.1 typical from 1953 to 1955. Photo by John Stein.

are long gone, too, but at least we know the framework of events on which those missing details were hung.

The setting for the tale is northern Webb County's Apache Ranch, where Henderson made his historic kill. But, the story actually began a few days earlier, just across the fence on the La Mesa

———◆———

Even back in those days, before trophy deer had become a national obsession, Claude was single-mindedly in search of a braggin' buck.

———◆———

Ranch, with a hunter named Claude King. Sadly for him, he and his .30-30 would play an unwitting role in Henderson's monumental achievement.

Claude apparently was a pretty hardcore hunter himself. Even back in those days, before trophy deer had become a national obsession, he was single-mindedly in search of a braggin' buck. His timing couldn't have been much better. Texas was nearing the end of a relatively wet climate cycle that had done wonders for the deer habitat. The Lone Star State was about to enter a long stretch of horrifically dry weather, but for now, times were good and Claude hoped to cash in. To do so, he had decided to focus his efforts on a huge thicket on the La Mesa Ranch. Sure enough, he found a trophy—a 13-pointer with antlers spreading far wider than the buck's body!

While the exact circumstances of their meeting have been lost, the outcome hasn't. Somehow, the buck escaped Claude's bullets unharmed. We can imagine that when Claude got back home from that disappointing encounter he lamented having missed a "30-inch buck." We can just as confidently assume

that nobody believed him. Deer with racks spreading 2 1/2 feet wide have always been among the rarest members of the whitetail world.

Later that same month on the evening of December 27, Henderson Coquat was laying out his strategy for hunting the neighboring Apache Ranch. He, too, was hoping to kill a big buck, but unlike Claude, he was going to enlist help in doing so. Henderson's buddy, Mike Williams, would accompany him into the brush the next morning in an attempt to lure a trophy into range with the sounds of a fake buck fight.

Rattling is now one of the most popular whitetail tactics across North America, but in those days, it was virtually unknown outside the borders of Texas. To be honest, its origins still aren't clear. Some claim white settlers picked up the idea from Indians who had been doing it for millennia; others suggest cowboys probably tried it after watching bucks come running to a real deer fight in the brush. Whatever the case, it seems "modern" rattling began in Texas and then spread elsewhere, largely due to the well-chronicled exploits of such expert rattlers as Murry Burnham and Bob Ramsey.

Rattling with a partner—one person to work the antlers, another to shoot—is among the best ways to hunt the Brush Country during the rut. The reason it works so well is that before smart bucks rush onto the scene of a "fight" they commonly circle downwind, trying to get a whiff of the combatants before barging in. With so much thick thornbrush growing within four feet of ground level, it can be quite difficult for the rattler to see his quarry before he himself is seen or smelled. By setting up some distance downwind of the rattler and remaining motionless, the second hunter often can get a shot at a circling buck.

On this particular hunt, we frankly don't know if Mike was the "designated rattler" and Henderson the "designated shooter" or whether they traded those duties back and forth. All we are sure of is that they got a leisurely start on the morning of

Veteran hunter Henderson Coquat displays the shooting form that helped him down his world record on the run at 200 yards. Photo courtesy of John Stein.

haps 200 yards away…coming right at him!

The hunter's .270 was plenty of gun, even at that distance…if he could hit the buck. What really complicated matters was the fact that Henderson and the buck had seen each other at virtually the same time. As you might imagine, the buck wasn't waiting around to make things easier for the hunter—he was leaving, pronto!

We can only imagine what a buck with long, dark tines and an outside spread of 30 2/8 inches must have looked like as he ran away through the brush. Even normal-sized racks look big from behind, and this one was far from normal size! Perhaps that incredible image is why Henderson missed his first shot, and as Texans are fond of saying, "the second one hit him in exactly the same place." Moments later, however, Henderson's luck took a turn for the better and the third bullet slammed home. In less time than it takes to tell it, the great buck tumbled to the muddy ground.

If Henderson and Mike feared a degree of "ground shrinkage" as they hurried to reach the deer, their concerns quickly disappeared. What they found lying there in the brush must have astounded even these old hands. The greatest Christmas present of Henderson's life had come three days late that year, but he probably didn't mind!

At that time, there was no universal means of judging deer racks. That would come a year later, when B&C implemented its modern scoring system, initiating a mad scramble to measure trophies from across the continent. Some fine typicals were entered from that first round of scoring.

Henderson's buck, however, wasn't entered in time to get into the third edition of B&C's *Records of North American Big Game,* which came out in 1952 and listed the 180 6/8-point New Brunswick buck profiled in Chapter 2 as the world record. But, the wide-racked Texas trophy would eventually get its turn. On March 25, 1953, B&C named Henderson's buck the new world-record typical on the strength of a net score of 183 7/8.

December 28, since a cold rain the night before led the hunters to believe the bucks would be late in rising. The men planned to try rattling in a few choice spots. If nothing happened, they would head back to camp and weigh their options.

Despite their late departure, Henderson and Mike still seemed to be ahead of the deer because they saw nothing of note during their first few rattling sessions. Should they head back to camp or give it one more try? Fortunately, they opted for the latter and began walking toward another area of the ranch. They never got that far. As they left the scene of their last rattling session and began easing through the brush, Henderson looked up and spotted a wide-racked buck, nose to the ground, per-

Actually, the score should have been even higher. Under the original rules, the credit for inside spread couldn't exceed the length of the shorter main beam, which was 25 3/8 inches. The rule later was changed so that the spread credit could not exceed the length of the *longer* main beam. The net effect of the rule change pushes the final score of Henderson's buck to 185 1/8 points.

It is also interesting to note that, despite B&C's concerted efforts to find and measure as many trophies as possible in the early days, the stunning Coquat buck was at that time the world's biggest typical only on paper. As we'll see in the next three chapters, in later years the hunting community would learn that even higher scoring typicals had been taken long before Henderson's 1949 trophy. Indeed, in South Texas alone, at least four other typicals from earlier in the century would outscore his ultra-wide deer. Basil Dailey's buck from 1903 would eventually be scored at 192 2/8, while Milton George's monster from 1906 would come in at 196 1/8. (They still rank No.2 and No.4 all time in Texas; see Chapter 28.) In 1945, Charles Edwards got a buck netting 187 5/8. Donald Rutledge followed a year later with a 187 7/8-point brute he rattled up. Then in 1950, one year after Henderson shot his deer but prior to it being measured, C.P.

Claude King missed a shot at Henderson's wide buck early in the 1949 season, but his disappointment turned to elation when he downed this 212 2/8-point non-typical later that year! Photo courtesy of John Stein.

Howard bagged a 190-pointer.

Any of those Brush Country trophies, as well as other contenders from across North America, theoretically could have beaten out Henderson's deer to become a world-record typical; however, none was entered in time to do so. Such is the nature of the record books, and chance played a larger role than usual in those early days.

What of poor Claude King? Did he spend the rest of his years berating himself for having blown a chance at hunting immortality? Maybe…but maybe not. For you see, only days after missing that super-wide typical, Claude made amends for his poor shooting display in a very big way.

While still-hunting through the thick brush on the La Mesa Ranch, the scene of his earlier disappointment, he heard a buck raking his antlers ahead of him in the thicket. The cover was so nasty that walking straight to the deer was out of the question. Claude literally had to crawl through the brush for a long way, listening as best he could for more of the rubbing sounds. Even as the hunter inched toward this "unknown" deer, haunting thoughts of that wide-racked buck must have swirled through his mind. Before he knew it, Claude was coming down with what he claimed to be his first-ever case of buck fever, and a bad case at that.

Eventually, the hunter reached a somewhat open spot where he could stand and get his bearings. As he rose, he discovered he had done almost too good a job of homing in on those rubbing sounds – the big buck making them was only 50 feet away, eyeing this intruder in his thorny sanctuary! In the anxious moments that followed, Claude's shooting failed him again as the first two shots from his saddle gun went astray. Luckily, though, the third bullet found its mark, striking the buck in the neck and dropping him instantly.

———◆———

Just how close did Claude come to taking two official B&C whitetails in a single season?

———◆———

When Claude walked up to his trophy, it is probably safe to say he at least temporarily forgot about that 13-pointer he had missed because the buck he had just shot sported far more inches of antler on his head! Indeed, when officially measured, this buck would net out at a whopping 212 2/8 B&C points, 27 1/8 inches more than Henderson's trophy! However, whereas the Coquat buck was a typical, this one was a non-typical 24-pointer.

It is interesting to ponder the course whitetail history might have taken had Claude been a better (or simply luckier) marksman and downed that "30-incher" he missed, putting himself into position to become a record holder in the typical category. Then again, there's a real chance he wouldn't have had the buck scored during the short window in which it would have been No.1. Apparently, it was some time before Claude either heard of or got enthused about the B&C scoring system because his non-typical wasn't measured for a number of years. Had he shot the other buck and then waited years to get that one measured, the window of opportuni-

ty to become No.1 would have already been closed. So all things considered, maybe things worked out for the best.

Here is another potential scenario to mull over: Just how close did Claude come to taking *two* official B&C whitetails in a single season —something apparently never done before or since anywhere on the continent? Even back in those days, it was quite legal in Texas to shoot two bucks so it could have happened. Then again, after you had just shot either of these tremendous deer, would you have felt motivated to keep hunting for another one that year? In Claude's case, we'll never know.

Henderson or Claude, which of these old-time Brush Country hunters really came out ahead back in 1949? Heck, that's easy: They both did!

Henderson Coquat, Texas, 1949

Measurements	Right	Left	Difference
No. of points	7	6	
Main beam	25 6/8	25 3/8	3/8
1st point (G-1)	7 0/8	6 5/8	3/8
2nd point (G-2)	10 5/8	9 5/8	1 0/8
3rd point (G-3)	9 3/8	9 6/8	3/8
4th point (G-4)	9 1/8	7 4/8	1 5/8
5th point (G-5)	5 6/8	4 0/8	1 6/8
1st circ. (H-1)	5 0/8	4 6/8	2/8
2nd circ. (H-2)	n/a	n/a	2/8
3rd circ. (H-3)	n/a	n/a	5/8
4th circ. (H-4)	n/a	n/a	1 7/8
Total	88 4/8	80 6/8	8 4/8
Greatest spread		30 2/8	
Inside spread		27 0/8	
Gross typical score		195 0/8	
Assymetry deductions		-8 4/8	
Non-typical deductions		-1 3/8	
Net typical score		185 1/8	

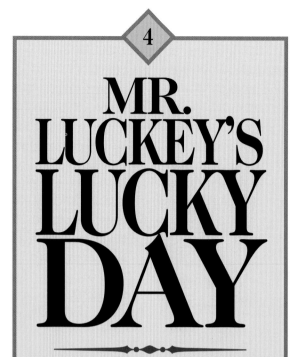

4

MR. LUCKEY'S LUCKY DAY

Not even a thief could spoil the amazing story of the greatest typical ever taken in the Northeast...but that didn't stop him from trying.

TITLE: THIRD B&C TYPICAL WORLD RECORD

SCORE: 198 3/8

HUNTER: ROOSEVELT WILLIAM LUCKEY

LOCATION: ALLEGANY COUNTY, NEW YORK

YEAR: 1939

O h, the potential is there, as you'll see in this story, but excessive hunting pressure and, oddly enough, too many deer are today's nemesis's of trophy buck production almost everywhere east of the Mississippi River. In much of the East, bucks simply can't escape the bullet long enough to the reach the age needed to realize their full potential. Even 2 1/2-year-old bucks are rare in some places. And for much too long, too many mouths have vied for too little food. No wonder many Eastern hunters are skeptical about finding big, mature deer in their own state.

The search for better trophy prospects has led many to the far corners of the continent. From the remote ranches of Mexico's Rio Grande region to the farms of the Midwest and the "big bush" of Canada, Eastern hunters today comb every part of

North America's broad backcountry, hoping to stumble onto one of those special spots where bucks get a chance to show what they're made of. But, a half-century ago you could find one of those heavenly deer havens in a remarkably convenient location, and it could be accessed for only the token price of a hunting license. The trophy haven I'm speaking of was, of all places, western New York.

These days, the Empire State has a huge herd that supports one of the largest annual deer harvests in the nation but things once were much different. By the late 1800s, whitetails had been virtually exterminated from most areas, leading to an almost total ban on hunting them. To satisfy the public's taste for venison in the early part of this century, the Department of Environmental Conservation (DEC) did allow deer hunting in certain areas, including the Adirondack Mountains in the state's northeastern corner. There, thanks to the rugged and remote habitat, deer had managed to survive in huntable numbers and hunting camps were an honored tradition. Sportsmen would come from great distances to hunt these mountain deer, traveling by whatever mode they could muster for the sometimes arduous journey.

It is almost certain that one of those hunters drove a Ford to the Adirondacks. His name was Roosevelt William Luckey, a Ford dealer and garage owner in the town of Hume, way out west in Allegany County. "Bill," as he was known by family and friends, was a serious deer hunter, having taken his first Adirondacks buck in 1926. Each fall, he would make that long trip to the mountains where he and the rest of his hunting party had a cabin on an island in a remote lake. During the short deer season, Bill's place of business stayed open, but only to pump gas. Those who needed repair work had to wait for the hunting

Although shot nearly 60 years ago, the 198 3/8-point Luckey buck remains the highest-scoring typical ever from the Northeast. He easily became the B&C world-record typical whitetail when measured in 1955 and held that ranking for five years. Photo courtesy of New York State Department of Environmental Conservation.

party to return from the mountains!

While the Adirondacks are a legendary hunting area, it was in Bill's home county, not the mountains, that New York's best-known whitetail of all time would be harvested. It happened near Hume on November 25, 1939, during only the second legal day of deer hunting in Allegany County in many years.

The biggest problem in researching long-ago hunting stories is finding living eyewitnesses who can separate fact from fiction. In that regard, I started working on this story none too soon. Although Bill had passed away in 1991 after a long, full life that included three decades of retirement in Florida, I was able to interview his nephew, Beverly ("Bev") Luckey, who had direct knowledge of the historic hunt. I contacted Bev in the summer of 1997, and he revealed some interesting details that had never appeared in print. Then in early November of that year, I received from him the accompanying portrait of his uncle Bill taken in 1924. Sadly, that photo turned out to be one of the last pieces of correspondence Bev ever mailed. A week later, he passed away.

Some of the fine points in what follows were gathered during my all-too-brief phone conversation with Bev. The bulk of the story, though, comes from information laboriously compiled by New York State Big Buck Club founder Bob Estes, who tracked Bill down during the 1960s and recorded the hunter's own memories of the hunt. Bill later checked over Bob's information and gave him his blessing to have it published in a 1968 issue of the DEC's *Conservationist* magazine.

The second day of that 1939 season was, Bill recalled, "a cool but very nice" day to be in the woods. As was frequently the case in that era, the hunt would be a group affair, with Bill and his brother, Alden, teaming up with Gerald Thomas, Richard Gayford and another sportsman whose name never was recorded. We don't know if any of them had shot a deer on opening day, but by the second afternoon of the short season, there was talk of needing to make something happen. With so much manpower available, a series of deer drives seemed to be the logical choice.

Even working in concert, these guys embarked on a difficult task – you see, the area they were going to hunt was seven miles long by a mile wide with pastures and brushy thickets scattered throughout. Even in small cover, it can be tricky to push deer to predictable spots. In an area the size of

Roosevelt Luckey —known to family and friends as "Bill" — was 23 years old when he posed for this portrait in 1924. Fifteen years later, he would shoot the most famous whitetail in New York history. Unfortunately, no photos exist of him with either the dead deer or the mount. Photo courtesy of Beverly Luckey.

this one, the challenge would be daunting indeed. On the plus side, these deer were about as naive as they possibly could be, having never dealt with hunters before (at least not legal hunters).

Nobody in the group knew for sure what was lurking in those big woods, but around 4 p.m., after a couple of short pushes had been made, a tremendous buck was seen leaving the cover far ahead of the drivers. That's when the shooting broke out. Bev claimed one of the men had what seemed to be a good opportunity at the buck, but his shot hit a sapling instead. In the minutes that followed, as the huge buck ran through the cover, several other hunters also touched off their shotguns and missed. Then, it was Bill's turn.

"On the third drive, I was on watch, taking what was left and feeling like there was no chance for a deer to come by," he said. "I was standing in a bunch of thornapples when I caught a glimpse of a deer coming my way. There was an opening he would go through. The big buck was taking 20-foot leaps. My first impression was that the deer had caught some brush on his antlers. I took a fast shot at the heart-and-lung area."

That shot came at a range of roughly 100 yards. As soon as Bill's Model 11 Remington roared, he knew immediately the slug had connected. The deer's front legs came out from under him and he stumbled. But, he wasn't yet down for the count. Even though the shot had been a good one, within moments the clearing was vacant. All that remained was a tremendous blood trail.

"We tracked the deer for what seemed to be a half-mile," Bill remembered. "At 4:30 p.m., we found the buck, with a massive set of antlers! He had been shot through the heart." No doubt the harried buck had made it so far on sheer adrenaline.

According to Bev, Bill's brief account of the events left out one important and amusing part of the story. During the long time it took to trail the buck, it seems the buck had yet another encounter with a hunter. This fellow wasn't a member of Bill's hunting party, but in a rather embarrassing fashion, he managed to become part of whitetail history anyway.

"The deer came running down in front of this guy, who was shooting a double-barreled shotgun," Bev explained. "He shot, and as soon as he did, the buck fell to the ground. When the guys who had been following the blood trail got there, the fellow was saying, 'I got him! I got him!' But, there was only one hole in the deer so it was clear that my uncle was the only one who'd hit him. The buck just happened to fall over dead as soon as that guy shot!"

Once the Luckey (or just plain lucky?) party had recovered the trophy buck, they hauled him out of the woods and headed to Bill's house in Hume. "The hometown buzzed with excitement that night, and anyone interested in hunting came to see the big deer," the hunter later recalled. "It weighed 195 pounds dressed out."

What Bill had assumed was "brush" hanging on the antlers turned out to be the rack itself. A wall of long, thick tines adorned each side of the rack, and the sweeping main beams formed a fitting crown for this king of deer. All told, there were 14 scorable points (12 typical), plus several non-scorable stickers and forks coming off the typical tines. Everyone was amazed that such a buck had been taken in the area.

Today, if a whitetail of this magnitude were shot, someone almost certainly would measure the rack and come up with a rough B&C score within a week, if not hours. But that system didn't even exist in 1939. So while the Luckey buck was much celebrated in the Hume area, no official scoring of the rack occurred until Grancel Fitz put a

Bob Estes hoists the Luckey buck's massive sheds for a comparison to the actual rack. Joe Merwin found the fresh sheds in the spring of 1938, meaning the buck grew them two years prior to the deer's death. At better than 200 net typical points, the sheds outscored the buck's final rack. Photo courtesy of Bob Estes.

Immediately after the stolen sheds were recovered in March 1994, Lt. Robert Lucas of the DEC handed them over to their rightful owner, Mrs. Joe Merwin. Shortly afterward, Mrs. Merwin and her family opted to give the sheds of the former world record back to the DEC so the antlers could be seen and admired by New York hunters for years to come. Photo by Bob Estes.

tape to it on May 6, 1955. When that happened, the net score of 198 2/8 typical was enough to easily push the New York deer past every other known typical, including Henderson Coquat's world record from Texas (Chapter 3). The delay in measuring didn't cost him his world-record title, but it did cut into the time he stood atop the rankings before being knocked off by the next No.1 typical in 1960 (Chapter 5).

Bill kept the mount of his great deer tucked away in his garage for many years, but once the rack's true significance was realized, the hunter decided such a historic animal should be shared with all New York sportsmen. He elected to give the mounted head to the DEC so it could be displayed not only in the agency's headquarters but also at various public functions. As of this writing, the rack remains in the possession of the state and occasionally is displayed at public events, though only in tightly controlled settings.

It was an unfortunate incident in 1978 that

caused the DEC to become more cautious about the security of the Luckey buck. The incident didn't involve the record-book mount, but rather, the closest thing to it – a pair of the buck's shed antlers, which are at the core of this story's strange epilogue.

In 1976, a pair of measurers for the New York Big Buck Club—Ray Minnick and Grant Shattuck—located an enormous set of sheds in an old Allegany County barn. Their research finally uncovered the history of the antlers and led to the inescapable conclusion that they were sheds from the same deer Bill had shot 37 years earlier!

They discovered that the antlers had been picked up in April 1938 by Joe Merwin, then a 13-year-old farm boy who had been sent to the pasture to round up some livestock. One of the horses turned out to be a bit unruly, so Joe reached down to the ground for a branch to throw at it. But, what he picked up wasn't a branch; instead, it was a massive whitetail antler!

Remember, in those days many people didn't even know that deer actually dropped their racks every year. Fortunately, Joe did. He immediately started looking around for the other side of the buck's rack. Sure enough, he found it lying only 50 yards or so from the first. Joe took his prizes home and drilled a hole between each burr and brow tine so that he could attach the antlers to a board. They apparently were hung in an old barn, which is where Ray and Grant found them in 1976, nearly four decades after they had been picked up.

At first, there was some doubt that the antlers had come from Bill's deer. When the measurers pressed for details, they learned that the sheds had been found in the Hume area. In fact, Joe had picked them up near Claybed Road, meaning the buck had dropped them no more than a mile from where the deer was shot 19 months later! Besides, anyone with an eye for antlers could tell the two racks were amazingly similar, too much so to have come from different deer.

Even though the sheds (grown in 1937) are 7x7

typical with a single abnormal point and the actual rack (1939) features a 6x6 mainframe and two abnormals, it is obvious they're from the same animal. (The antlers grown by the buck in 1938, the year in between those racks, apparently were never found.) With an estimated 18 1/8-inch inside spread (the same as the buck had when he was shot), the sheds would have a net B&C score of 205 6/8 points! As such, they are one of the largest matched typical sets of all time and by far the most impressive ever found in the northeastern U.S. The sheds from the Luckey buck were mounted onto a solid base covered with leather, the significance of which we'll see shortly.

In 1978, two years after Ray and Grant discovered the sheds, officials at the annual Erie County Fair asked if they could display the mount of the state-record Luckey buck. Since the mount was unavailable from the DEC at that time, New York State Big Buck Club founder Bob Estes borrowed the sheds from Joe's family and sent them instead, along with some other trophies from around the state. That was fine…until the morning the mounted sheds and a shoulder mount of a solid-white buck (from Seneca Army Depot) turned up missing!

Bob immediately reported the theft to those in charge of security at the fair, and an investigation began. Unfortunately, law-enforcement officials drew a blank at every turn. Bob suspected that it might have been an "inside job" of some sort, but he couldn't prove it and no leads turned up. As days turned into months and months into years, Bob reached the conclusion that he would never see either trophy again.

Then in March 1995, some 17 years after the theft, an anonymous phone caller suggested that the DEC send an officer to a specific location to pick up a "big pair of deer horns." The caller claimed the antlers were tied to the post of a stop sign but noted that they wouldn't be visible to passersby because of the deep snow. Curious to check out the tip but

fearing a possible ambush, the DEC dispatched a game warden to watch the area overnight before approaching the stop sign where the antlers reportedly had been left. Finally convinced there was no ambush, the game warden went to the stop sign and did indeed find a "big" set of antlers tied to the post. The base of the rack was covered with, you guessed it, leather.

When Bob got word of this strange find, his heart skipped a beat. This rack had to be the long-missing sheds from Bill's state-record buck! Sure enough, the massive antlers were those stolen nearly

———◆———

Some 17 years after the theft, an anonymous phone caller suggested that "a big pair of deer horns" could be found tied to the post of a stop sign.

———◆———

two decades earlier. After a lengthy investigation, charges were filed against Nicholas L. Gumhalter, who had worked as a security guard at the county fair back in 1978. By this time, Gumhalter was retired from a lengthy career as, of all things, a state trooper! While it couldn't be proved that he had actually stolen the antlers from the show, he was found guilty of possessing them and transporting them to the site where they were dumped on the roadside. He paid a fine of $500.

Later, the story came out that the so-called "security guard" had kept the mounted sheds in the top of his garage, telling his son they were an old rack from a deer his grandfather had shot years earlier. The boy had even allowed many of his childhood friends to view the rack secretly, never realizing the big antlers were stolen property. (Incidentally, as of this writing, the mount of the white buck hasn't turned up, though authorities reportedly have a lead on it.)

According to Bob, the happy ending was the result of nothing more than a guilty conscience on the part of Mr. Gumhalter. The reason for committing such a crime is anyone's guess, but as Bob told me, "I'm just thankful the guy didn't panic and destroy the rack. Anybody could steal something, but it takes a pretty big man to return it."

Naturally, Joe Merwin's widow was elated to get the antlers back after 17 years. Graciously, she transferred permanent ownership to the DEC so all the citizens of New York could enjoy seeing the two biggest sets of typical antlers in their state's history.

Just how old the buck was when Bill shot him is a topic still up for debate. According to the hunter, DEC biologists studied the jawbone and proclaimed the animal to have been just 4 1/2 years of age. That age seems highly improbable in light of the buck's 200-plus-point

Bill's world record wasn't the only trophy shot in Allegany County during that historic 1939 season. In fact, Bill's buck didn't even have the highest-scoring rack! That distinction belongs to Homer Boylan's 244 2/8-point non-typical, which still holds the state record in that category. Amazingly, the colossal bucks were shot only one day and 24 miles apart. Photo courtesy of Bob Estes.

sheds from two years earlier! Perhaps there was a mix-up of some kind, either among the jawbones examined or in Bill's recollection of what he had been told. Bev told me he remembered the buck as having been clearly past his prime when Bill shot him. "His teeth were worn down to nothing," Bev noted. "He wouldn't have made the winter, for sure." (By the way, the winter of 1939-40 was quite severe, with heavy deer losses across much of New York. It's a good thing Bill got him when he did!)

The twists and turns of this tale make it one of the more intriguing stories of any world-record whitetail. Just the saga of the sheds is a strange one for a buck of any size, much less a No.1 B&C buck. There are other curious points to ponder as well.

First, Bev told me there was some speculation that the buck had been released into that area as part of a DEC restocking program. "The deer had a hole in one of his ears, where it looked like maybe a tag had been," he noted. I have no reason to doubt the buck had a hole in one ear, but from what I've been able to determine, it is unlikely that it came as the result of ear-tagging. DEC records do not indicate any releases of deer in that part of the state in that era. The expansion of the herd seems to have been the result of a natural buildup of remnant pockets of local deer and immigration from surrounding areas, including northwestern Pennsylvania. Adult bucks everywhere commonly have torn (and less commonly) perforated ears, usually from the slashing tines of rival bucks. It is possible that Bill's deer merely showed the scars of a long, hard life in the wild.

Another interesting point is that while this hunter always signed documents —including the paperwork for his B&C entry—as Roosevelt Luckey, he apparently didn't like his first name one bit. In fact, "If anyone called him 'Roosevelt,' he would get mad," Bev told me. The irony of this revelation is that, while no living person knows for sure, Bill likely was given that first name to honor Theodore Roosevelt, who was sworn in as the nation's 26th President in 1901, the year Bill was born. Only 14 years prior to that, Roosevelt and friends had banded together to form the Boone and Crockett Club, the organization that ultimately would make the Luckey buck a well-known part of whitetail history. If Bill were indeed named in honor of the club's founder, you'd think he would have liked the name —particularly after his deer became No.1!

And, here's a final fascinating fact: While Bill's trophy is the only official B&C world record ever from New York, the buck isn't the overall highest-scoring whitetail ever shot in Allegany County. In fact, it isn't even the biggest buck shot in that county *that week!* Instead, that honor goes to the Homer Boylan buck, a 13x13 giant that to this day remains New York's top non-typical at 244 2/8 points. Homer's buck was shot on the November 24 opener, just one day before Bill took his trophy. Over the years, there has been speculation that perhaps the

two trophies were related since their racks are superficially similar. According to Bob, however, the kill sites were some 24 air miles apart, minimizing the chances of a close genetic link.

No other county in North America can match Allegany's claim of having produced a pair of whitetails that have stayed atop the state rankings for as long as the Luckey and Boylan bucks have. While some observers think they might even last for a full century or more as New York's No.1 deer, common sense tells us the great genetics that produced these monsters are still there. If we somehow could recreate the days of old, when many bucks reached their prime and balanced deer numbers assured plenty of nutritious food, who is to say New York couldn't produce even bigger trophies?

ROOSEVELT WILLIAM LUCKEY, NEW YORK, 1939

Measurements	Right	Left	Difference
No. of points	6	8	
Main beam	29 5/8	29 4/8	1/8
1st point (G-1)	3 0/8	3 0/8	–
2nd point (G-2)	10 4/8	11 6/8	1 2/8
3rd point (G-3)	13 0/8	14 1/8	1 1/8
4th point (G-4)	11 1/8	12 3/8	1 2/8
5th point (G-5)	7 1/8	5 7/8	1 2/8
1st circ. (H-1)	4 6/8	4 6/8	–
2nd circ. (H-2)	4 6/8	4 6/8	–
3rd circ. (H-3)	6 5/8	6 3/8	2/8
4th circ. (H-4)	6 3/8	5 4/8	7/8
Total	96 7/8	98 0/8	6 1/8
Greatest spread		21 0/8	
Inside spread		18 1/8	
Gross typical score		213 0/8	
Assymetry deductions		-6 1/8	
Non-typical deductions		-8 4/8	
Net typical score		198 3/8	

5

GIANT OF THE NORTH WOODS

◆────◆

When a world-record typical steps out of the brush, even the most devout "meat" hunter will rearrange his priorities.

◆────◆

TITLE: FOURTH B&C TYPICAL
WORLD RECORD

SCORE: 202

HUNTER: JOHN BREEN

LOCATION: BELTRAMI COUNTY,
MINNESOTA

YEAR: 1918

When we reflect on the early days of the 20th century, it is only natural to be envious of the opportunities enjoyed by deer hunters back then. With vast woodlands and relatively few hunters, sportsmen in those days must have had it made...or did they?

In many cases, the reality of that era was far different than today's idealized image of it. True, modern deer woods are smaller and more crowded with hunters, but they're also far more crowded with whitetails. In fact, current deer numbers are many times what they were 100 years ago. Most hunters in those days didn't expect to see deer every day, something most of us now take for granted.

Offsetting this relative lack of game was the fact that if you did see a deer chances were it would be big. Of course, for most hunters back then, "big" carried a somewhat different meaning than it does today. Whereas we now tend to think of rack size over body size, it used to be just the opposite. Meat on the table was worth far more than antlers on the wall. Bringing home v enison was serious business, and many hunters were willing to devote considerable effort to making it happen.

Minnesota's John Breen was cut of that cloth. Over the years, he spent a lot of time afield and returned with plenty of venison to show for it. Perhaps it's ironic, then, that this old-time hunter is remembered not for the tons of meat dropped by his .30-30 Winchester but for a few pounds of bone adorning the head of a buck no one could eat.

John was 37 years old when, in 1903, he moved his family to the northern Minnesota town of Bemidji, roughly 100 miles south of massive Lake of the Woods on the Ontario border. There, he got a job as a clerk and set about raising a family that eventually would grow to include five sons. With so many hungry mouths to feed and with the region's logged-over timberlands harboring a fair number of whitetails, it is little wonder John availed himself of every chance to hit the woods. He shot a number of deer during his first 15 years in the area.

You might assume that in such a remote setting as early-20th-century northern Minnesota a guy could pretty much shoot a deer whenever he encountered one. However, that wasn't the case. By the time World War I began, there was already a sense that the herd needed some level of legal protection. As a result, deer could be hunted only during a short fall season. It opened in mid-November so a hunter could take advantage of fresh snow to help him literally track down a winter meat supply.

Getting to where you wanted to hunt was the first obstacle since there was no well-developed road system in northern Minnesota back then.

John Breen's legendary buck, shot 33 miles north of Bemidji, Minnesota, in 1918, is the favorite typical of all time for many antler enthusiasts. He was the B&C world-record typical from 1960 to 1966 and the first typical ever to net score over 200 points. Photo courtesy of Dr. Charles "Chuck" Arnold & Duncan Dobie.

Automobiles were just coming into common use, so many residents still made their everyday rounds with horse and buggy. On longer trips, they often rode the train, even to the deer woods. Many old stories tell of hunters in Minneapolis and other large cities climbing aboard trains for long journeys north in search of game, then heading back south again with their supply of venison.

One of these rail lines ran from Bemidji northeastward to International Falls on the Ontario border, cutting through prime deer country en route. It was about 33 miles up this line from Bemidji, near the village of Funkley, that whitetail history would be made in the fall of 1918.

Among the occasional customers at the store where John worked was a fellow named Knute Wick, who lived near Funkley in the even tinier community of Hopt. (It is no longer even on the state highway map.) Knute was a deer hunter and knew John was, too.

When the November season rolled around, Knute asked the store clerk if he would like to join

When John returned home from his November "meat" hunt, he brought with him a deer far better suited to admiring than cooking. John's son, Ray, later recalled that the meat was so tough nobody would eat it! In this historic photo, John admires his awesome buck. Photo courtesy of Duncan Dobie.

him in trying a good spot he had staked out in the Funkley area. John's two eldest sons were in Europe at the time fighting in World War I, but three Breen boys still lived at home. Fresh meat would indeed be welcome. John eagerly agreed to go. Only a day or two later, he returned with the biggest-racked buck anyone in those parts had ever seen!

Details of the hunt itself are somewhat cloudy, as is usually the case with outdoor exploits of that era. Because John didn't live to see his buck's rack recognized as any sort of record, he apparently was never interviewed about the events so we have no eyewitness account of the hunt. Years later, his son Ray, who was 12 at the time of the historic hunt, would recall the facts as he understood them.

"The story that I always heard was that he was on his stand with his .30-30 rifle when a bunch of deer came by," Ray said. "Several does were being

He was the first typical ever known to crack the magical 200-point barrier.

chased by a buck. He raised his rifle and started to shoot the buck. All of a sudden, he saw this great rack of horns coming through the woods (on a different buck) so he took aim and shot this big buck instead."

If this sketchy account is indeed accurate, several points are interesting. First, John would have been among a surprisingly small percentage of people who have taken world-record-class bucks while hunting from a stand as a result of natural deer movement. Most such deer have come as a result of some sort of forced movement, like that imposed upon the deer by deer drives, snow-tracking and active still-hunting, all common practices back then. Much less common was waiting in ambush. Also worth pointing out: While John was a "meat hunter," when he spotted a buck with an enormous rack he suddenly forgot about the other, smaller buck, a decision that proved to have both good and bad consequences.

On the positive side, the hunter immediately received recognition for having shot a rare trophy, as the antlers dazzled even fellow "meat" hunters. "When he got the buck home, everybody came by to see it," Ray recalled. "A lot of people made a big fuss over it. The rack was so big that even in those days everybody knew that it was something special. Dad took his buck to a nearby vacant barn, hung it up and skinned it out. The rack was so wide that we had a hard time getting it through the front door of the house."

The only disappointing aspect of John's decision to shoot the deer became apparent as soon as the first piece of that venison was carved up on the Breen dinner table. "The deer was thin and gaunt when Dad brought him home, despite the size of his antlers," Ray noted. "He was a big-bodied deer, and I think I remember people saying that he weighed well over 200 pounds. Dad tried to give away some of the meat, but it was so tough that nobody wanted it. We ate on that buck for so long that I hoped Dad never would shoot another one like him!"

Despite John's disappointment with the quality of venison, he did appreciate the beast as a unique trophy that should be preserved. Not long after the hunt, he sent the antlers and cape to a taxidermist named Story in Duluth.

By the time this fascinating photo was taken, the original neck mount already had begun to fall apart. But, even a deteriorating mount could not detract from a set of antlers nearly too wide to fit through a doorway! Photo courtesy of Duncan Dobie.

"Mr. Story took one look at those antlers and offered him $50 cash for them," Ray recalled. "Now, $50 was a lot of money back in those days, probably equal to about half a month's wages. Dad turned him down flat. That deer meant too much to him. But even then, the rack was worth a lot."

The straight-on neck mount of the buck was finished in due time, but sadly, the quality of the work didn't approach the quality of the animal. John was so disappointed that he eventually had another taxidermist remount the antlers on a new cape, this time using a left-turn, head-down form to produce a much more flattering shoulder mount. (The deer has since been remounted several more times.)

John's two eldest sons returned safely from World War I, and he kept hunting deer in the years that followed. His family still needed meat, and for him, that was the most important reason for heading to the woods. Although history failed to record any of the deer John undoubtedly shot in later years, we must assume this veteran hunter got his share. He probably once again concentrated on meat-hunting; after all, he already had one of the world's most impressive typicals on his wall!

John was 81 years old when he passed away in 1947, just as the B&C Club was trying to decide how to structure its new scoring system. By the time the Breen "boys" gave in to the urging of friends to have John's monster scored by this new system in 1960, the 198³/₈-point Roosevelt Luckey buck from New York (Chapter 4) had moved into the top spot in the typical category. That proved no obstacle for the Minnesota monster. Despite more than 40 years of shrinkage and the presence of six abnormal points that cost him 9³/₈ inches of net score, the Breen buck still came in at an astounding 202 net points, the first typical whitetail ever known to crack the magical 200-point barrier! (As we'll see in Chapter 6, several years later the world would discover he had actually not been the earliest 200-point whitetail after all.)

The Breen mount stayed with the family for more than another decade, despite the best efforts of New Hampshire antler collector Dr. Charles ("Chuck") Arnold to purchase it. His first stab at acquiring the historic deer came in the late 1960s with a letter to the Breens. "He wasn't sure whether we spoke English or not so he wrote to us in both French and English," Ray recalled. "He said he collected antlers, and he offered us $1,000 for the rack. After talking it over, we decided not to take his offer because we didn't want the antlers to leave northern Minnesota. After all, Dad's trophy was Minnesota's largest typical whitetail of all time and we felt it should remain in the state. However, by this time

When John's buck was recognized as B&C's official world record in 1960, the hunter himself had long since passed away so sons Ray (left) and Art proudly accepted their dad's award certificate. The rack is now part of Larry Huffman's "Legendary Whitetails" collection. Photo courtesy of Duncan Dobie.

the old mount was beginning to show its age. For a while, we let it hang in a local store but most of the time it hung in our house."

———◆———

"Dad tried to give away some of the meat, but it was so tough that nobody wanted it...I hoped Dad would never shoot another one like him."

———◆———

Even today, Minnesota's most famous deer might still be on display in the state had anyone in an official capacity tried very hard to keep it there. Amazingly, the Breens couldn't find any organization that wanted to put the mount on public display! "We talked to several museums about possibly taking the trophy, but at the time, no one seemed to have much interest in it," Ray said.

That seems hard to fathom today. Many antler connoisseurs claim this buck's combination of extremely long main beams, impressive spread, great mass and overall beauty remains unmatched even today. But, the snubbing by those museums perhaps proved to be a blessing in the long run, for it gave Chuck one more chance to approach the Breens about purchasing the rack. In 1970 he did just that, this time offering the family $1,500 for the mount. "He promised us that he would take good care of the trophy and that he would see to it that it got the kind of recognition it deserved," Ray noted. "We talked it over and decided to take his offer. We packed up the head in a big crate and shipped it to him."

So, out of Minnesota passed the whitetail that is still the one most closely identified with the state. Chuck did his part to keep the deer in the limelight. For years, the Breen buck was one of the center-pieces of his magnificent trophy collection. Then in

the early 1990s, Larry Huffman of Wisconsin purchased this entire collection, along with some other huge racks from across North America, to form the backbone of his "Legendary Whitetails" collection.

Because Larry has displayed the Breen buck at numerous hunting shows around the nation, the antlers have been viewed by many more serious hunters than otherwise would have been the case even had the mount been accepted for display in a Minnesota museum. While John's sons now have all passed on, their wishes continue to be honored. And, you can be sure the Breen buck still is big enough to stun even the most jaded antler enthusiast, just as it did to a bunch of "meat" hunters in Bemidji so long ago. 🦌

JOHN BREEN, MINNESOTA, 1918

Measurements	Right	Left	Difference
No. of points	8	8	
Main beam	31 2/8	31 0/8	2/8
1st point (G-1)	5 6/8	6 3/8	5/8
2nd point (G-2)	12 4/8	11 6/8	6/8
3rd point (G-3)	12 4/8	13 2/8	6/8
4th point (G-4)	9 4/8	11 3/8	1 7/8
5th point (G-5)	–	–	–
1st circ. (H-1)	5 7/8	6 0/8	1/8
2nd circ. (H-2)	5 6/8	5 5/8	1/8
3rd circ. (H-3)	6 1/8	6 1/8	–
4th circ. (H-4)	5 3/8	5 2/8	1/8
Total	94 5/8	96 6/8	4 5/8
Greatest spread		26 7/8	
Inside spread		23 5/8	
Gross typical score		215 0/8	
Assymetry deductions		-4 5/8	
Non-typical deductions		-8 3/8	
Net typical score		202 0/8	

6

JIM JORDAN'S BITTER·SWEET BUCK

---◆---

When a young Wisconsin hunter downed a giant whitetail in 1914, he unwittingly began a 64-year odyssey of triumph and tragedy

---◆---

TITLE: FIFTH B&C TYPICAL WORLD RECORD

SCORE: 206 1/8

HUNTER: JIM JORDAN

LOCATION: BURNETT COUNTY, WISCONSIN

YEAR: 1914

How can you feel sorry for Jim Jordan? After all, he is one of the most famous whitetail hunters in history, a true legend of the sport. The fabulous buck he shot so many years ago remains one of the greatest of all time and in many hunters' minds epitomizes the classic trophy typical whitetail better than any other deer.

There is, however, a tragic side to Jim's story. Once you hear how cruelly fate intervened in his life after that historic hunt, I think you'll agree that he deserves our sympathy more than our envy.

His poignant story began with no hint of glory, before dawn on the cold morning of November 20, 1914. Just south of the small town of Danbury along the Yellow River in northwest Wisconsin, Jim and friend Stuart Davis set out from the farmhouse with a horse and wagon for a day of deer hunting. By the time shooting light arrived, they were in the riverbottom itself, which was covered in fresh snow. Conditions seemed perfect, and the two young friends hoped to make the most of the opportunity.

As usual, garnering a winter's meat supply was the order of the day. Before long, Jim had downed a fat doe. After she was field-dressed and loaded onto the wagon, Stuart decided to head back to the farmhouse with her. Jim, though, was of no mind to quit just yet. The day was young and there was plenty of country left to hunt. As Stuart returned with the doe, Jim walked farther into the riverbottom.

Soon, he found what he had been hoping to see —the fresh tracks of several deer plowing through the snow. One set of tracks was stunningly big, even by the standards of northwest Wisconsin. The hunter quickly fell in behind the tracks and began scanning the terrain ahead for sign of the deer. Jim

With his huge body and rack to match, the Jordan buck must have ruled his stretch of Wisconsin's Yellow River valley. Ron Van Gilder's painting, "The Jordan Buck," helps us visualize what this stately whitetail must have looked like in all his glory back in 1914 when the deer was taken. Print courtesy of the artist and Wild Wings, Inc.

determined that the tracks were leading along a railroad line that ran close to the river. He just kept easing along, ever alert, hands clutching his .25-20 Winchester in anticipation of a possible shot.

And then, the train whistle blew.

Most of us would resent such an interruption of our hunting day, even if we weren't following a fresh set of huge tracks. If that's how Jim felt, he never got much of a chance to think about it. As the whistle blared out across the riverbottom, four deer jumped from their beds in a nearby weed patch. Three were does, but the fourth was clearly the one whose tracks Jim had been dogging—a buck the size of which he had never seen!

Amazingly, all of the deer stopped within rifle range. Jim, recognizing this rare opportunity for what it was, took careful aim and squeezed off a shot at the huge neck of the buck. But to Jim's horror, all four deer all bolted at the sound of the shot,

with the buck heading one way and the does another. He quickly emptied his gun at the departing buck, but there was no indication of a hit.

Jim's heart fluttered as he assessed the chaotic chain of events. Had he missed with every one of those shots? He didn't think so. The buck's bounding trail was easy enough to follow so the hunter once again fell in behind, hoping to find the deer or at least some traces of blood. Soon, it occurred to him that he had a problem: He had fired all of his cartridges at the buck and now was walking around with an empty gun!

After digging around in his various pockets, Jim managed to find a single cartridge, which he quickly shoved into his lever-action rifle. Now the trail could be taken up again without having to return to the farmhouse for more ammo. Jim pressed on without further delay, easily following the huge buck's "plow" marks in the snow.

Finally, as the tracks neared the river, Jim noticed a few flecks of red on the snow, proving that he had indeed drawn blood during his initial flurry of shots. But, there wasn't any indication that the deer was giving up, even though the hunter felt that he was closing the gap between them. As time passed, Jim started catching glimpses of the buck in the brush ahead but was never close enough to risk expending his single cartridge. The chase continued, drawing nearer the river with every passing minute.

As Jim narrowed the distance to his quarry, he realized that both he and the buck were almost to the water's edge. The wounded whitetail seemed to slow, apparently weighing his options. Jim now could see him clearly. Just as he drew a bead with his final cartridge, the buck began to move again, this time heading straight into the flowing water. In short order, he managed to make it the other side of the narrow river, where he stopped to look back. Jim decided to aim for the spine. At the gun's report, the massive buck fell in the very tracks in which he stood.

No other buck in history is more legendary than Jim Jordan's former B&C typical record. The buck is not only huge but amazingly well balanced, with a mere 3 2/8 inches deducted for asymmetry. The great Wisconsin deer officially ruled the B&C record book for 29 years, longer than any other whitetail to date. Photo by Duncan Dobie.

Wisconsin rivers don't make for pleasant wading during mid-November, but Jim wasn't deterred by such minor inconveniences as potential hypothermia. Into the shallow water he plunged, wading across the river to the buck of his dreams. Soon, the soggy hunter was standing over the great deer, confirming that those massive 10-point antlers and the steer-like body were just as big up-close as they had looked at a distance. Whether Jim had been primarily in search of a trophy or just looking for more winter venison, we can't be sure but this buck had delivered both—in spades!

There would be plenty of time later to admire the rack, of course. Right now, standing wet and cold on the riverbank, Jim's first priority was to field-dress the deer. It was then that the hunter realized Stuart had the knife. Back to the farm he went, both to retrieve the blade and to recruit his friend's help in packing out the nearly 400-pound whitetail.

When Jim and Stuart returned with the horse and wagon, the immense buck was nowhere in sight! Bewildered, the hunters tried to figure out what had happened. Could the animal somehow have come back to life? Jim saw there were no deer tracks leading from the scene, so there could be only one answer: The buck had slipped into the shallow river and had been swept away! That theory was proved correct a few minutes later when, as Jim and Stuart reached the first bend downriver, they spotted the dead buck lodged against a rock in midstream. Once again, Jim eagerly waded out to retrieve his trophy. Eventually, he and his buddy got the massive animal gutted and back home.

In 1914, taxidermy was still in its early years but there were a few guys around who could mount deer heads. Among them was George VanCastle, a railroad employee who lived in the small town of Webster, roughly 25 miles from Danbury. As one of the many locals who came by to see the great animal, he detected Jim's pride in the trophy buck. The two men soon struck a deal for George to produce a neck mount of the deer. The fee would be $5.

Now, this is mass! Even today, the Jordan buck remains one of the most massive typicals ever killed. Photo by Duncan Dobie.

With the exception of having had to wade the icy Yellow River several times, Jim's involvement with the buck had been nothing short of wonderful to this point. He had not only shot the biggest deer he or anyone else around had ever seen, but now everyone was talking about his huge trophy. All that remained was the short wait for George to get the head mounted, and a special chapter in Jim's hunting career would be complete. There was no such thing as a record book for trophy deer in those days, but over the coming years, the hunter knew he could look forward to countless hours admiring his massive

memento of a great day afield.

Unfortunately, the wait for the finished mount proved to be *much* longer than the taxidermist had indicated. Shortly after George picked up the deer head from Jim, the taxidermist's wife passed away. George decided to move to Hinckley, Minnesota, roughly 30 miles due west of Danbury. He took the buck's rack and cape with him. A few months later, Jim finally traveled to Webster to check on how the mount was coming and learned of George's move to Hinckley. But, the hunter didn't follow him there because there was no bridge along that stretch of the St. Croix River, which separates Wisconsin from Minnesota. Rather than use an alternate means of getting to Hinckley, Jim decided to bide his time.

Patience is a wonderful quality for any trophy deer hunter to possess; however, in this case, it didn't pay off. While Jim was awaiting the completion of a bridge between Danbury and Hinckley, George was remarrying and moving again—this time to Florida! Jim learned of this development when he finally did make it over to Minnesota, and he surely must have started having serious doubts about the "good deal" he had struck with George. Jim was in no position to go halfway across the nation looking for his lost rack, so he returned home to Danbury a frustrated man.

Even under the best of circumstances, waiting for your deer head to be mounted at a taxidermy shop can seem to take forever. Imagine how Jim must have felt at this point. If anyone asked him about the big buck he had shot, he had nothing to

This historic photo shows Jim proudly lifting the antlers of his great buck in the early 1960s, roughly a half-century after he had lost track of the trophy. But, Jim was soon to discover that his frustrations regarding the deer were far from over. Photo courtesy of Duncan Dobie.

show. Jim apparently didn't have any photos of the deer, and now, no one knew for sure where the rack was. The taxidermist was long gone, and Jim assumed his deer head was as well.

The remainder of the hunter's lengthy life would be spent along his beloved Wisconsin-Minnesota border engaged in various pursuits. For many years, he was a tavern operator. In fact, a few years after Jim shot the massive buck, he and wife Lena actually moved to Hinckley and started a "watering hole" there. We can well imagine that the subject of Jim's trophy buck came up whenever the talk turned to deer hunting (which probably happened frequent-

ly). But, nothing ever happened that gave Jim any hope that he would ever see his treasured buck again. Years of frustration turned into decades. Then in 1958, 44 years after that memorable day on the Yellow River, fate intervened again.

In Sandstone, Minnesota, less than 10 miles north of Hinckley, the decrepit mount of an "antique" deer head turned up in a rummage sale. One of the customers at that sale was a local man named Bob Ludwig, then an employee of the Minnesota Department of Natural Resources and an avid deer hunter. Despite the ragged condition of the mount, Bob knew it was no ordinary whitetail. A deal was struck and he bought the rack for $3, "as is."

This mysterious deer head remained in Bob's possession for several years. Then one day, he chanced upon a magazine article that detailed the B&C Club's system for measuring racks. Out of curiosity, Bob decided to take a stab at scoring the old antlers. When he did, he was amazed to find that the unofficial net score tallied to 205 points – well above the 202-point world record, Minnesota's own John Breen buck! (Chapter 5.)

Could it be true? Could a $3 whitetail of unknown origin really be the greatest in history? Bob could hardly imagine that such good fortune was possible, but from the scoring instructions he had read, there seemed to be no way he could have made a mistake in measuring this classic 5x5 rack. Perhaps someone with more experience in such matters should check it out, he decided, so he mailed his score sheet to official measurer Bernard A. Fashingbauer down in the Twin Cities.

Once Bernard saw the staggering numbers Bob had recorded, he quickly called the trophy owner and asked to schedule an official scoring session. But for some reason, that didn't happen. Months passed with no action taken.

Fortunately, Bernard sometimes found himself in Bob's area. In August 1964, almost a year after first hearing about the buck, the measurer was driving down a road near Sandstone when, miracle of miracles, he spotted Bob's name on a mailbox! Figuring it had to be the home of the trophy owner, Bernard pulled in and checked. Sure enough, it was the right Bob Ludwig and the measurer was invited inside to see the deer for himself.

When Bernard laid eyes on the dilapidated mount, he was glad he had stopped. The 5x5 had tremendously long beams and tines and was ultra-massive…and had a degree of symmetry virtually unseen on world-class racks. In short, he was exactly the type of trophy for which the B&C system had been designed. Bernard's official measurements yielded an entry score of 206 5/8 points, even higher than what Bob had come up with. The mysterious "Sandstone" buck really was a potential world record!

Getting B&C to crown this buck as king of the typicals proved to be little more than a formality. The old mount was shipped to Carnegie Museum in Pittsburgh. There, on February 28, 1966, a panel of judges headed up by George Church, Jr., certified the deer at its final score of 206 1/8 net points.

The outdoor media immediately began publicizing the new record, but some key questions surrounding the Sandstone buck remained unanswered. First, there was no verified kill date, though the writing on the back of the old mount suggested the buck might have been killed in 1914. Secondly, there was no hunter's name to list in the record book. As a result, nobody held out much hope that the hunter or the kill location ever would be known.

This story might well have ended there, except for one more bizarre development—indeed, perhaps the most ironic twist in the history of trophy hunting. As it turns out, not long after his first attempts to measure the rack Bob showed the mount to his uncle. To Bob's amazement, that uncle immediately claimed that the deer was the same one he had shot back in 1914 on Wisconsin's Yellow River! Yes, Bob's uncle was Jim Jordan! Even though a half-century had passed since Jim had last seen the gigantic 10-pointer, he was adamant that this was

the buck he had spent most of his life trying to relocate!

Not surprisingly, Bob was stunned by this claim. He had never imagined that the person who had shot the buck ever would be found—much less that he would be a relative! Even so, Jim's claim wasn't enough to convince Bob that this really was Jim's missing trophy. For one thing, Bob had heard there was a bullet hole in Jim's rack and no such blemish marred this golden crown of antlers. Nor could Jim produce anyone to vouch for his account of the story. There simply wasn't any real proof that this rack was from the monster Jim had lost a half-century earlier. Thus, Bob saw no clear reason to hand over the trophy.

At this point, Jim didn't know what to think. On the positive side, he felt sure his great deer had been found. On the other hand, he didn't know how to prove the antlers were from that buck. Bob had told him about how he had bought the old mount in Sandstone several years earlier. But how had it come to be there?

In time the truth came out, and what a shock it must have been to Jim. The mount had never been taken to Florida at all. Instead, it had been "hiding" all those years in the attic of George's former home in Hinckley! Of course, there was no way for Jim to have known this since he had lost all contact with the taxidermist. Only after a subsequent owner of the property stumbled across the old mount and decided to peddle it for a few dollars did the hunting world have a chance to learn of this amazing animal. Had that not happened or had a fire or other disaster struck during those four decades of storage, we would likely never even have heard of the buck many whitetail hunters still call the most perfect typical in history.

Putting these scattered pieces of the truth back together was no quick or easy job. There was little verifiable proof that the buck had lived and died in Wisconsin, and Minnesota wasn't anxious to relinquish its claim to a second consecutive B&C world record. Among those who believed Jim's claims were Bernard A. Fashingbauer, the man who had first officially measured the rack, and antler collector Dr. Charles "Chuck" Arnold, who had purchased it from Bob in 1968. These men, and others, provided what documentation they could find to support Jim's story. However, there were frustratingly few pieces of evidence upon which to build their case.

About 1970, the newspaper in Grantsburg, Wisconsin, received a letter seeking support for Jim's claim that the new B&C world-record typical was the same buck he had shot in 1914. The letter had been written by Jim himself, who still lived just up the road in Danbury. Larry Huffman, who now owns the original letter, has graciously granted permission to reveal its contents here, with only minimal editing for spelling, punctuation and clarity:

This is the true story about the big buck I killed. The guy I hunted with that hunting season in 1914 was Mr. Stuart Davis. We got a nice doe in the morning, and he put his tag on it and took it home, and I went after the big buck. Stuart helped me pull the deer out of the river and dress it out. Stuart was with me a lot. He got well acquainted with the big deer. I showed him the picture

As a bartender for many years, Jim undoubtedly heard his share of hunting tales but none could match the one Jim himself told. After all, he had killed the greatest typical of all time and couldn't receive credit for it. Bernard A. Fashingbauer, the first official B&C measurer to score the buck, campaigned long and hard to get the old man proper recognition, but the tide was very slow to turn. Bernard took this rare photo of the hunter on April 4, 1978, just a few months before B&C finally accepted Jim as the person who had bagged the world record. Photo courtesy of Bernard S. Fashingbauer.

of the horns, and he said he would never forget them. He said, "They are the horns off the buck you killed and I helped you drag out of the river." I talked to Jim Hegge. His son-in-law has the horns, and they were on a mounted head. They found it in an old, abandoned house up in the attic. The rats and mice had all the hair off the head, and it looked awful. And there was some writing on the board: "killed in 1914."

The head was bought at a rummage sale at Sandstone, Minnesota. Bob Ludwig bought it and dismounted it and just saved the horns and the top of the skull. I talked to another fellow that saw the head when it was mounted, and he said the head never had much neck, about 7 or 8 inches. And I remember that when I butchered the buck, I skinned the neck and cut it off close to the head.

So I know this is the same buck as I killed south of Danbury, Wisconsin, in 1914. And I am sure someone around Danbury or Markville (Minn.) or Webster must remember it. I would like to hear from someone that remembers it. These horns were crated and sent away and came back the world's largest buck deer. I do not want the horns, all I want is the name of killing it.

The guy that has the horns is my nephew. I heard

the guy that mounted the head was VanCastle of Webster.

> *Thank you,*
> *(signed)*
> *James Jordan*
> *Rt. 1, Box 71*
> *Danbury, Wisconsin 54830*

Despite this and other efforts to find anyone who could corroborate his story, Jim continued to have trouble rallying support for his claim. But gradually, the tide began to turn in his favor. When B&C's records committee convened its annual meeting in December 1978, the club finally decided enough evidence had been presented to support Jim's argument. When that meeting ended, the decision was made public: Jim Jordan was the holder of a B&C world record!

Under normal circumstances, this would have prompted an immediate letter to the hunter, notifying him officially of the good news. In the days and weeks that followed, he would have found himself besieged by well-wishers from all corners of North America. But, these were not normal circumstances. You see, there was no hunter to whom such a letter could be sent. Only a couple of months prior to the committee's announcement, Jim had passed away!

At the tender age of 22, he had shot the greatest typical whitetail the world had ever seen. Yet, despite living another 64 years, he would come up just two months short of seeing his efforts to prove what he had done that cold morning in 1914 come to fruition.

Jim did not fail the system; rather, the system failed him. Yes, it's easy to argue that had he never let the antlers out of his sight he could have become the record-holder as soon as the modern B&C scoring system was implemented in the early 1950s. That would have made him a living record-holder for more than a quarter-century. But, can we blame a young woodsman for wanting to have his greatest trophy mounted? Can we blame him for never having sought out a camera to record his achievement before the deer was turned over to George? Can we really gauge the wisdom of any of Jim's decisions regarding this deer? Remember, at the time he shot it, there wasn't even a record book. Jim just did what most of us would have done in the same situation. The fact that fate later dealt him bad cards doesn't necessarily mean he made poor choices.

While nobody since Jim has shot a 200-plus typical in Burnett County, hunters there occasionally get trophies big enough to remind us that the potential still exists. So, who knows? Perhaps someday another world-record whitetail will stand on the edge of the Yellow River and look back at a hunter who is down to his last bullet. If that ever happens again, let's just hope the guy's aim is as good as Jim's was…and that in the years following, his luck is a whole lot better.

JIM JORDAN, WISCONSIN, 1914

Measurements	Right	Left	Difference
No. of points	5	5	
Main beam	30 0/8	30 0/8	–
1st point (G-1)	7 6/8	7 3/8	3/8
2nd point (G-2)	13 0/8	13 1/8	1/8
3rd point (G-3)	10 0/8	10 4/8	4/8
4th point (G-4)	6 0/8	7 5/8	1 5/8
5th point (G-5)	–	–	–
1st circ. (H-1)	6 2/8	6 1/8	1/8
2nd circ. (H-2)	6 2/8	6 4/8	2/8
3rd circ. (H-3)	7 3/8	7 4/8	1/8
4th circ. (H-4)	7 0/8	6 7/8	1/8
Total	93 5/8	95 5/8	3 2/8
Greatest spread		23 6/8	
Inside spread		20 1/8	
Gross typical score		209 3/8	
Assymetry deductions		-3 2/8	
Non-typical deductions		–	
Net typical score		206 1/8	

7

THE FARMER WHO GREW... FAMOUS

Breaking the world record established by the Jordan buck was the dream of every deer hunter...every deer hunter, that is, except the modest Saskatchewan resident who ended up doing it.

TITLE: CURRENT B&C TYPICAL WORLD RECORD

SCORE: 213 5/8

HUNTER: MILO HANSON

LOCATION: BIGGAR, SASKATCHEWAN

YEAR: 1993

Milo Hanson never meant to be a folk hero. The fact that he became one anyway just goes to prove one thing: The spotlight of fame decides when, where and upon whom it will shine.

Before 1993, you would have been hard pressed to find anyone outside the small town of Biggar, Saskatchewan, who had ever even heard of Milo. He and his wife Olive were just another couple of anonymous farmers in a region full of them. Nothing newsworthy had ever happened to the Hansons, and there was no particular reason to think anything would. That was fine with them, for they enjoyed the quiet life they had made for themselves.

But, that anonymity disappeared in the blink of an eye on the morning of November 23, 1993. As the report of Milo's .308 Winchester echoed across the snow-covered prairie, the history of whitetail hunting—and the lives of the Hansons—were forever altered in a way the hunter and his wife never could have imagined. Milo had just shot the highest-scoring typical of all time, a buck that would blow away the long-standing mark of Wisconsin's Jordan buck (Chapter 6) and turn a farm family's peaceful world upside down.

Today, the Hanson buck—all 213 5/8 net B&C points of him—is a well-established part of history, perhaps the most famous deer ever shot by a hunter. Because both hunter and hunted have been featured in scores of magazine articles, videos, television shows and books, sportsmen everywhere recognize Milo and his trophy on sight. And why not? If the goal in trophy hunting is to shoot a great buck, what greater accomplishment is there than shooting the greatest buck of them all—a world-record whitetail?

To fully understand how significant it is for someone to harvest a B&C world-record whitetail, you have to examine the story not only from the hunting world's perspective, but also from that of the hunter himself. Remember, Milo was no jet-set sportsman on a high-dollar hunt. In fact, he says that prior to taking his world-record deer he had never once thought about what it would be like to shoot one. That statement alone provides a hint to just how unprepared he was for the events that would envelop him.

The story of how the huge deer was taken is somewhat involved. While Milo was no jet-set sportsman and had no world-record ambitions, he was an experienced hunter and his story indicates a more serious approach to hunting than is so with many of the other record-holders included in this book. Nonetheless, it is also apparent that fate still played a major role. It was Milo who ultimately got the deer, while several

When North American WHITETAIL *publisher Steve Vaughn and I arrived at Milo's rural home on December 2, 1993, we found a happy hunter who was just coming to grips with what he had achieved. The phenomenal buck, taken by "pushing the bush" on the morning of November 23, 1993, has everything it takes to be a B&C world-record typical —extreme symmetry, tremendous main beams, few non-typical deductions and a wall of long, well-matched tines to go with a most impressive 27 2/8-inch inside spread. Photo by Gordon Whittington.*

other local hunters, arguably no less deserving, did not. Once again, we are reminded that when pursuing a world-class buck it never hurts to have luck in your corner, regardless of how skillful and dedicated you might be.

In this case, Lucky Stroke No.1 obviously was the fact that a deer of such magnitude lived in Milo's hunting area. Throughout modern times, Saskatchewan's rolling farmlands, pastures and conifer forests have been consistent producers of trophy bucks, but even there, a 200-class typical is extremely rare. According to B&C's listings as of this writing, only Bruce Ewen's 202 5/8-pointer from Archerwill (1992) and Pete Swistun's 200 2/8-pointer from Spiritwood (1983) had officially cracked that barrier before Milo's buck came along. So despite Saskatchewan's well-deserved reputation as a hotspot for world-class whitetails, nothing in its history suggested the province was likely to produce a 213 5/8-point typical. Nor was this deer's true size known

Ron Van Gilder's painting, "The Hanson Buck," captures Milo's world-record buck as he might have looked traveling across the farm-country landscape near Biggar, Saskatchewan, early in the fall of 1993 when Milo finally caught up with the wide-racked deer. Painting courtesy of the artist and Wild Wings, Inc.

prior to Milo's historic hunt, though the animal had been seen on a number of occasions.

Perhaps the first known sighting occurred during the 1992 rifle season, when local school bus driver Jim Angelopoulos reported seeing an exceptional buck in the area. Because Jim wasn't a hunter, nobody in Biggar was sure he had really seen a world-class buck, even though he later said he had spotted the animal again on his bus route. For the rest of 1992, there were no other sightings of the deer.

Word of a huge buck began circulating again the next summer; however, this time the source was one of the Hansons' closest neighbors. In mid-summer, the man told Milo he had seen a tremendous, velvet-racked whitetail not far from his home, which lay within the overall area Milo and friends hunted. Still, the buck's true size remained a mystery, not only because of the velvet on the rack but also

because the man who had spotted the deer wasn't an avid trophy hunter. Even so, Milo knew it would take a major-league buck to get the guy's attention, as this one clearly had.

The farming life offers many advantages, to be sure, but having plenty of free time during late summer and early fall isn't one of them. Milo was eager to pursue the buck his neighbor had told him about, for he felt there was a good chance the deer spent at least some time in Milo's traditional hunting area. Unfortunately, that pursuit couldn't begin until the November 15 rifle opener because of the many farm projects to be finished in the meantime, including harvesting the wheat crop and working the cattle before winter arrived.

The early archery and muzzleloader seasons began without Milo. All he could do as he took care of business was listen to reports to see if anyone else had taken the deer, which by now was being discussed by many hunters in the area. Lucky Stroke No.2 for Milo came when September and October passed without the buck having been shot. By the time November 15 rolled around, Milo and Olive had finished the bulk of their field work and the big buck apparently was still on the loose. At long last, it was time to hunt.

The tactics most widely used by U.S. whitetail hunters are still somewhat novel in western Canada's wide-open country. Whereas an American might pursue a specific buck by scouting for likely stand locations and then trying to execute a successful ambush, resident gun hunters in the prairie regions of Saskatchewan, Alberta and Manitoba often have more faith in forcing the action. Due both to the typically frigid weather and the fact that a few deer are scattered over a huge area, the customary Canadian practice is to cruise the backroads in search of deer or their fresh tracks. Once located, deer pushes (drives) on foot are then conducted through likely cover whenever the bucks aren't moving on their own. For many hunters, these mobile tactics are much more enjoyable than turn-

At 213 5/8 points, Milo Hanson's current B&C world-record typical is in a league of his own, beating Jim Jordan's long-standing former record by 7 4/8 inches. That's particularly amazing when you realize that bucks 2 through 10 on the list all are bunched within 5 7/8 inches of each other! Photo by Gordon Whittington.

ing into a human Popsicle while on-stand and under certain conditions they can be far more productive.

This is exactly the tactic Milo and his hunting buddies had employed for many years. They typically drove the roads early in the morning hoping to catch a big buck away from the security of cover. If they failed to find the right deer or couldn't get a shot, they then conducted small, well-organized drives (a tactic commonly called "pushing the bush") through scattered pockets of cover during the bright-light hours. Late afternoon, the party would spread out again to ride the roads hoping to spot bucks heading out to feed or chase does.

This is a very effective strategy, and Milo had taken many bucks, some quite respectable, while employing it. In fact, he had filled a tag every season since the age of 16, when he started deer hunting near his birthplace of Eastend in southwestern Saskatchewan. Most of the other guys in his hunting party had enjoyed similar successes over the years, so much so that they really didn't worry if there was little time to scout before hunting season began. The "ride-and-push" approach had been good to them, and they were once again counting on it to come through.

On Monday morning, November 15, a handful of guys met at Milo's place as usual, eager to discuss the game plan for the season opener. The party that day consisted of Milo, Walter Meger, Adam Evashenko, Walter Gamble and Gerry Yaroshko. Talk centered around the huge buck known to inhabit the area, even though none of these men had ever laid eyes on the animal itself. A decision was made to hunt that buck until he was bagged or the plan proved useless. As dawn broke that gun season in the North Country, the guys paired up and headed out.

What nobody in the party could imagine was that Milo's Lucky Stroke No.3 was about to occur. At 8 a.m. on that opening morning, another local hunter spotted the deer everyone was looking for. Dwayne Zagoruy was the young man's name, and he was a friend of the Hansons. In fact, he had previously shot a big buck with a .243 rifle borrowed from Milo's wife, Olive. On this day, however, he was using his own weapon—a rifle that, unfortunately for him, was soon to deliver one of the most infamous misses in whitetail history.

Dwayne spotted the big buck going into a large "bluff" (woodlot) in the area. The deer was travel-

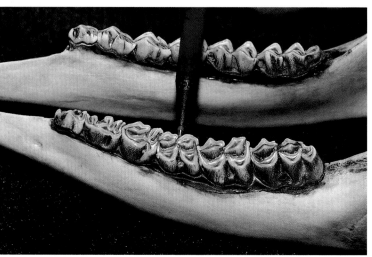

Many hunters were surprised to learn Milo's world-record typical wasn't an oldtimer. By comparing this buck's jawbone (above) to those of known-age deer, whitetail expert Dr. James Kroll concluded that the animal was no more than 4 1/2 years of age. As the photo clearly shows, the buck's molars were still quite sharp, i.e., lightly worn, when he was harvested, indicating relative youth. Photo by Gordon Whittington.

ing alone, but because there was too much brush in the way, the hunter didn't feel he could sneak close enough for a shot. So, Dwayne sneaked out of the spot and went to the home of friend Bill Litwinow, who wasn't yet back from working the night shift at a nearby salt mine. Dwayne waited for Bill to get home and told him what he had seen. Though tired after working all night, Bill eagerly agreed to help push the buck out for a shot.

The plan nearly worked to perfection…almost. Dwayne hid in an ideal spot at the end of the patch of cover while Bill flushed the deer in his direction. When the monster broke cover, he was just 50 yards from Dwayne but hardly presented an easy target. The hunter tried his best to get his crosshairs on the rapidly moving target, but the deer was zigzagging all over the place. Frantically, Dwayne fired a shot but failed to connect. The buck bounded over a hill and onto a tract of posted land, cutting off any chance of further pursuit.

Milo and his friends were in the same general area at the time but had no idea another hunter had shot at the buck. They hunted all morning without noting any evidence of the huge whitetail everyone had been talking about. All they saw were other hunters, who clearly had invaded the area en masse.

"I think the deer must have spent most of the

day on that posted ground because we never got a look at him," Milo later reflected. "Then late in the afternoon, Walter (Meger) spotted him way off coming out of that area. All Walter could see was the antlers sticking up in the sky on the horizon, from about a quarter-mile away."

In this situation, the buck didn't offer a reasonable shot. Even so, from the perspective of Milo's hunting party, the good news far outweighed the bad. They now knew that the deer was still alive and

---

Late in the afternoon, Walter spotted him…all Walter could see was the antlers sticking up in the sky on the horizon, from about a quarter-mile away.

---

in the area, and not just a rumor. Walter was a veteran trophy hunter who knew a big buck when he saw one, and he now could confirm that this one was a giant. No wonder everyone was after him!

The next morning, Milo and friends went afield hopeful of getting a crack at the buck but their early patrol turned up nothing. Finally, they decided to check the snow for sign that the deer had moved off the posted ground during the night. Sure enough, a set of fresh tracks led from the edge of the posted property toward an uncut rye field owned by Rene Igini, one of the guys who frequently hunted with Milo's party. At the time, Rene was in northeastern Saskatchewan hunting moose with John Yaroshko but had told the guys it was all right to hunt his land when he wasn't there. So, Milo's party went to check out the rye field.

There really was nothing special about the size of the buck's tracks. In fact, the deer's feet—and his body, for that matter—were much less impressive than anyone might expect of a world record. "You

would think a buck with a rack like that would be really big-bodied but he wasn't," Milo said. "His track was about the size of a big doe's. Many tracks in our hunting area were much larger than his. That's one of the reasons this buck ended up being so hard to hunt."

When the hunting party checked Rene's field, they found it laced with great numbers of deer tracks of every description. Sorting out which tracks might have been made by the small-footed buck was impossible. The hunters found themselves stalemated. "We didn't know where to go from there," Milo admitted. "There were lots of other hunters out, and we couldn't seem to get on the buck's track. So, we just moseyed away to some other areas we had permission to hunt. Walter Gamble ended up shooting a nice 4-pointer (8-pointer by Eastern count). Late in the afternoon, we came back and sat on some good vantage points trying to catch a glimpse of the big buck but didn't see him."

Wednesday, the third day of rifle season, began in more promising fashion when Walter Meger again spotted the buck at long range. Unfortunately, any hopes of catching up with the trophy animal were soon dashed. The deer's trail once more was lost in the track-littered rye field. Despite spending the rest of the day pushing bush in the area surrounding that field, Milo's party turned up no more traces of the buck.

As the hunt progressed, guys came and went. On Thursday, Adam and Gerry left to hunt moose in another part of the province. On Friday, Rene and John Yaroshko returned from their own moose hunt. Through it all, the one frustrating constant was the party's inability to get a shot at the big buck. In fact, after Walter's sighting early on Wednesday morning, no more was seen of the animal the remainder of opening week.

Still, there was an important development, and one that had absolutely nothing to do with luck. On Thursday, while acting as a stander on a drive, Milo had a chance at another good buck that was just standing there within easy shooting range. Milo pondered whether or not he should shoot and end his season. As if aware what glory the future held, he put his gun down and let the deer escape.

By law, there's no Sunday hunting in Saskatchewan. In this case, it was probably just as well. Everyone in the hunting party was tired, and there was no new snow for tracking. For his part, Milo also had an extra-long list of chores to do. He not only spent Sunday catching up on them but Monday as well. The other guys hunted on Monday but saw nothing of the monster deer.

Come Monday night, Milo still had plenty of work to keep him busy on Tuesday. However, between a bit of new snow and strong winds, he knew the old deer tracks would be covered. Milo considered his options. He then made what later would prove to be the best decision of his deer-hunting career: He called up his buddies to tell them he would be joining them for the Tuesday hunt.

The next dawn found Walter Meger and Rene watching from one vantage point and Milo and

History being reported to a stunned whitetail world! In the February 1994 issue of North American WHITETAIL, *we broke the story of the new world record, changing the longstanding whitetail-record landscape forever and launching Milo on his path to becoming a true folk hero to millions of whitetail hunters. Cover courtesy of Game & Fish Publications.*

John from another. Not long after dawn, the party got a huge break when Walter and Rene spotted the big buck. They even managed to get off several shots at him at long range but none connected, representing Lucky Stroke No.4 for Milo. The buck, as well as the two does with him, promptly disappeared into heavy cover. When the four hunters met up a few minutes later to discuss strategy, the mood was distinctly upbeat since the odds finally had swung their way. The men knew where the buck was; they had fresh snow to track him; and they had nearly a full day to devote to the chase. This was the opportunity every deer hunter in the area had hoped for.

Rene, an expert tracker, drew the assignment of bird-dogging the buck's trail. John, Milo and Walter moved into likely positions for an ambush. It didn't take Rene long to determine that the tracks were heading northward. This was Lucky Stroke No.5 since it meant the deer was moving away from the posted land and into an area all of the hunters knew quite well. To ensure that the buck didn't double back onto posted property, Milo set up at the south end of the cover in which Rene was tracking. John went to the southeast side and Walter to the northwest.

Almost immediately after Rene entered the south end of the thick stuff, the buck made a run for it, heading out the north end and flagging all the way. "I could see him over the willows from where I was, maybe a half-mile away," Milo noted. "I figured it couldn't be him flagging like a doe but it was. By the time he came into view, he was a long way from me and nobody could get a good shot at him. But, he was making a mistake, going north all the time."

The men saw that the buck had gone into another small bluff, and they moved on ahead to set up another drive. Not long after Rene entered that cover, on what he assumed was the buck's trail, a quandary arose. The track he was on led to an old road where several deer recently had crossed. Was the buck one of them? The guys all studied the sign and decided he had indeed crossed the road, meaning he was heading toward Rene's rye field. Despite the recent snow, they knew that field was likely full of fresh deer tracks, which figured to once again confuse the pursuers.

Over the next couple of hours, the men looked for the buck in various parts of Rene's pasture but turned up nothing. Milo eventually checked for tracks on a road circling the entire area but saw no fresh tracks to indicate that any deer had left the block. After hearing this, Walter suggested the hunters keep plugging away because the buck was in there somewhere.

Sure enough, around 10:30 that morning Walter caught another glimpse of the big deer, this time heading onto the Hansons' land. "The buck ran into 30 or 40 acres of willow and small poplars (aspen)," Milo recounted, "an area we've always called the 'willow run.' I'm sure he had been in there before because it's thick and hard to hunt."

The deer still was moving northward so Milo and John looped around to the north end of the cover. Walter covered the west side, and Rene fol-

lowed the track into the bluff's south end. Then, Lucky Stroke No.6 occurred.

"If the deer had wanted to stay in that willow run and hide, I don't know that we could have gotten him to come out," Milo admitted. "But, he wanted to get out of there and loop back around to a similar patch of willows on my neighbor's land. He came out, trying to get over there, but he spotted me standing there. Before I could get off a shot, he turned back to the north. Now he was about 150 yards from me, broadside but running flat out. I missed him and so did John (Lucky Stroke No.7). It was a tough opportunity because the deer was really moving."

The hunters reconvened, plotted strategy and conducted another drive on the piece of cover into which the buck had disappeared. What they didn't know was that he had gone through that bluff without stopping. The drive turned up nothing except a set of tracks. It was on to the next bluff to do it all over again. This time, they hoped for better results.

That's exactly what the hunters got!

———◆———

"Now he was about 150 yards from me, broadside but running flat out. I missed him and so did John…"

———◆———

Milo and John set up on the west side of the bluff. Walter covered the north end. Minutes after the push began, as Rene was sneaking along the buck's trail, a shot rang out. It came from the west edge of the bluff, courtesy of Milo's Model 88 Winchester.

"The buck came out and turned, giving me only a shot at him running straight away," Milo said. "He was probably only about 100 yards from me when I touched the trigger. As soon as I shot, I could see steam pouring off his back. That's when he went down to his knees, and I thought he was dead."

John had been close enough to see these events unfold but hadn't been in position to shoot. (Lucky Stroke No.8 for Milo.) "You got him!" John hollered to his friend, and both men put down their rifles. Milo even left his spent .308 cartridge in the chamber, assuming he wouldn't be needing to fire another shot. That assumption was dashed only moments later when the buck scrambled to his feet and bolted for the next bluff...without either man getting off another shot!

Unknown to anyone at that moment, Milo's Lucky Stoke No.9 had just occurred—though it perhaps could better be classified as a lucky "non-break." You see, a large chunk of the bullet that had knocked the buck down had continued on, striking and becoming lodged in the back of the buck's right main beam just below the G-2 tine! The impact had blown out some small antler fragments and created a significant crack in the antler. Had the beam actually snapped, as might have been the case with a direct hit or a deflected hit from a more powerful cartridge, the rack would have been rendered unscorable for B&C. Instead, it held fast.

Taking up the buck's trail, Milo entered the next bluff and scanned the cover from a high vantage point. Soon, he spotted the wounded deer and squeezed off another round, striking the animal in the neck and angling back into the shoulder. The buck dropped.

Walking up to the buck, Milo realized he had downed the biggest whitetail of his life but never pondered the possibility of a world record. For now, he just wanted the deer dead. Because he could see

the buck's head was still up, he knew the job wasn't quite finished. He decided to shoot once more, this time at the right side of the head!

Lucky Stroke No.10 was another *"non-break."* Instead of hitting the skull with full impact as intended (and possibly snapping the rack's skull plate), the bullet went a bit to the left, striking near the ball joint at the junction of the skull and neck. The magnificent buck's head dropped to the ground at the sound of the shot with no further damage to the antlers or their support structure. Finally, around 11 a.m. on Tuesday, November 23, 1993, the greatest typical whitetail in history was dead!

My own involvement in this story began around 10:15 a.m. Eastern Standard Time on Wednesday, December 1. That's when the phone rang in my office at *North American WHITETAIL* in Marietta, Georgia, and I found myself listening to a distinctly Canadian voice. "Mr. Whittington," the man said, "my name is Jim Wiebe, and I've just measured a whitetail rack that will be a new world record in the typical category." In a decade of chasing down tales of trophy bucks, this certainly wasn't the first time that I had heard talk of a potential No.1 typical. The difference here, however, was that this rumor was true! Jim's description of the rack was offered with such clarity and conviction that I quickly found myself believing his story. In fact, I was so certain of it that I didn't even bother to write down all of the rack measurements he was offering me.

I asked Jim if representatives from our magazine could meet with the hunter the next day, provided we could get more than halfway across the continent on such short notice. He checked with Milo and confirmed that a meeting would be fine. So, less

————◆————

"You got him!" John hollered, and both men put down their rifles. But the buck scrambled to his feet and bolted for the next bluff...without either man getting off another shot!

————◆————

than three hours after the first phone call about the deer had reached our office, *North American WHITETAIL* publisher Steve Vaughn and I settled into our seats on a jet bound for Canada.

Early the next day, we met up with Jim at his home northwest of Saskatoon and then followed him to the Hanson farm, where we arrived in mid-morning. When Jim knocked, Milo and several of his hunting buddies came to the door. As I reached out to shake Milo's big right hand, I asked him, "Is this the magic trigger finger?"

"Yeah, that's the one!" he responded with a hearty chuckle.

Steve and I stepped inside and instantly felt welcome. Several minutes of pleasant conversation followed, but the anxiety inside us must have shown. Finally, Milo decided we had suffered long enough. "I guess you'd like to see the deer," he said. With that, he started toward a closed door in the basement.

Just as Milo will undoubtedly never forget his first glimpse of the buck, I'll never forget mine. As we walked through that door, my eyes focused on an image no one in the outdoor media had seen in decades—the rack of what was sure to be a new world-record typical whitetail. Few words were spoken for several minutes, and I can't recall what any of them were anyway because I really wasn't paying attention to anyone in the room. Perhaps I had been secretly dreading this moment, fearful that we had come all this way only to learn the buck had been horribly overstated. Perhaps it was just the sheer adrenaline rush of knowing I was on the scene of history in the making. Whatever the case, I felt a tingle come over me as my eyes locked onto a rack

Milo and Olive had begun to experience just what life in the fish bowl was all about… they had an answering machine installed for the first time in their lives.

the likes of which I had only imagined.

You would figure that anyone who has just flown most of the way across North America on a moment's notice to see a potential No.1 whitetail rack would want to verify its size with a tape measure and some serious number-crunching. It's a logical assumption, but that isn't what happened. Instead, Steve and I simply strolled around the rack, which was still on the uncaped skull, and marveled at what could only be described as a miracle of nature. We never asked for a tape, pencil or pad. We didn't need to. Any experienced whitetail chaser could tell this was world-record material, a rack clearly big enough and balanced enough to beat the Jordan buck with inches to spare. Our trip had not been in vain.

The first authorized magazine feature on this phenomenal animal appeared only a few frantic weeks later in the February 1994 issue of *North American WHITETAIL*. Along with the story of the hunt and details on the potential score, we published a number of exclusive photos from the scene. Unfortunately, Milo's own efforts to get photos of himself with the dead deer hadn't been very productive—only one frame had turned out—but we had enough shots to get by.

Even before that first story rolled off the presses, Milo and Olive had begun to experience just what life in the fish bowl was all about. No sooner had Steve and I left the farm on December 2 that the Hansons' phone began to ring off the farmhouse wall. Nobody in the family could get much work done, so they had an answering machine installed for the first time in their lives. Even while walking down the street shortly afterward in Saskatoon, an hour from his home, Milo was occasionally recognized by passersby as "the man who shot the big deer." Slowly, the once-private farmer began to realize he was becoming a public figure.

The response to our magazine's exclusive first feature on the buck was as gratifying as it was immediate. The hunting public was overjoyed that the "impossible" had happened! A jolt of excitement surged through the whitetail community at warp speed, and the clamor for Milo's time hit a new high. Steve and I had already arranged for the Hansons to attend the January 1994 SHOT (Shooting, Hunting & Outdoor Trade) Show in Dallas as guests of *North American WHITE-TAIL.* There the happy hunter graciously autographed hundreds of copies of our magazine for attendees. Naturally, all of them had to shake Milo's meaty right hand—trigger finger and all—and ask him to tell the story just one more time. To his credit, in every case he did.

In all of whitetail history, such immediate fame had never before come to any person. After all, Milo's deer was the first hunter-killed buck big enough to become a B&C world record since the "golden age" of serious trophy deer hunting began in the early 1980s. As a result, there was a pent-up craving for a new "hero" on the whitetail scene. Milo's good fortune had made him the chosen one —willing or not.

Grand are the thoughts of having people ask you to recount the story of how you, the mighty hunter, toppled the greatest typical buck the world has ever seen. Visions of such glory doubtless keep some sportsmen awake since taking a world record is arguably the pinnacle of hunting achievement, just as scoring the winning touchdown in the Super Bowl is the ultimate football fantasy. But while every football player prays for a chance to shine in front of the crowd and the cameras, the same can't be said of every hunter. Most simply like to spend time in the woods. While all of them probably hope to shoot the biggest buck around, true sportsmen appreciate trophy deer for what they are, not for what such animals can do to enhance a person's reputation or bank account.

That description fits Milo perfectly, for he has been a reluctant hero from the start. This isn't to say he dislikes dealing with the public. To the contrary, since having his buck officially recognized as No.1 at B&C's June 1995 banquet in Dallas, Milo has hauled the mount to numerous hunting shows and other functions, most of them at least a thousand

Milo has traveled countless miles to outdoor shows to display his world-record buck, and he and sidekick Ron Boucher (left) drive the trophy to each and every show—whether in North Carolina, California or anywhere in between! Photo courtesy of Ron Boucher.

miles from his home. This is a particularly serious undertaking since the head's special display case (which, like the shoulder mount itself, is the outstanding work of taxidermist Bub Hill) weighs more than 200 pounds! This beautiful but bulky assemblage has a built-in lighting system and must always be driven to show sites, even those on the other end

---◆---

In the end, history's top-ranked typical whitetail was shot by a man who had no world-record ambitions, traveled nowhere and had only the price of a resident permit invested in the hunt.

---◆---

of the continent. All this travel and time away from family and home, plus the occasional hassle with U.S. customs agents, certainly hasn't made cashing in on the clamor for the world-record typical quick or easy for a farmer living in western Saskatchewan.

The only simple way to make big money with any world-record deer is to sell the rack to a collector. As of this writing, Milo has showed no serious interest in doing so, despite offers of up to $125,000 in U.S. funds. By all indications, he's perfectly content just to keep displaying the mount at hunting shows, as long as none of this "celebrity" business gets in the way of family, friends or farming.

Now that Milo's story has become part of whitetail lore, it's hard not to find a bit of humorous irony in the way it played itself out, given the sometimes high-stakes atmosphere of trophy hunting today. You see, for years tens of thousands of us serious whitetail enthusiasts from around the globe have traveled to the prairie provinces of Canada and to other great trophy regions and spent thousands

of dollars, each dreaming that perhaps we would be the one to shoot a new world record. Indeed, for a crack at a buck netting 213 5/8 points, many hunters would have traveled anywhere in the solar system and paid any fee. Yet in the end, history's top-ranked typical was shot by a man who had no world-record ambitions, traveled nowhere and had no more invested in the hunt than the price of a resident deer permit.

For a folk hero, perhaps that is the way it should be.

MILO HANSON, SASKATCHEWAN, 1993

Measurements	Right	Left	Difference
No. of points	8	6	
Main beam	28 4/8	28 4/8	–
1st point (G-1)	6 5/8	6 0/8	5/8
2nd point (G-2)	12 4/8	13 1/8	5/8
3rd point (G-3)	13 6/8	14 0/8	2/8
4th point (G-4)	11 4/8	11 5/8	1/8
5th point (G-5)	5 0/8	7 0/8	2 0/8
1st circ. (H-1)	4 6/8	5 0/8	2/8
2nd circ. (H-2)	4 2/8	4 2/8	–
3rd circ. (H-3)	4 3/8	4 2/8	1/8
4th circ. (H-4)	4 2/8	4 2/8	–
Total	**95 4/8**	**98 0/8**	**4 0/8**
Greatest spread		29 0/8	
Inside spread		27 2/8	
Gross typical score		**220 6/8**	
Assymetry deductions		-4 0/8	
Non-typical deductions		-3 1/8	
Net typical score		**213 5/8**	

8

LEGEND
OF THE
ROCKIES

Jim Brewster's list of achievements made him a key figure in the history of western Canada. But, it was the whitetail he shot in 1905 that made him a legend among deer hunters.

TITLE: FIRST B&C NON-TYPICAL WORLD RECORD

SCORE: 245 7/8

HUNTER: JIM BREWSTER

LOCATION: ELK RIVER, BRITISH COLUMBIA

YEAR: 1905

Perhaps nowhere else in North America are the views as stunning as in the Canadian Rockies, a string of rugged peaks angling northwestward from southern British Columbia and Alberta. Every year, visitors from all over the world come here to ski, hike, fish, hunt or simply take in some of the greatest scenery imaginable.

It wasn't always such a popular place, though. In fact, less than a century ago, most of the rugged region was still largely unexplored by the white man and only the hardiest of souls dared venture deep into this wilderness. Skyscraping mountains, unbroken forests, surging rivers, often-harsh weather and formidable predators, including grizzly bears, wolves and mountain lions, conspired to make any foray into the backcountry a true challenge. Some early explorers returned with horrific tales of close calls with nature's cruel side; others never returned at all.

Such stories made the Canadian Rockies one of the continent's last wild regions to be explored and settled, and perhaps rightly so. However, if the potential rewards are great enough, some folks will go anywhere. Jim Brewster apparently was just such a man.

Just after the turn of the century, Jim was among the brave souls who blazed a trail through this wilderness and opened it up to outdoorsmen from around the world. Today, the Brewster name is well known in and around the mountain town of Banff, Alberta, now a well-developed tourist destination. Still, his trailblazing exploits are not what earned him a place in this book. What we really care about here is the fact that one day in 1905, while in the vicinity of Elk River, British Columbia, Jim raised his rifle and shot a world-record whitetail.

As the first non-typical buck officially recognized as a world record under the modern B&C scoring system, the animal occupies a particularly noteworthy place in deer-hunting lore. When I began researching this story, I assumed it wouldn't take long to learn the facts. After all, Jim was a historically significant man and many members of the Brewster family still live in that region. However, it turns out that few of them are avid deer hunters and that details about where and how Jim shot his amazing deer apparently were never well chronicled.

Though time has obscured much about Jim's monumental hunt, we can get to know the man, thanks in part to the May 1947 commemorative issue of *Trail Riders of the Canadian Rockies,* the official bulletin of the organization of the same name. Jim, one of that group's most prominent members, had died suddenly on February 11 of that year, just one day after

Hanging without fanfare on its original mount in the dining room of the Mount Royal Hotel in Banff, Alberta, Jim Brewster's wide buck from 1905 was B&C's first-ever non-typical world record. The buck achieved his net score of 245 7/8 points despite a whopping 31 4/8 inches of deductions for asymmetry! Photo by Tom Foss.

celebrating his 65th birthday in Banff. Because he had been such a key figure in the Trail Riders since its inception, the entire bulletin was devoted to his memory. It is clear from this publication, as well as from other information, that he was one of Canada's most influential and respected figures of that era…and a true credit to hunting.

Jim was born in Kingston, Ontario, on February 10, 1882. When he was two, parents John and Isabel

Brewster moved the family west to Winnipeg, Manitoba. Three years after that, following the Riel Rebellion, they traded the flatland life for one in the mountains, moving farther west to the then-remote outpost of Banff. It was in this scenic region that the Brewster fortune would be made.

Even at the tender age of 10, Jim knew western Canada's natural resources had commercial potential. He and brother Bill already were hiring-out to guide fishing parties. Not long afterwards, the boys became full partners in their own guiding and outfitting business. By the turn of the century, they had formed a livery business known as Brewster Brothers. In 1910, Bill sold out to his brother, who kept the company going for another five years.

During this period, Jim began the successful conversion of his business from "horse power" to "horsepower," acquiring buses and automobiles to help him take tourists where they wanted to go. That was the beginning of what would become Brewster Transport Company, which is still a thriving Banff business owned by the family. By the time of Jim's death right after World War II, the company had a number of buses and cars, along with "fleets" of saddle and pack horses, in such scattered locations as Lake Louise, Emerald Lake, Calgary,

Golden, Watertown and Field. What's more, Jim owned Sunshine Ski Lodge, Columbia Icefield Chalet and Mount Royal Hotel, three facilities that catered directly to the ever-growing flow of tourists into the Canadian Rockies.

You would gather from these facts that Jim was a man of considerable clout, and you would be right. He was described as a "personal friend" of the Duke of Windsor, and he met all of the male members of the British Royal House. In 1901, at the ripe age of 19, he assisted the visiting King George V, who needed someone to act as his interpreter in conversations with the local Indians. Jim also accompanied the king and queen of Siam on a horseback ride during their visit to Banff. It is even said that the Will Rogers film, *So This Is London,* was in reality based on Jim's adventures while he was in England as a guest of the Earl of Suffolk.

Such honors and deeds are the stuff of legends, and Jim clearly was one. Yet, according to the bulletin, while he was a man who participated in great adventures, he was "never one to talk about them." It seems he left that to others, who were only too happy to recount his rich life. Unfortunately for today's deer hunters, that thorough documentation apparently did not include his 1905 trip into the wilds of southeastern British Columbia, leaving us to speculate about the events surrounding the greatest of his many big-game trophies.

In recent years, there has been increasing interest

By the early days of the 20th century, when this photo was taken, young Jim Brewster had already established a successful expedition company to carry sportsmen into the rugged wilderness of the Canadian Rockies on horseback. It was somewhere around this time that Jim shot his world-record whitetail near Elk River, British Columbia. Photo courtesy of Whyte Museum of the Canadian Rockies, Banff, Alberta.

in whitetail hunting in the northern Rockies. Because this part of the world has traditionally been regarded as the home of mule deer, elk, moose, bighorn sheep and mountain goats, many hunters think whitetails have only recently moved into the region. That's hardly the case.

This animal has lived in the northern Rockies for thousands of years — long enough, in fact, to have developed into an identifiable subspecies, the northwestern whitetail *(Odocoileus virginianus ochrourus).* This refutes the modern idea that the species gained a foothold in the region only after settlers began clearing timber. Also, the artifacts and lore of native peoples in the northern Rockies suggest that the whitetail has been in the region for a very long time.

It is unlikely that southeastern British Columbia was overrun with deer in Jim's day. Even now, densities there are relatively low. Still, many of the whitetails that did inhabit the region at that time undoubtedly had a chance to reach prime age. After all, there were very few hunters around and most of them were searching for more glamorous big-game species.

While whitetails can be found at elevations as high as timberline in the northern Rockies, they are generally concentrated in the drainages, where there is better food and more protection from the often-harsh elements. Elk River, lying just west of the Continental Divide, fits the description of a prime mountain whitetail area. The Elk begins right along the Alberta-British Columbia border southeast of Banff and flows almost due south for better than 50 miles before angling off to the southwest, eventually entering the Kootenay River only a few miles above the Montana border. For much of its length, the Elk River valley is still pristine glacial country. Elk Lakes Provincial Park, which today encompasses the upper end of the valley, is one of North America's wildest places. You can be sure that the entire area was even wilder back in 1905 when Jim, then only 23, downed what would become his most celebrated trophy.

The young hunter almost certainly shot the deer during one of his countless horseback forays into this rugged backcountry. He and brother Bill were then partners in their outfitting business, and they spent much more time in the woods than in Banff. Jim clearly had big dreams for his business and must have spent untold hours searching for new trails and potential sites for camps. The phenomenal mountain scenery – and tourism potential – of the Elk River basin probably lured him there, though speculation has it that he might have been prospecting

During Jim's lifetime, the huge non-typical hung in plain view of his easy chair. Around the time this photo was taken, the king and queen of England paid a visit to the Brewster home and admired the hunter's many big-game trophies. Photo courtesy of Whyte Museum of the Canadian Rockies, Banff, Alberta.

for gold when he encountered the giant buck. But, I have no evidence that was the case.

This we do know. Quite a few years after the buck was shot, Jim decided to register him with B&C, though the club had not yet published any sort of record book at the time. But by 1932, Prentiss Gray had indeed put together the 1st edition of *Records of North American Big Game.* When that first book came off the press, the top listing for whitetails belonged to Jim Brewster with a deer shot in 1905 near Elk River. (The entry actually listed James G. Brewster as the hunter but that was an error. Jim's middle name was Irvine.)

By today's standards, it would not be totally correct to call the Brewster buck an official "world record" on the basis of that listing since there was not yet a scoring system per se. Bucks were simply ranked according to "length of outside curve," which we would now call "length of main beam." This deer's "outside curve" was shown to be 30 3/4 inches. The next nine racks listed had beams ranging from 30 1/2 inches down to 28 inches. Also provided in the listings was the "circumference of main beam," (4 3/4 inches for the Brewster

With tines as long as 17 2/8 inches, great mass and an inside spread of 25 3/8 inches, Jim's buck is truly magnificent. The left antler has a gross typical score of 108 5/8 inches, perhaps the highest such total ever for a basic 5-point side! Photo by Tom Foss.

buck); "greatest spread," (33 1/2 inches); and "number of points on each horn," (12 on one side and 14 on the other).

(Interestingly, listed at 29 1/8 inches "outside curve" was the C.B.D. Garrett buck, a 10x8 non-typical, shown as having been shot at Cranbrook, British Columbia, in 1908. Cranbrook lies only a few miles west of the lower Elk River, adding still more evidence that whitetails have long been entrenched in the area.)

When the 2nd edition of *Records of North American Big Game* was published in 1939, Jim's huge buck again was listed as No.1. It is fortunate that the hunter had these few measurements of the rack recorded when he did because he died five years before the 3rd edition came out in 1952. That volume listed Jim's deer as the first world-record non-typical according to the modern scoring method. Nearly a half-century after the animal had last walked the Elk River valley, Jim's buck received a net score of 245 7/8 points, blowing away all known challengers to his title of "world's biggest whitetail."

We now realize that at the time this deer was announced as a world record he was no longer the biggest buck known. In fact, several with higher scores already had turned up but hadn't yet been officially measured. (One from the 1890s is profiled in Chapter 9; another from around 1940 is discussed in Chapter 28.) While Jim unfortunately did not live long enough to see his buck recognized as No.1 by the modern scoring system, he actually was lucky none of these other monsters was measured any sooner.

It is only fitting that the most historic whitetail ever to come from the Rockies was taken by someone the Stony Indians knew as "Yaha Dun Skun," which means "Mountain Child."

While most world-record bucks are hidden away from the eyes of the public, that is not the case with Jim's outstanding deer. At this writing, the original mount still hangs in the dining room at Banff's Mount Royal Hotel, an establishment once owned by the hunter. That mount, along with some of Jim's other trophy animals, is on loan from great-nephew Joe Brewster. Most guests dining at the hotel never realize they are in the presence of such a

Because Jim did so much to promote the beauty of the Canadian Rockies, a peak overlooking Banff was named in his honor. Here, the legendary outdoorsman poses with Mount Brewster towering in the distance. Photo by N. Morant, courtesy of Canadian Pacific Archives.

historic trophy, but that might be just the way the modest hunter would have wanted it.

Of course, you can't keep a secret of this sort from everyone and local legend has it that the Brewster buck occasionally has been targeted by burglars. In fact, I heard from one source that a thief once slipped into the dining room after it had closed, grabbed the mount off the wall and then actually called a taxi to take him out of the area. The cabby, to his credit, is said to have recognized the old mount and, rather than whisking the guy out of

---

A lofty peak overlooking Banff has been named Mount Brewster.

Banff, drove him straight to the local police station instead! Such tales, whether fact or fiction, certainly add to the mystique of this enormous deer.

We do know that when Great Britain's King George VI and Queen Elizabeth visited Banff in

1939, it was Jim who chauffeured them around the area in a horse-drawn buggy. The royal couple even visited the Brewster home informally where, according to published reports, they "viewed and expressed admiration for his large collection of big game and other trophies." We can only assume that the huge non-typical buck was among the mounts for which they showed their appreciation.

It is only fitting that the most historic whitetail ever to come from the Rockies was taken by someone the Stony Indians knew as "Yaha Dun Skun," which means "Mountain Child." Jim was indeed that, a man who was just as much a part of the land as it was of him. In fact, a lofty peak overlooking Banff has been named Mount Brewster, helping to ensure that his name is memorialized forever. But given this legendary outdoorsman's many contributions to the region he loved, it is unlikely he ever would have been forgotten anyway.

JIM BREWSTER, BRITISH COLUMBIA, 1905

Measurements	Right	Left	Difference
No. of points	11	14	
Main beam	31 2/8	27 6/8	3 4/8
1st point (G-1)	5 7/8	10 4/8	4 5/8
2nd point (G-2)	14 1/8	17 2/8	3 1/8
3rd point (G-3)	11 1/8	14 2/8	3 1/8
4th point (G-4)	4 5/8	13 4/8	8 7/8
5th point (G-5)	–	5 4/8	5 4/8
1st circ. (H-1)	5 5/8	5 6/8	1/8
2nd circ. (H-2)	4 6/8	4 7/8	1/8
3rd circ. (H-3)	7 0/8	5 2/8	1 6/8
4th circ. (H-4)	4 6/8	4 0/8	6/8
Total	89 1/8	108 5/8	31 4/8
Greatest spread		35 6/8	
Inside spread		25 3/8	
Gross typical score		223 1/8	
Assymetry deductions		-31 4/8	
Non-typical additions		+54 2/8	
Net non-typical score		245 7/8	

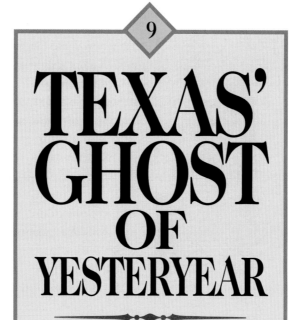

TEXAS' GHOST OF YESTERYEAR

The deeper we dig into the strange story of this amazing buck, the less we're sure we know.

TITLE: SECOND B&C NON-TYPICAL WORLD RECORD

SCORE: 284 3/8

HUNTER: UNKNOWN

LOCATION: McCULLOCH COUNTY, TEXAS

YEAR: CIRCA 1892

Trophy whitetails are renowned for doing the unexpected. But once a buck is dead, we generally assume he has no surprises left to pull. Perhaps that is why the former Boone and Crockett world-record non-typical from Texas is so remarkable. Even now, a century after this great deer's death, his story still contains more questions than answers. Indeed, whenever one of the mysteries surrounding him is solved, a new one seems to emerge.

It is understandable that the details regarding this giant are a bit sketchy. After all, evidence indicates that the deer lived in the 1890s when Texas was still largely wild. In some areas, ranchers and farmers were only a few years removed from open conflicts with Indians. Despite the fact that barbed wire was beginning to divide the countryside into private holdings, the land remained rugged and untamed. Men with big dreams wanted to stake their claim on the future, and they knew Texas was

one place where it could be done—if they had enough guts and guile.

In an era like that, documenting the facts about a big deer was pretty low on the list of priorities. We have been left to piece together the truth about this buck as best we can, working from 100 years of stories, clues and speculation.

We know the deer exists, of course, but what else is certain? No one has ever produced photos or eyewitness accounts to support the generally accepted story that a ranch foreman named "Papa Jeff" Benson either shot the buck or found him dead. Nor can we can say with conviction that the deer died in 1892, as has been assumed for decades now. For that matter, I'm not even sure we can assume the buck was killed in McCulloch County, as the B&C record book has always indicated. I do know that two very different accounts of the deer's origins have been told through the years. Let's begin with the older and better-known of these versions.

THE TRADITIONAL VERSION

To get to the bottom of this particular story version, you must travel back more than a century to the Ford Ranch, a big spread several miles southwest of the small town of Brady in Central Texas. The ranch has long been a fixture in McCulloch County. Even today, it remains a working cattle operation of more than 32,000 acres. A commercial hunting program on the ranch attracts clients from all over the nation who are eager to sample the property's well-managed whitetail herd. And, printed on the ranch's brochure is the image of a gigantic buck – the same one that was once a world record.

Legend has it that the deer spent at least part of his life on this property and that he was either shot or found dead in 1892 by Papa Jeff, who by then had been ranch foreman for four years. According to a book from the Buckhorn Hall of Horns in San Antonio (the significance of which I'll explain later), "The buck had been seen on a number of occasions on a certain hill on the Ford Ranch. One day, a cowboy rode into town and claimed he had shot a buck with antlers 'like Yosemite Forest' but couldn't find it."

Official measurer John Stein displays the rack of Texas' former world-record non-typical, a buck that, despite a century of investigation, remains clouded in mystery. All we know is that the buck died in the 1890s. More than a half-century later, his score of 286 made him an easy B&C world record, but for reasons explained in this chapter, he is now listed at 284 3/8. Photo courtesy of John Stein.

The story goes that Papa Jeff was the only person hearing the tale who didn't think the old cowboy had been staring too long at the sun. Why did Papa Jeff buy into the tale? While we can't know for sure, some believe the foreman either had seen the buck himself or had heard stories about it from other cowboys. According to current ranch manager Forrest Armke, the hill in question was known to be a deer hotspot back then because it was covered with far more oak timber and brush than most other parts of the county. After hearing the report that the deer had been shot (or at least shot at), Papa Jeff apparently decided to investigate the scene of the shooting. In doing so, he eventually found what the cowboy couldn't—an enormous dead buck.

Whether he found the deer soon enough to salvage its carcass, or merely recovered its skull, is unknown. Decades later, a local man named Ben Smith told an interviewer that he himself had seen the deer's skull at the Ford Ranch, where it was hanging in a tree after Papa Jeff had retrieved it. Ben reportedly was a lad of only 11 years when this happened, which would have put the year of recovery at 1892.

Most information suggests that while Papa Jeff

was proud of the huge rack he had recovered he was also favorably disposed toward financial gain…and in the former, he saw great potential for the latter. We can assume that those who saw the antlers must have been impressed, fueling Papa Jeff's notion that big money was to be made by selling them. But, there was no established monetary value for antlers in those days. Even if there had been, this remote part of Texas wasn't exactly the epicenter of whatever market may have existed. After a failed attempt to sell the rack himself, Papa Jeff realized he would need help in order to cash in.

He apparently found it in Jim Wall, who operated a feed store in Brady. Just what connection Jim had with potential antler buyers has never been explained, but Papa Jeff probably figured a storeowner in town had more marketing savvy than did a ranch foreman in the boondocks. Presumably, Papa Jeff brought the rack to the feed store and left it with Jim. They agreed that the asking price would be $100, to be split between them upon completion of the sale. Thus, the first known antler-consignment deal was struck.

The Ford Ranch's 32,000 acres consist of a mixture of open grasslands and low, brushy hills in Central Texas' McCulloch County. It was on one of these hills that the incredible non-typical is rumored to have been shot in 1892. Photo by Nick Gilmore.

What a bargain! Just $100 for a buck that would be the unchallenged world record for years! Of course, $100 was no small sum in the 1890s. For Papa Jeff and Jim to make a sale, they would need to find someone with plenty of money and the desire to own a set of big, bizarre antlers. In short, it would take a man named Albert Friedrich.

The Buckhorn Saga

Born the son of a German immigrant, Albert was an innovative entrepreneur. In 1887 when he was just 23, he opened the Buckhorn Saloon in downtown San Antonio. This new watering hole immediately became a favorite meeting place for locals, as well as cowboys and others passing through town. By every account, the saloon had a charm all its own, due in no small part to the great number of interesting wildlife trophies lining every wall. Throughout the establishment were hung all manner of deer and other racks, many of which Albert had acquired by trading discounts on alcoholic beverages. Then as now, Texas was home to many trophy whitetails, so the tavern owner soon acquired some spectacular deer, including many that exhibited freakish antler growth.

There is no known record of how Albert heard about the buck Papa Jeff had found, but I think we can assume that a story about some unbelievable antlers traveled quickly in those days, just as it does now. Perhaps a cowboy unwinding at the Buckhorn after a long trail ride mentioned having seen the rack up north in Brady. Or, maybe Jim Wall had heard of the saloon's many big racks and sent word to Albert about the special trophy he had for sale. Whatever the reason, in the late 1890s Albert reportedly traveled north across more than 100 miles of cattle country in hopes of acquiring this crazy-looking rack. Given the time and difficulties involved in such a trip, we can only assume he was confident it would not turn out to be a wild-goose chase.

Albert's own memoirs state that he actually made *two* trips from San Antonio to Brady in his quest for the antlers and that he finally acquired them in 1899, apparently for the asking price of $100. It is hard to imagine that he had to see the rack twice to convince himself that it would be a worthwhile addition to the Buckhorn, but for some reason, he apparently didn't buy the antlers on his first trip.

Papa Jeff never again saw that set of antlers after Jim made the sale to Albert, nor did he live long enough to know the deer had assumed the No.1 position in the B&C record book. He might never even have known (or cared) what became of it once he had his half of the money, which he reportedly later took and used to purchase two city lots in Brady, along with a second-hand surrey. He lived a long, full life and is survived by a number of relatives who still live in the area.

Albert's new rack was destined to become the centerpiece of his Buckhorn collection. We know the saloon owner soon had the antlers placed on a neck mount. Right after the turn of the century, Buckhorn promotional materials included photos of the finished trophy. A plaque in the shape of a five-pointed star was attached to the rear of the

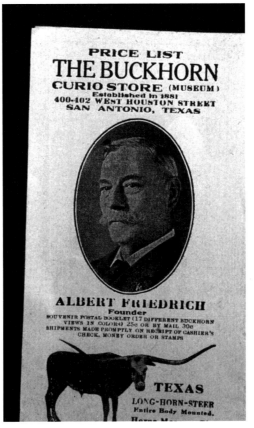

Albert Friedrich was a shrewd entrepreneur who turned San Antonio's Buckhorn Saloon into one of the city's most popular attractions. Much of the allure came from his huge collection of wildlife trophies, including two mounted racks of the so-called "Brady" buck. Photo courtesy of the Buckhorn Hall of Horns.

mount, and the letters T-E-X-A-S each were painted on the star's points. Beneath the deer was painted "78 points," indicating how many countable projections were considered to be on the rack. Back then, hunters figured a "point" was any antler projection you could hang a ring on, and this buck had them in spades— sticking upward, downward, inward, outward, forward and backward. Since there was no formal scoring system for whitetails at that time, Albert came up with a system of his own, using the rack's point total as a way of quantifying its size.

Albert's memoirs show just how happy he was to have bought this trophy. "It has 78 prongs, and I feel the greatest pride in its possession," he wrote. Later, he added, "Growing from the head is a unique cluster of horns, which wrap the beholder in astonishment and admiration. The curator of the Smithsonian Institution says, 'The antlers are the most remarkable I have ever seen. In the number of points, it far exceeds any specimen of which I have knowledge.'"

The Buckhorn prospered thanks to Albert's ceaseless efforts to make it a one-of-a-kind establishment. Shortly after the turn of the century, he was asked what had prompted him to build a business around such unusual décor. His answer confirmed that he understood what his customers wanted: "The decorations of the saloon are essential as well as beneficial. Some 29 years ago, the idea of decorating my place with mounted horns forced itself upon me. During that period, time, money and energy have been spent and I am proud to state that I now possess the grandest and largest collection of horns existing, native as well as foreign."

While Albert may have been a bit ignorant of proper terminology —he lumped both horns and antlers together as "horns"— nobody can question his business acumen. He was a marketing visionary, willing to try almost anything to drum up business.

This is the set of sheds that mistakenly stayed atop the B&C non-typical listings from 1955 to 1983. We'll never know if Albert believed this was an actual rack, but he displayed the mount as though it were, claiming it had 78 points. By B&C's stricter definition of a "point," the count really is 49, still an incredible tine count. Photo courtesy of John Stein.

In 1905, for example, he attached electric light bulbs to the elk and deer racks in the saloon. Eventually, putting colored lights on the trophies became a Christmas tradition at the Buckhorn. Vaudeville performers headlining at the nearby Majestic Theater frequently ducked into the Buckhorn for a quick drink and to gawk at the trophy mounts and to play assorted games. The saloon was the first business in San Antonio to feature coin-operated machines, some of which played music, told fortunes or made mechanical birds sing. It was a unique place operated by a unique man.

Albert's wife helped out with the decorating as well. One of her specialties was making mosaic designs from the rattles of Texas rattlesnakes, and perhaps her most impressive effort was a mosaic of a deer, comprised of an astounding 637 rattles. The piece, still on display at the Buckhorn Hall of Horns in San Antonio, apparently was a tribute to the nation's 26th president, Theodore Roosevelt. (The irony of that shouldn't be lost on students of whitetail history. Here was Albert's wife actually making a "deer" for one of the founders of the Boone and Crockett Club, the organization whose scoring system would many years later recognize her husband's most prized deer mount as the world record —long after both Roosevelt and the Friedrichs were dead and gone.)

Although Albert's establishment flourished for years, in 1919 it hit a snag—the Eighteenth Amendment to the U.S. Constitution, which outlawed the sale of alcoholic beverages. Suddenly, prohibition was forcing saloon owners to make the tough choice of either shutting their doors or converting into speakeasies, which sold booze on the sly. Rather than take either of those routes, Albert opted to turn the Buckhorn Saloon into the Buckhorn Curio Store. In short order, he added a soda fountain and all manner of unusual items for sale to tourists, who by now were pouring into San Antonio.

A brochure describing the store painted a fascinating picture of the place. Its cover was adorned with a black-and-white photo of the "78-pointer" while the interior contained two seemingly contradictory poems: "Hell in Texas" and "Texas, a Paradise." Oddly, they

John Stein holds up the mount of the 284 3/8-point antlers the deer was wearing at the time of death. The 286-point shed rack (right) is almost identical to the real thing. Ultimately, it took X-ray equipment for John to prove the wrong rack (the 284 3/8) had been removed from the record book nearly 40 years ago. Photo courtesy of John Stein.

were said to have been penned by the same unnamed person. The mail-order listing in the brochure offered such curiosities as armadillo-shell baskets ($2), jumping beans (25 cents) and "Mexican dressed fleas" (35 cents a pair, in box). We don't know exactly where Albert got the fleas or their wardrobe, but we do know he continued to seek out unusual wildlife specimens. In fact, he acquired many new curiosities during the prohibition era—including his greatest whitetail rack ever, though he apparently never realized it!

Mystery Times Two

If that seems confusing, let me explain. As Albert was building the Buckhorn Saloon into a San Antonio landmark, a man named Bill Keilman was doing much the same thing in another part of town with an establishment called the Horn Palace.

Apparently, it was just as lavishly decorated as the Buckhorn. Perhaps the Horn Palace was more of a dance hall than was Albert's establishment, but both places were popular hangouts for the more adventurous types in town…until fate intervened in 1921 when a rowdy Horn Palace patron shot Bill in the face, wounding him badly. The next year, Bill sold his entire trophy collection to Albert. Now, the Buckhorn's walls were even more crowded with big, unusual critters, including whitetails.

When Bill died in 1926, he took with him the story of the biggest deer in the bunch, a "72-pointer" bearing an uncanny resemblance to the "78-pointer" on display in the Buckhorn. It is hard to fathom why Albert failed to note the great similarity between the two racks, though, as we'll see, other antler experts later made the same mistake. Albert hung the "72-pointer" in his curio store without putting it on a plaque or otherwise drawing attention to it. The "78-pointer" was still king, at least in his mind, perhaps because that rack had more "points."

Only two years later, Albert passed away. After his death, his family kept the Buckhorn Curio Store open and, after prohibition ended, began selling alcohol again. But, the

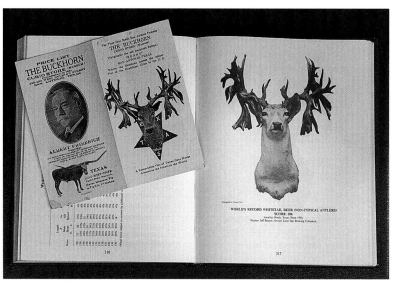

San Antonio's Buckhorn Hall of Horns (the former Buckhorn Saloon and Buckhorn Curio Store) frequently used the Brady buck to promote the business, as it did in the prohibition-era mail-order catalog on the left. All of these promotional efforts featured the 286-point sheds rather than the buck's 284 3/8-point actual rack. For years, even B&C was confused about which was the true rack. B&C record books as recent as 1981 (right) erroneously listed the sheds as No.1. Photo by Gordon Whittington.

Friedrich estate, Lone Star decided to see how its "new" bucks would stack up against those from the rest of North America.

Official B&C measurer Grancel Fitz was granted the honor of stretching a tape over the two biggest racks in the Buckhorn collection. When he did, he came up with numbers never before seen on a

heyday of the enterprise was over. In 1956, Albert's surviving son and daughter accepted an offer from Lone Star Brewery president Harry Jersig for the contents of the saloon. The brewery soon announced plans to display the materials on its grounds several miles south of downtown. So was born the Buckhorn Hall of Horns, as it has been called ever since. (As this book was going to press, the collection had been purchased by one of Albert's grandchildren and was being moved back downtown to become a self-supporting tourist destination once again.)

By the time Lone Star Brewery purchased the various racks and began creating its museum to house them, B&C had implemented its modern scoring system and had published the 3rd edition of *Records of North American Big Game* (1952). It listed the 245 7/8-point Jim Brewster buck (Chapter 8) as the non-typical world record. So, soon after acquiring the huge collection of trophies from the

whitetail score sheet – 286 net points for the "78-pointer" and 284 3/8 for the "72-pointer!" The Brewster buck had been a fitting world record, but here were *two* Texas bucks that would blow him right off the throne! Indeed, when the 4th edition of *Records of North American Big Game* came out in 1958, the two racks in the Hall of Horns were ranked Nos. 1 and 2, respectively. However, B&C didn't know who, if anyone, had taken either of these trophies, so the hunter names were simply listed as "unknown."

Grancel's comments in the 4th edition of the record book clearly noted as much. "In the non-typical whitetail class, we know nothing of the two very old and strikingly similar specimens which stand at the top, except that they are Texas bucks from the old-time Buckhorn Saloon collection in San Antonio," he wrote. "But, both of these remarkably symmetrical freaks are far ahead of any other trophies in their class."

Who's The "Real Deal"?

With the incredibly close inspection given world-class racks today, there is no way two racks of such similar size and shape would be assumed to have come from different deer. Back then, however, it took awhile before someone noted how alike the two racks really were. Sometime between the publication of that 1958 record book and the next edition in 1964, speculation began to spread that both of the Lone Star Brewery racks must have come from the same buck, meaning one must be a set of sheds! All antlers entered into the B&C records must be naturally attached to a skull plate, of course, and one of these sets obviously wasn't. The decision was made to drop the 284 3/8-pointer from the official rankings, leaving the 286-point rack as the unchallenged world record. What's more, for some reason B&C also decided to name Jeff Benson as the hunter who had shot the animal and list 1892 as the year it happened.

We don't know exactly why B&C opted to remove the 284 3/8-point rack from the record book and leave the 286. All we know is that this decision was incorrect. The 284 3/8-point rack was, in fact, the one still naturally attached to the skull plate! The 286-pointer, for so many years considered the biggest legitimate whitetail rack in the world, was really just a pair of sheds, albeit from the same buck!

Dropping the wrong antlers from the records has to rank as one of the greatest gaffes in the history of any record book. Still, it is hard to be too tough on whoever botched the call. Remember, few hunters in those days had even heard of the B&C scoring system. The network of measurers was just being developed, and there were no specialty deer magazines to question such a move. Also, it would have been considered inappropriate to pull the capes off two mounted heads in a museum to check the skull plates, which would have answered the question conclusively. None of the principals were around to question. Perhaps somebody figured that because both racks belonged to the same owner it didn't much matter which set was the sheds so the rack with the higher score might as well remain in the book.

From Nos. 1 And 2 To Near-Omission

The credit for ferreting out the "real" rack goes to John Stein of San Antonio, an official B&C measurer who knows more than anyone else about Texas' greatest bucks. He is, after all, the publisher of the *Big Rack* books, a series of highly detailed volumes depicting the Lone Star State's top whitetails. While conducting research for the various editions of *Big Rack,* attending deer shows and measuring antlers for fellow hunters, John sifts through reams of information about trophy deer. Some of these tidbits caused him to wonder about the real story behind the "Brady" buck.

In the spring of 1996, with the blessing of Buckhorn Hall of Horns curator Bill West, Hal John arranged for a team of technicians to bring their gear to the museum and X-ray both the 286 and 284 3/8-point mounts. That testing confirmed a suspicion John had held for some time—the wrong set of antlers had been removed from the B&C records prior to the publication of the 1964 record book! The X-rays clearly showed screws were holding the 286-point rack in place while the skull plate was naturally attached to the 284 3/8-point antlers.

That was big news in the whitetail world. But, John's investigation also revealed another shocker— the skull plate of the 284 3/8-pointer was cracked and had been wired back together! It may not seem odd for such an old mount to have a cracked skull, but that revelation becomes pretty sobering when you realize B&C's stated policy is to reject the entry of any rack in such condition. There was no predicting exactly how B&C would rule on this stunning new information when it came to light. The worst-case scenario was that Texas could go from once holding the top two positions in the record book to having neither of those historical racks included in the book at all!

Fortunately, B&C's Records Committee decided at its June 1996 meeting to remove the 286-point rack of the "Brady" buck from the book and to replace it with the 284 3/8-point rack from the same deer, even though the latter had a cracked skull plate. There was, after all, no way to know whether the crack had occurred before or after Grancel measured the mounted head more than 40 years earlier (he had long since passed away). Given that, the committee ruled in favor of reinstating that rack at its former score, which seems the only fair way to resolve the situation. To have tossed out the 284 3/8-pointer would have called Grancel's expertise into question, and doing so would have been an act of disrespect to one of the scoring system's founding fathers. At the same time, Grancel apparently never realized that both racks were both from the same highly recognizable buck, even though he made the original measurements of each rack.

More Questions

Before we get too hung up on these questions, let me hasten to say there are still plenty of other questions surrounding this buck. For starters, John's investigation turned up some very old photos of the 286-pointer that clearly reveal the rack had more points then than it does today. Some are still missing even now while others appear to have been glued back on. Who made those repairs and when? Did it happen before Grancel measured the rack? True, it doesn't really matter because this rack should have never been in the record book at all. Fortunately, the 284 3/8-pointer shows no such repairs so its legitimacy appears to be beyond any question.

But none of these revelations cast light on the most important question of all —when and from whom did Bill get the 284 3/8-point "real" rack? (We know Bill, not Albert, originally owned the 284 3/8-point "real" rack because John Stein's research actually turned up a photo of it on the wall of the Horn Palace.) The answer to that question might provide the clues necessary to solve the mystery of who, if anyone, actually shot the "Brady" buck, but scanty details of the early days of the Horn Palace leave us to speculate through the fog of an entire century.

It seems logical to assume that this rack was purchased from Papa Jeff or someone else working on the Ford Ranch. After all, we know it came from the same deer that produced the 286-point sheds. John's best guess is that sometime in the 1890s on or near the Ford Ranch Papa Jeff or another local cowboy

If James Arnwine (inset) was involved in killing the Brady buck, whitetail history is far different from what we have been led to believe over all these years. In that case, the deer would have come from the Neches River bottoms, now a state game sanctuary, some 250 miles east of the area from which he has long been assumed to have lived. Inset photo courtesy of Jimye and Lloyd Pipes; sign photo by Gordon Whittington.

shot the 284 3/8-point buck. John speculates that in the process of looking for the shot buck perhaps the previous year's sheds were also found. Finally, John says, there is always the chance that Papa Jeff

◆

Texas could easily have gone from holding the top two positions in the record book to having neither of those racks included in the book at all.

◆

believed the old cowboy's tale of shooting a buck with a rack "like Yosemite Forest" because he had already discovered his sheds, though no reference to the "72-point" rack or any shed antlers could be found in the old stories about Papa Jeff, Jim or Albert.

Obviously, the story of the former world record from Texas is full of mystery and uncertainty, even following these latest revelations. But, there is yet another twist to the tale that muddies the water even further. You see, there is an entirely different scenario regarding the history of this buck, one that almost completely contradicts everything you have just read!

AN ALTOGETHER DIFFERENT TALE

On Thursday, December 10, 1959, the now-defunct *Houston Press* carried a tantalizing outdoor column written by Zane Chastain and Keith Ozmore entitled "How 'Record' Rack Was Found on River." This column was sent to me many years later by Joe Moore of Palestine, Texas. It focused on questions surrounding the two racks that had just been listed as Nos. 1 and 2 in the 1958 B&C record book. At the time, no location or hunter's name was given for either rack so there was considerable speculation regarding their origins. Rather than try to paraphrase the content of this newspaper column, I'll provide the text verbatim (misspellings and grammatical errors included):

Houston police lieutenant A.W. Rainey, who spent his boyhood days hunting big whitetail bucks near Jacksonville, revealed today that Texas can't possibly claim the second place standing it holds in the Boone and Crockett Club for whitetail deer with non-typical (freak) antlers.

"Simply because that deer was never killed," he said. "So how can they claim second place among world records?

"You see, the rack they measured is the same one now in the old Buckhorn Saloon collection which the Lone Star Brewery of San Antonio owns … and back in January of 1896, Mr. Marion Stewart and Will Miller, with whom my dad hunted, each found one side of those antlers laying in the woods just outside Jacksonville, where some buck had shed them."

Those two men —who found one side in Cherokee County and the other across the Neches River in Anderson County—then sold the points to owners of the Buckhorn Saloon, in Palestine at that time.

"They, in turn, had the two sides mounted," the 68-year-old police officer continued, "and to this day, folks up there swear they came off the same buck claiming the world record that was killed in that locale."

Rainey, who inspected the Boone and Crockett record book, was surprised and disappointed that the publication didn't list where the record deer in that category was killed, nor by whom it was killed. He quickly cleared up that mystery.

"Three hunters were responsible for that deer's death," he said. "Samuel Benge, Brice Burrett and James Arnwine. All three of them are dead now.

"They were chasing deer with dogs near the Dunica Bend area on the Cherokee County side of the Neches River when they jumped it. Mr. Burrett

wounded it first with a shotgun, breaking the deer's leg. Then Mr. Benge hit it with an old Winchester .32, and the deer fell in Pails Creek. That's when Mr. Arwine finished off that buck."

This, he said, was in the fall of 1896, and after leaving the deer antlers at James Arnwine's home, Mr. Burrett learned he could sell the rack.

"Got $25 from the owners of the Buckhorn Saloon," Rainey recalled his father's recollection of the incident. "They kept it, along with the other rack, there in the saloon at Palestine."

The two racks stayed there in Palestine until the county became dry. Then the owners moved the saloon to San Antonio, taking the racks with them. That was the last Rainey had heard of them, except for the tales told time and time again by his father of the hunt that produced them.

There, in San Antonio, the racks gathered much notice from tourists.

Finally, when the Lone Star Brewery of San Antonio bought out the world-famous collection in 1956, officials of that firm had the racks measured for possible consideration as records. They weren't disappointed when the Boone and Crockett Club notified them they were the top two.

The racks had gone virtually unnoticed for 60 years.

Now, though, one must possibly drop from the ranks following the revelation of an innocent human error on everyone's part.

To appreciate just how stunning Mr. Rainey's claim was, you must understand that the Neches River bottoms described in the newspaper article are, as the crow flies, 250 miles east-northeast of the Ford Ranch! One or the other, or both, of the stories of this deer's origin is certainly outright fiction.

Two Buckhorns?

In this later version, the Buckhorn Saloon connection is intriguing…if there was indeed a Buckhorn Saloon in Palestine, Texas, in the 1890s.

And, guess what—there was, on Spring Street in the heart of the railroad town's thriving business district. But, was that establishment operated by Albert Friedrich or even Bill Keilman? Of that, there is neither proof nor reasonable suspicion.

To start with, Albert and Bill were both born of German families who had immigrated directly to the San Antonio area in the mid-19th century. Palestine's history is exceptionally well-documented, and nothing there, including census records, shows that either Albert or Bill ever lived in the area. In fact, there is no proof Albert or Bill ever set foot in Palestine, which is almost 300 miles northeast of San Antonio. Perhaps most importantly, however, is the fact that a Palestine city directory from the 1890s lists the proprietor of that town's Buckhorn Saloon as a J.H. Hewlett.

————◆————

Yes, there were two Buckhorn Saloons…but who ran the one in Palestine?

————◆————

Apparently, the Buckhorn Saloons in Palestine and San Antonio were two completely different establishments that simply happened to share the same name. This isn't to say J.H. Hewlett couldn't have packed up and headed to San Antonio for a new start after Anderson County outlawed liquor sales early in the 20th century. Unfortunately, I have not been able to pick up his trail in San Antonio. Even if he did open a tavern there, it would have made no sense to have continued to call his place the "Buckhorn" since Albert already had a well-established saloon by that name in San Antonio. (Just to further confuse the issue, there is also an antler-filled Buckhorn Saloon in D'Hanis, a small town roughly an hour west of San Antonio, but its origins have been traced to the 1800s, and its proprietor was a fellow named Pete Koch.)

The Place Revisited, Family Stories Recounted

While first glance provides no obvious path of this buck's origin back to Palestine, that doesn't mean he couldn't have come from that area. In a last-ditch effort to find out if the East Texas angle has merit, in October 1997 I interviewed two children of J.W. Arnwine, one of the hunters A.W. Rainey said had shot the buck on the Neches River 101 years earlier.

My first stop was at the home of 99-year-old J.H. Arnwine, who was born less than two years after his father, along with Sam Benge and Brice Durrett (misspelled as "Burrett" in the *Post* column), reportedly shot the deer. J.H. had been a deer hunter himself, and he told me he had often heard his father speak of having shot a deer with "40-something" points. Unfortunately, he said he had never seen the rack himself since it had been sold before he was born in February 1898.

Interestingly, he showed me a well-preserved 12-gauge Model 97 Winchester shotgun, with which his father presumably had shot the buck. If that gun was present on the historic hunt, however, we have a timing problem—the Model 97 wasn't even introduced until November 1897, a year after the deer is rumored to have been shot. However, James had other guns as well so he might have used one of them on that particular hunt. Likewise, for all we know, the Neches River deer in question might really have been shot in 1897 or even later.

A San Antonio Connection For The East Texas Giant!

After visiting with J.H., I drove eastward to Rusk to visit with his younger sister, 79-year-old Jimye Pipes. J.H. told me she had a photo of their father, though not with the big deer, and perhaps could tell me more. When I got to the Pipes home, Jimye and her husband, Lloyd, showed me the photo of James and shared one of the most intriguing tidbits of information I've yet heard regarding the buck. You see, Jimye told me she had actually seen the mount

This column from the December 10, 1959, issue of the now-defunct Houston Press *started the rumor that the Brady buck might not have been shot near Brady after all. Unfortunately, anyone who might have verified the East Texas story had already passed on before further investigation of the newspaper's claims was made.*

of the deer her father had shot … and she had seen it in San Antonio!

"When I was very small, my father took our family to San Antonio," she said. "I was too young to remember that trip, but I was told about it. Then in the 1930s, when I was a student at Lon Morris (Junior College in Jacksonville, Texas), he took us down there again. We were there on vacation to see the Alamo and other things, but I remember that part of the reason we went was to look at this deer. We went to this place that was like a drugstore, and there on the wall was this big deer head. My father said it was the one he'd shot."

———◆———

Jimye told me she had actually seen the mount of the deer her father had shot…and she had seen it in San Antonio.

———◆———

This revelation floored me. After so much searching for the truth regarding this buck, at last I had found someone who claimed to be able to connect the deer to a specific hunter and a specific place…and it wasn't McCulloch County's Ford Ranch! I told Jimye that during the era of prohibition, Albert's Buckhorn Saloon in downtown San Antonio had been converted into a drugstore/curio shop with a wide array of offerings. I asked her if that might have been where she saw the deer head. She thought about it for a few moments and replied, "That sounds like the place."

I had with me a copy of John Stein's book, *Big Rack IV,* which contains not only a photo of the 286-pointer but also those of several "anonymous" B&C non-typicals that have been in the Hall of Horns since the early days of the collection. Unfortunately, Jimye's 60-year-old memories of the mount were quite vague; all she could recall was that it was a "big deer." Hoping to jar her memory

of the mount, I asked if perhaps it had been on a star-shaped plaque, as the sheds had been until they were remounted in the 1950s. She said she couldn't remember such a plaque. "I was a girl in college, and all I knew was it was a deer head on a wall, and my father had taken us into that drugstore to see it because it was the big one he'd shot," she concluded.

"Mr. Arnwine was a very matter-of-fact person," Lloyd noted of his late father-in-law. "If he told you something, that was the way it was. So if he said he shot that deer, you could believe it."

During my East Texas investigation, I also checked in Palestine to see if there was any documentation that the antlers had once been in the Buckhorn Saloon there. In the process, I became acquainted with the Chamber of Commerce's Kathy Rainbolt, who took an interest in my unusual request and kindly agreed to let me know if she found anything that might be of help. Sure enough, a few weeks later Kathy informed me that she had run into a dairy farmer who said he knew something of the buck. His name was Rodney Newman, and he lived outside Maydelle, near the old Arnwine homestead on Tails Creek (misspelled as "Pails" Creek in the *Houston Press* column).

"My whole life I've heard that story about the buck really having been shot down on the river here," Rodney told me. "But, you really should talk to my dad, Lionel. He knows a lot more about it than I do."

———◆———

"…if he said he shot that deer, you could believe it."

———◆———

My call to Lionel revealed that he had never been told anything about shed antlers having been found, but he did say that his own maternal grandfather, George Ball, had been a member of the hunting party that got the buck!

Around the turn of the century, Palestine's Spring Street was a hub of commerce in the bustling railroad town. If rumors suggesting the Brady buck came from East Texas are true, the deer's sheds and actual rack might well have been hanging somewhere within range of the photographer's lens in this circa-1900 shot. Unfortunately, no one has been able to produce a photo showing the interior of Palestine's Buckhorn Saloon, which might reveal if either set of antlers ever were displayed there. Photo courtesy of Palestine Chamber of Commerce.

"From what I always heard, they were all hunting with dogs down near a place called the 'Wilson Patch' pretty close to where Tails Creek runs into the river," Lionel said. "That 'Dunica Bend' in the newspaper column would have been what was often called the 'Dunica Hole,' where the stage used to cross the river before there was a bridge. That is in the same area we're talking about. Anyway, the story was that when the deer ran out he had rattan vines hanging from his rack. He was supposed to have been a fairly small-bodied deer. I guess Mr. Arnwine shot him, and later, there was a lawsuit over the deer."

A lawsuit?

"Well, supposedly there was a dispute over who would get the head," Lionel explained. "I guess it was handled by the justice of the peace, but I'm not sure. Anyway, whoever settled it apparently sided with Mr. Arnwine and he ended up selling the head to the Buckhorn Saloon in Palestine. He got $25 for it, which was nearly a month's pay back then, so it must have been an unusually big set of antlers."

Since Lionel wasn't born until a number of years

after this all reportedly took place, he never saw the rack himself and, thus, couldn't identify it precisely. And he, like so many others in East Texas, had always assumed the Buckhorn Saloon in Palestine became the Buckhorn Hall of Horns in San Antonio, though history shows otherwise.

What's The Truth?

I have no reason to doubt that one day back in the 1890s several hunters teamed up to kill a huge buck along the Neches River. I can't dispute the claim that this was the same buck whose sheds Samuel Benge, along with Marion Stewart and Will Miller, reportedly had picked up the previous spring. I will not deny anyone's claim that these sheds, as well as the real rack, were later sold to the owner of the Buckhorn Saloon in Palestine. And for all I know, in the 1930s James Arnwine really did walk into a drugstore in San Antonio and show daughter Jimye the deer he had killed years before mounted on the store's wall.

Still, I have no real *evidence* that the mount James pointed to was, in fact, the buck later to become the official world record. We can't even say for certain that the "drugstore" Jimye told me of was Albert's Buckhorn, though that seems likely. We just don't have enough information, and with the deaths of key players, even the indirect ones, we may have missed the window of opportunity for unraveling the mystery. James lived until 1968, but as far as I know, no one followed up with him regarding the details of that hunt described in the 1959 newspaper column. Even A.W. Rainey, whose version of the story led me to explore the East Texas angle, died before I could interview him.

It seems the only way to verify an East Texas origin for the "Brady" buck is to come up with a photo or highly detailed sketch of the interior of Palestine's Buckhorn Saloon because no field photos of the deer apparently were taken. Desperate to find anything visual on the old saloon's interior, I even asked for help through Palestine's daily newspaper, the *Herald-Press*. As of this writing, no leads of any substance have emerged. Unlike Albert's Buckhorn in San Antonio, the one by the same name in Palestine was neither heavily promoted nor well documented.

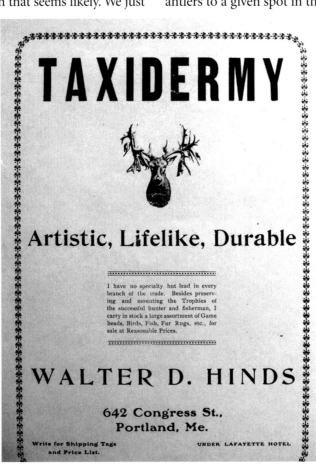

This ad ran in Maine Sportsman *back in 1904 and features the mount of the 286-point Brady sheds from Texas! While there is no reference to the deer in the ad, the photo certainly implies that the buck was mounted by a taxidermist in Portland, Maine. It seems more likely, however, that the taxidermist "borrowed" the image from Albert Friedrich's printed materials promoting the Buckhorn Saloon in San Antonio.*

Barring the unlikely discovery of photos that would undeniably link at least one of these sets of antlers to a given spot in the Lone Star State, we are left only with speculation. The majority of experts continue to believe the buck was from Central Texas. If I had to wager one way or the other, that is where I would put my money. In the end, one of the greatest problems with the East Texas scenario is that it contradicts Albert's own memoirs about how and where he purchased the rack. And remember, there is evidence, albeit anecdotal, to support claims that the antlers did indeed come from the Ford Ranch.

Still, I believe I'm the only person who has ever researched the East Texas angle to any extent. One thing it does have going for it is that it is the only known scenario specifically mentioning the possibility of shed antlers to go along with the deer's actual rack. Based on my interviews with J.W. Arnwine's son and daughter, there is now reason to at least question the claim that the buck came from Central Texas. We may never know the truth. All we can say with confidence is that the so-called "Brady" buck came from somewhere in Texas, right?

More Confusion

Well, maybe not. Even *that* fact may be up for debate!

In 1996, taxidermist Tad Proudlove showed me a photocopy of an old magazine ad that featured a photo of this deer's mounted 286-point sheds. The magazine had been printed in 1904, and the taxidermist who was using this trophy to advertise his work was Walter D. Hinds…of Portland, Maine!

Could this deer possibly have come from somewhere other than Texas? You would naturally assume that Walter was showing off one of his own mounts in that *Maine Sportsman* ad, which would suggest the buck was from Maine since taxidermists

---

…I am left with the rather hollow conclusion that the many players in this story took the truth with them when they died.

---

back then depended almost entirely on local business. But, we know that in the early 1900s the 286-point rack was in Albert's saloon in San Antonio. There is no indication that he ever sent any antlers all the way to Maine for mounting. Also, the photo of the mount in Walter's ad is the spitting image of the one used in the Buckhorn's early promotional materials, suggesting that perhaps the taxidermist merely "borrowed" that photo of the impressive whitetail for his ad. (The mount in Walter's ad isn't on a plaque, but not all of Albert's promotional materials showed it on the plaque either.) Again, we are unlikely ever to know why the buck showed up in that 1904 magazine ad a half-continent away from Texas, but there has never been a single rumor about the deer ever having been anywhere outside the Lone Star State. With that, Texas remains his

state of origin until proven otherwise.

Despite having invested vast amounts of time, effort and money in my quest for the truth about the "Brady" buck, I am left with the rather hollow conclusion that the many players in this story took the truth with them when they died. With their demise went the real story of when and where the animal lived; who (if anyone) shot him; who found his sheds; who originally mounted the two sets of magnificent antlers; who damaged (and repaired) the 286-point sheds; and who decided to list the sheds rather than the real rack as the world-record non-typical.

Yet, in the final analysis, let's not let the cloud of uncertainties detract from the one thing we *do* know—the "Brady" buck was among the greatest deer of all time and a deserving member of the ranks of world-record whitetails.

UNKNOWN, TEXAS, CIRCA 1892

Measurements	Right	Left	Difference
No. of points	21	26	
Main beam	21 4/8	19 6/8	1 6/8
1st point (G-1)	8 0/8	8 1/8	1/8
2nd point (G-2)	10 5/8	9 7/8	6/8
3rd point (G-3)	8 5/8	7 4/8	1 1/8
4th point (G-4)	6 4/8	4 3/8	2 1/8
5th point (G-5)	–	–	–
1st circ. (H-1)	4 4/8	4 4/8	–
2nd circ. (H-2)	4 0/8	4 0/8	–
3rd circ. (H-3)	4 5/8	4 3/8	2/8
4th circ. (H-4)	4 4/8	5 0/8	4/8
Total	72 7/8	67 4/8	6 5/8
Greatest spread		26 6/8	
Inside spread		16 2/8	
Gross typical score		156 5/8	
Assymetry deductions		-6 5/8	
Non-typical additions		+134 3/8	
Net non-typical score		284 3/8	

10

A WHITETAIL FOR THE AGES

The world's highest-scoring non-typical died of natural causes in a county populated by nearly a million people. What does that tell us about the survival instincts of a mature buck?

TITLE: CURRENT B&C NON-TYPICAL WORLD RECORD

SCORE: 333 7/8

HUNTER: PICKUP

LOCATION: ST. LOUIS COUNTY, MISSOURI

YEAR: 1981

Let's say it is my job to convince you that suburban woodlands hold great potential for producing trophy deer. How will I do it? Simple. I'll take you on a little trip. Our destination? The top of towering Gateway Arch standing alongside the Mississippi River in downtown St. Louis, Missouri.

From our vantage point more than twice the height of New York's Statue of Liberty, I want you to face upriver so you can appreciate some of the unique features of the surrounding landscape. See that broad expanse of land just a few miles north, near where the Mississippi and Missouri rivers merge? That's Columbia Bottoms, a huge floodplain that boasts some of the most fertile farmland in North America. See that higher ground to the west? That's the limestone tableland through which these two mighty rivers

carved their path. Now, see where the lowlands and uplands join? Well, congratulations, my friend—you're looking at the very spot that has provided all the evidence necessary to prove that the suburbs are worth hunting. For it was there that the whitetail world was changed forever, thanks to a titanic non-typical living almost within the city limits.

I'm talking about the 333 7/8-point "Missouri Monarch," officially the highest-scoring whitetail of all time. He was found dead in northern St. Louis County on November 15, 1981. His stunning discovery did more than awaken folks to the possibilities of suburban hunting, it also forced deer experts to revise their thinking on just how big a rack can grow!

At the time the Monarch turned up, there was

no reason to think a whitetail could score more than 300 points. Hunters and collectors had been accumulating gigantic racks for decades, but nobody had yet brought such a beast to light. Indeed, rarely had Texas' ancient Brady buck, dating back to the 1800s and scoring in the 280s (Chapter 9), even been challenged as the world record. Most observers figured the Brady buck's mark was safe. But, the Missouri Monarch blew away all such notions, for his rack is *much* bigger than that of his predecessor. The Monarch's heavy crown features 44 scorable points, with almost as many of them pointing downward as upward. An outside spread of 33 3/8 inches helps the buck show off everything he grew. Whether you look at him from the front or back, left or right, you are aware of one salient fact: What this rack doesn't have, a hunter doesn't need!

Though the Monarch confirmed that not all trophies live far from city lights, he raised several new questions. What were the circumstances of his mysterious death? How did he manage to grow old in a county containing almost a million people? And, should he even have been allowed entry into the B&C record book?

Wild-looking bucks and wild-sounding stories seem to go hand-in-hand. (If you haven't yet been convinced of that fact, you will be before you finish this book.) The rumor mill kicks into overdrive whenever one of these monsters turns up, leading to a string of "facts" that often prove untrue. So, I would be surprised only if the Monarch *wasn't* surrounded by intrigue. Still, his story is more puzzling than most…and despite the fact that he is the highest-scoring buck of all time, one of the most obscure.

As a trophy hunter, you probably know even less about the Missouri Monarch than any of the other current world records. The Monarch simply has not received that much play in the media. This seems amazing given the enormous attention heaped upon such animals as B&C's typical world record, the Hanson buck (Chapter 7). There are, however, reasons for the lack of fanfare.

Found dead near St. Louis in 1981, the 333 7/8-point Missouri Monarch is officially the highest-scoring whitetail in history. Photo by Jim Rathert, Missouri Department of Conservation.

Ron Van Gilder's "The Missouri Giant" shows the world-record buck in the Columbia Bottoms he called home. Imagine seeing this sight in real life. Print courtesy of the artist and Wild Wings, Inc.

The first is that the Monarch was not shot by a hunter, so there is not much human involvement to discuss. The second is that the rack has seldom been displayed at hunting shows, particularly outside Missouri. (Plus, practically all "appearances" have been of replicas, not the original rack.) But, perhaps the greatest reason for the relative anonymity of the Missouri buck has its roots in Ohio. You see, just a few months after B&C anointed the Monarch the official world record in 1983, a deer rumored to be still bigger—Ohio's mysterious "Hole-in-the-Horn" buck—came to light and diverted the attention of the hunting community. While the Hole-in-the-Horn ended up scoring 328 2/8 points (Chapter 28), thus falling just short of unseating the Monarch, he did steal much of its thunder and legitimately brought into question which of these two deer is the world's biggest whitetail.

When you combine all of these facts, it's easy to see why, despite the Monarch's unprecedented offi-cial score and great visual appeal, he has remained largely out of sight and out of mind. As a result, most hunters know little more about the Missouri buck today than they did early on…and that wasn't much. Let's read what Dick Idol had to say in one of the earliest magazine articles about the animal in the February 1983 issue of *North American WHITETAIL:*

"The whitetail hunting fraternity predicted and expected that Jeff Benson's 286-point non-typical world-record whitetail, which he found dead near Brady, Texas, in 1892, would never be broken. They were wrong.

It was not only broken but shattered on November 11, 1981, when a hunter named Dave Beckman first spotted a dead buck near the highway. He reported the find to Mike Helland, a Missouri conservation officer, who picked up the buck and eventually turned him over to the Missouri Department of Conservation.

After being scored by official measurer Dean Murphy, the 44-point giant tallied a new world-record score of 325 7/8. Although not official yet, the score is expected to end up very near 325 points.

Although the breaking of the 90-year record was unexpected, its location was even more surprising— within 20 miles of downtown St. Louis, Missouri. Fortunately, the 250-pound buck had been dead 24 hours or less and the cape was still in good condition. No definite cause of death has yet been determined. ...”

While that's pretty much how the events unfolded, there is a fair bit more to the story. Let's go back to the beginning and set the record straight on what happened and what did not.

St. Louis resident Dave Beckman *did* find the buck...while returning from a successful day of deer hunting in the riverbottom, not while actually hunting as some reports had it. As he drove along, Dave's eye caught something unusual near an intersection. The object appeared to be a deer's antler sticking up on the far side of a security fence bordering the highway. Unsure of what he was seeing, he decided to check it out. When he walked over to the spot, his curiosity turned to pure amazement. It

This photo shows the Monarch hanging in the Rockwoods Conservation Area check station on the night of November 15, 1981. Game warden Mike Helland had just brought in the deer, and wildlife biologist David Wissehr (shown) was about to examine it for evidence of the cause of death. Photo by Mike Helland, courtesy of David Wissehr.

◆

...Dave was out of luck... legally he couldn't do anything with this awesome whitetail lying before him.

◆

---

was not merely a deer's rack —it was one bigger and stranger than any the hunter had ever imagined! The buck was lying next to the fence and was somewhat bloated, suggesting he had been there for a number of hours.

Missouri wildlife regulations precluded anyone

from recovering a found deer unless the person had an appropriate hunting permit to use on the animal. Dave was out of luck in that regard. Earlier that day, he had used his permit on a nice buck. Legally, he couldn't do anything with this awesome whitetail lying before him but he knew who could.

In those days, Missouri Department of Conservation (MDOC) game wardens would check harvested deer in the field as opportunity allowed, saving many sportsmen long drives to official check stations. Only minutes earlier, Dave had checked in

Whitetail enthusiast Roger Selner poses with the Missouri Monarch and Ohio's Hole-in-the-Horn, the two largest whitetails in history! The Ohio buck was discovered soon after the Missouri buck was crowned No.1 and stole much of the limelight. At first, an official B&C scorer taped the Horn-in-the Horn at world-record proportions, but the B&C judges' panel later lowered the score to 328 2/8, putting the Horn-in-the-Horn in second place to the Monarch. Still, the controversy over which is bigger continues. Photo courtesy of Roger Selner.

his harvested buck with warden Mike Helland. Dave decided he would go back to Mike with news of his improbable discovery.

When they returned to the spot, Mike was just as amazed by the incredible buck laying before him as Dave had been. The property on which the deer lay was a fairly large tract belonging to a local steamfitters' union, whose members used it for recreation. As best the men could tell, there was no evidence the animal had been shot. Even if it had, the buck had clearly been lost since the condition of the body

suggested it had been dead for a day or so.

A hole was cut in the fence so Mike and Dave could drag the buck out to the warden's pickup. Once the beast was loaded, Dave—by all accounts, none too happy about losing possession of the rack—drove home to St. Louis. Meanwhile, Mike headed to Rockwoods Conservation Area near his own home in the western part of the county. At the time, Rockwoods was the only official MDOC check station in the county. The warden knew his coworkers needed to see this incredible animal.

Right at 8 p.m., as the guys at the check station were about to lock up for the night, the front door swung open. Mike ran in, shut the door behind him and leaned back against it, as if to prevent anyone from leaving. "What's the most points you've ever seen on a deer rack?" he asked those present.

"Eighteen," replied area manager David Wissehr, wondering why Mike was asking.

"Twenty-three," said Art Johnson, a veteran MDOC field agent who had seen his share of trophy bucks.

"Well, I've got one with forty-four!" Mike said.

David and Art were skeptical…and for good reason. Only one whitetail in history had ever managed to grow as many as 44 points, and that was the world-record Brady buck from Texas. The most points ever officially recorded for a Missouri buck was 26. "We really thought Mike was crazy," David told me.

The warden quickly led everyone out to his pick-up, which had been backed up to the front door of the building. After the floodlight had been turned on, the tailgate dropped…along with everyone's jaw.

As Mike told what had happened, the men began to inspect the buck from one end to the other. In addition to that monstrous rack, he had a big body—50 pounds ungutted, despite a fair amount of dehydration. David estimated the deer had been dead for perhaps a day. His eyes had begun to sink in; some bloating had occurred; and hair was on the verge of pulling loose from the hide. Even the meat wasn't salvageable.

Fortunately, David had a background in wildlife biology and an intimate knowledge of deer anatomy. Even though there didn't appear to be a mark on the buck, the biologist realized that skinning him out was the first step toward verifying that no arrow, bullet or antler wound (from fighting) had caused internal damage. David skinned the deer right down to his hocks, looking for any clue to cause of death. The biologist found no holes anywhere in the hide, and none of the organs were damaged.

What had been the cause of death? The only clue was a hematoma (pocket of blood) under the skin on the buck's left shoulder and the left side of his neck. David focused his attention on the buck's rut-swollen neck, where the blood had accumulated under the skin. Carefully cutting away one muscle at a time, he eventually worked his way down to bone and came upon what appeared to be the answer to the mystery. The third cervical vertebra, several inches behind the skull, had suffered severe trauma, leaving David "99 percent sure" the animal had died of a broken neck.

———◆———

"What's the most points you've ever seen on a deer rack? I've got one with forty-four!"

———◆———

How might that have happened? According to Mike, there had been no trampled brush or other evidence of a buck fight at the scene. That possibility ruled out, David opinioned that the deer simply got his huge antlers entangled in the fence, snapping his neck in the process.

We'll never be sure exactly what led to such an outcome, but there are theories. One possibility tossed around by locals was that free-ranging dogs had chased the buck into the barrier. David dismissed that scenario. "If dogs had been chasing the buck, we would have seen some evidence of that when we examined him," the biologist told me. "But, there was no sign that anything had chewed on him."

A more plausible scenario is that the deer fell victim to a fatal accident. The rut is generally well underway in that region by the second week of November. David speculates that the buck could have been using the security fence to help him "herd" a hot doe. Bucks commonly use physical barriers—cliffs, waterways, blowdowns and, yes, fences—to help them steer does in a certain direction or to hem them up. As David pointed out, the Monarch could have been chasing a potential mate along that fence when he accidentally snagged one or more of those thick points in the wires, whipping his head around so forcefully that the impact broke his neck.

One interesting side note is that the autopsy of the Monarch revealed no incisor teeth in the front of his lower jaw. "There was no evidence he'd ever had any," the biologist said. "He also had a very short muzzle. It was a birth defect of some sort." Is it possible that this abnormality somehow contributed to the wild growth of those huge non-typical antlers? We know that certain skeletal injuries and defects can lead to non-typical antler growth. An interesting question to ponder.

Another fascinating question involving this buck concerns his possible interaction with hunters in the area. From what I have been able to piece together, a pair of

From every angle, the Missouri Monarch is a giant. Each main beam practically "explodes" with long points reaching in every direction. While the typical frame isn't shockingly big—it nets 149 7/8 as a 4x4—36 abnormal points add 184 inches to the awesome rack's non-typical score. The mounted world-record buck is on display at the Missouri Department of Conservation's Runge Nature Center in Jefferson City. Photo by Gordon Whittington.

bowhunters reportedly saw an unbelievable non-typical during the 1981 bow season in the same vicinity. Their names never were recorded, but years later, Jim Holdenreid, another trophy bowhunter living near St. Louis, recalled having talked with them about the deer.

"I was competing in the weekly shoots over at Town Hall Archery in Belleville, Illinois, back in those days," Jim told me. "These two bowhunters from the north side of St. Louis also went over there to shoot. That year, I remember they kept talking about this huge buck that was in their hunting area. Every time we had a shoot in the fall, they would tell us how many times they had seen him the previous week. They apparently were seeing him pretty regularly, though not every time they went out."

Jim told me one of the guys claimed to have had him as close as 20 yards but thick brush prevented a clear shot. The monster eventually walked away from the treestand without a shot being taken. Rumor has it that the two bowhunters nicknamed the non-typical "Socrates" for the ancient Greek philosopher. Whether or not all this is true, or even that the reported non-typical was the Monarch, I can't say. The only way to verify the two bowhunters' possible involvement in this story would be to interview them, but thus far, they have not come forward.

———◆———

One of the guys claimed to have had him as close as 20 yards but thick brush prevented a clear shot.

———◆———

At the beginning of this chapter, I brought up the question of whether or not the deer even should be in the B&C record book. That is an issue because of two other persistent rumors surrounding the buck, making it necessary to deal with them here.

The first issue might have crossed your mind while reading of the Monarch's discovery: Was he "trapped" inside the fenced union property, thus disqualifying him as a free-ranging animal? If some artificial barrier (e.g., a high fence) limited the buck's movement, B&C could not accept him as a world record, period. The club has stringent rules against including an animal so confined.

That question clearly crossed the minds of B&C officials early on, for they asked MDOC to verify that the Monarch had freedom of movement. It turned out that there actually were a number of large holes in the chain-link fence so B&C accepted the entry. (Those sketchy reports of the mysterious bowhunters having seen a huge non-typical outside the property would lend credence to this if the reports could be verified …and it turned out to be the same deer.)

The second rumor holds that the Monarch was a

total fraud from the start. If you are wondering what that's supposed to mean, check out the letter that reached my desk at *North American WHITE-TAIL* in the fall of 1997:

Gordon,

I know you get a lot of letters proclaiming wild things in regards to large whitetails. Well, here's another!

About 7 or 8 years ago, I was in on a conversation, quite by accident, that really set me back. It has to do with the world-record non-typical whitetail from Missouri. It so happens this deer is not from Missouri at all! This deer was a pen-raised deer from Minnesota! He was purchased along with some other deer by someone in Missouri. The Minnesota deer farmer was attempting to deliver these deer without proper paperwork from either Minnesota or Missouri! During a routine stop and check of the animals, he found the big buck dead in his trailer. He panicked, thinking he would be in more trouble if he was caught with a dead deer, so he dragged the deer from the trailer and deposited him under the fence and drove away.

I personally saw pictures of this deer in an obvious pen with other deer. I know deer, and there is no doubt in my mind which deer I was looking at.

Now, you say you need proof! I have none. I don't even know where to tell you to start. I am not trying to take anything away from this deer. He is what he is, whether from a Minnesota pen or Missouri country-side! I just feel the truth should be known of his origin! I know you and the others at North American WHITETAIL *have better resources and connections than I. Please check it out, and if you find the truth, please publish it so the whitetail fraternity will know!*

Thanks,

J.V.W.

Whoa! Now that's a rumor! If true, we have got a

real story on our hands, wouldn't you say?

But, let's not grab the bait just yet. Rather, let's sit back and ponder what this letter claims and by whom it was sent.

"J.V.W.," whoever the nameless, addressless person is, unfortunately has a history of fabricating claims about trophy deer. This person's initials and handwriting, as well as the letter postmark, match those of another letter I received a few months later. In that second envelope was a photo of an obviously fake "world-record" typical, which the person claimed to be a buck one of his/her relatives had shot in Iowa! (A photo of that "rack" can be seen in Chapter 29.) This definitely causes me to question the veracity of the person's claim to have seen a photo showing the Monarch in captivity.

On the other hand, this wasn't the first time I had heard that the huge non-typical was a pen-raised buck that died en route to a private deer facility and was unceremoniously dumped on the side of the road. Indeed, variations of this story have been floating around in whitetail circles for many years. Still, I have many reasons for discounting these claims as pure fantasy, among them are the following:

1. Deer breeders don't often transport incredibly valuable breeder bucks a great distance, especially during the rut. (If they do so, they usually saw the

Dave Beckman appears depressed in this photo, and for good reason. He had just found the world's highest-scoring buck but didn't have a tag of his own to put on the animal! As a result, Missouri wildlife officials claimed the world-record antlers for the state. Photo courtesy of Jim Reimer.

antlers off, though I can see why that wouldn't have happened in this case.)

2. A deer breeder illegally transporting a live world-record buck across state lines would not dump him just because he died to avoid being caught with the dead animal in his trailer. It doesn't make any sense.

3. If someone dumped the buck, how did he place the carcass inside that security fence? There were no large holes nearby, and no evidence indicated that the deer had been dragged or carried to where it was found.

———◆———

Until hard evidence dictates otherwise, let's accept the Monarch for what he is— the highest-scoring whitetail of all time.

———◆———

4. A deer breeder who produced the world's highest-scoring buck would have every reason to let that fact be known throughout the whitetail community so he could cash in on the economic benefits of such a great breeder buck. Apparently, no one knew about such a buck in captivity.

5. Live photos of this buck have never found their way to any of us working in the whitetail media. Perhaps more than any other single point, this makes me question the existence of such photos.

6. David Wissehr, the MDOC biologist who went over the buck with a fine-toothed comb, specifically noted the presence of "sandy, alluvial-type soil" on the buck's hooves and lower legs similar (if not identical) to that found throughout that bottomland area. Also, David told me there was considerable "tannic staining" of lower leg hair, as would be expected for a deer spending most of his life in a damp riverbottom. While no DNA testing was done on the buck, the biologist indicated the deer had the look of a mature buck from that area.

It's only natural for questions to arise when the owner of a world-record whitetail also happens to be the agency responsible for investigating controversial issues about the deer. After all, MDOC officials would want the state to get credit for having produced a B&C world record. The mounted rack, which hangs in the department's Runge Nature Center in Jefferson City, is clearly a source of great pride for Missouri wildlife managers, as would be expected. But, the mere potential for conflict of interest is hardly proof that the "conspiracy theorists" are correct.

So until hard evidence dictates otherwise, let's accept the Monarch for what he is—the highest-scoring whitetail of all time. And, let's just be thankful this phenomenal buck was recovered, for he proved conclusively that the sky really is the limit on antler size. Oh, one more thing: You can be sure his discovery did wonders for the interest in suburban deer hunting!

PICKUP, MISSOURI, 1981

Measurements	Right	Left	Difference
No. of points	19	25	
Main beam	24 1/8	23 3/8	6/8
1st point (G-1)	8 1/8	7 0/8	1 1/8
2nd point (G-2)	7 1/8	8 1/8	1 0/8
3rd point (G-3)	6 3/8	7 6/8	1 3/8
4th point (G-4)	–	–	–
5th point (G-5)	–	–	–
1st circ. (H-1)	5 1/8	5 1/8	–
2nd circ. (H-2)	4 4/8	4 4/8	–
3rd circ. (H-3)	7 6/8	6 5/8	1 1/8
4th circ. (H-4)	3 1/8	3 7/8	6/8
Total	66 2/8	66 3/8	6 1/8
Greatest spread		33 3/8	
Inside spread		23 3/8	
Gross typical score		156 0/8	
Assymetry deductions		-6 1/8	
Non-typical additions		+184 0/8	
Net non-typical score		333 7/8	

11

NEW YORK'S OTHER WORLD RECORD

Before many of today's bowhunters had even been born, an archer bagged one of the most historic whitetails of all time. Too bad nobody knows it.

TITLE: FIRST P&Y TYPICAL WORLD RECORD

SCORE: 149 3/8

HUNTER: GEORGE FERBER

LOCATION: WESTCHESTER COUNTY, NEW YORK

YEAR: 1957

Back in the 1950s, before there was a Pope and Young Club, most bowhunters knew little, if anything, about scoring deer antlers. In those days, the idea of assigning a score to a deer was so foreign to the average bowhunter that some of the greatest trophies weren't widely publicized by outdoor magazines or fully appreciated by the public. By the time the bowhunting community had become familiar with the scoring system, many of these early record bucks had been supplanted by even bigger ones, which then received all of the attention. That, in a nutshell, explains why you've never heard of George Ferber.

To bowhunters hunters today, George's name should at least be familiar, if not legendary. Why? Because he did something that can never be dupli-

cated: He bagged the first buck that could legitimately be called a world record by bow. (At the time his deer was recognized, no non-typicals had been entered and George's buck stood alone as the only bow-kill world record in existence.) He did it during the 1957 season in southern New York's Westchester County. It was a noteworthy achievement—and one for which the hunter himself was justifiably proud —but never in his lifetime did he receive anything more than token credit for his accomplishment. In fact, so poorly were the details of George's historic hunt documented that the P&Y record book doesn't even list the county in which it occurred! (What makes this even more amazing is that of the 15,814 whitetails entered into the P&Y records as of December 31, 1996, George's is one of only *two* listed without a known kill location. The other is Everett Reid's 1962 buck from Iowa.)

How could George's world-record deer have been so slighted for all these years? Sadly, I never got to ask the hunter that question. He passed away in January 1996 at the age of 74. The good news is that some of the details still live in the recollections of George's widow, Gloria, who once was pretty handy with a bow and arrow herself.

During the 1950s, the Ferbers owned a bow shop near their home in Greenwich, Connecticut, just a few miles up the coast from bustling New York City. They were among the finest archers around, as borne out by the fact that in separate years each was crowned a state champion. Gloria never hunted, preferring instead to focus strictly on tournament shooting. Her husband, however, discovered that the skills he used in competition translated well in the deer woods.

After years of hunting whitetails strictly with a gun, George began bowhunting in 1953. According to Gloria, his success was immediate. "He would get a deer every year in bow season," she said. "He had

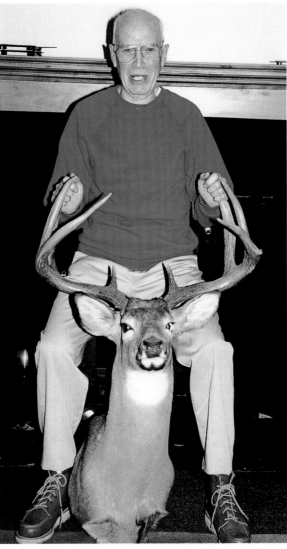

George Ferber's 149 3/8-point typical, shot during the 1957 season in southern New York, won the first-ever bowhunting competition based on the B&C scoring system. That made the impressive 4x4 the first "world record" by bow, though he never was widely promoted as such. Photo courtesy of Gloria Ferber.

tremendous patience and could sit for hours, waiting for a deer to come by."

On an historic day during New York's late bow season in December 1957, such patience proved unnecessary. That morning, according to Gloria, George and hunting partner Tony Angotta headed north across the state line into Westchester County and on to an area they frequently bowhunted near the town of North Salem. The men apparently hadn't been afield long when Tony decided to head off on foot to check out another spot. George liked where he was and picked out a place to sit.

The weather conditions were pretty nasty and seemed unfavorable for deer movement, but somebody forgot to tell this buck. We don't know the details leading up to the shot or where the cedar arrow hit (though the field photo shows either an entry or exit wound high on the deer's left shoulder). All Gloria remembers is that when Tony returned to check on his partner a bit later that morning, George told him, "I got my deer!"

And, what a deer it was! A wide, massive 8-pointer with long beams and long tines, it was certainly the best buck of George's bowhunting career. Gloria's impression is that the men had no idea such a trophy was frequenting their hunting area. Neither man had seen the buck before. Nonetheless, they immediately realized the trophy must be a record for bow kills in that area. What they didn't know was that he would prove to be much more.

In the spring of 1958, George received an invitation to bring the buck to the National Field Archery Association (NFAA) annual tournament and banquet in Grayling, Michigan. This was to be the NFAA's first-ever big-game competition, and based on the entry score of George's buck, he might turn out to be the top typical entered. Into the back of the Ferbers' vehicle went the trophy, which had just been mounted by New York's famed Jonas Brothers Taxidermy.

When George and Gloria reached Grayling, they weren't disappointed. The buck did indeed end up winning the competition, and in the process, he became the first bow-killed typical to be ranked No.1. While it is not clear that the label "world record" ever was *officially* applied to the buck, that's

George was just getting settled into his ground blind when the huge 8-pointer appeared that cold December morning. As it turned out, the deer made a bad decision—George was a Connecticut state archery champion! Photo courtesy of Gloria Ferber.

what he was since no whitetail taken by bow had previously been certified at such a high score on the modern B&C scoring system.

Many of the top bucks arrowed during the 1950s and early 1960s were taken in the farm country of the Midwest. George's buck is especially noteworthy in that he is one of only two No.1 bow kills ever from the East Coast, and the only one from New York. However, if the Ferber buck hadn't been shot, the Empire State might well have been credited with the first bow world record anyway. As unbelievable as it may seem, during that same 1957 bow season in which George bagged his 149 3/8-point world record, another typical netting 149 2/8 points was arrowed in New York. In fact, this buck was from Westchester County as well!

Joe Keeler was the hunter who claimed him. We can only imagine the thoughts that must have gone through his mind when he learned his trophy had been beaten out of the top spot by a buck scoring just 1/8 inch higher…and a buck not just from the same state but from the same county! In the history of bowhunting, few twists of fate are stranger!

George continued to operate his bow shop for a while after shooting the record buck, and during that time, he displayed the mount on the wall there. Although not one to brag, he clearly was proud of his great deer and, when asked, would happily tell the story of the hunt. Sadly, George suffered a heart attack in 1972, which immediately forced him to cut back on his outdoor activities. He underwent open-heart surgery two years later. At far too young an age, he had to walk away from deer hunting, a sport that had been a huge part of his life for years.

◆

George bagged the first buck that could legitimately be called a world record by bow…but never received more than token credit for his accomplishment.

◆

"He really loved nature," Gloria told me. "When he'd come back from a hunt in the evening, he would want to tell me every detail of a bird or animal he had watched that day. I saw him feed chipmunks and chickadees right out of his hand. George just enjoyed the peace and quiet of being in the woods. When his health became such that he couldn't go hunting any more, it was hard on him."

It is too bad that New York's only world-record buck by bow got so little media attention during George's lifetime and that this sportsman never saw his place in hunting history fully acknowledged. Perhaps this belated account of his hunt, sketchy though it may be, will help make amends. At least now, thanks to Gloria, we know where George killed his buck. That may help close the chapter on one of the whitetail world's most special trophies.

George Ferber, New York, 1957

Measurements	Right	Left	Difference
No. of points	4	4	
Main beam	26 6/8	25 4/8	1 2/8
1st point (G-1)	2 4/8	2 6/8	2/8
2nd point (G-2)	12 5/8	12 2/8	3/8
3rd point (G-3)	9 1/8	9 2/8	1/8
4th point (G-4)	–	–	–
5th point (G-5)	–	–	–
1st circ. (H-1)	4 6/8	4 6/8	–
2nd circ. (H-2)	4 4/8	4 4/8	–
3rd circ. (H-3)	5 0/8	5 0/8	–
4th circ. (H-4)	5 0/8	5 0/8	–
Total	65 2/8	64 0/8	2 0/8
Greatest spread		n/a	
Inside spread		22 1/8	
Gross typical score		151 3/8	
Assymetry deductions		-2 0/8	
Non-typical deductions		–	
Net typical score		149 3/8	

12

THE RECORD RACK THEY THREW AWAY

The only thing more unlikely than arrowing a world-record buck on the run is tossing the antlers into the woods afterwards. Amazingly, this North Dakota bowhunter did both!

TITLE: SECOND P&Y TYPICAL
WORLD RECORD

SCORE: 163 4/8

HUNTER: BOBBY TRIPLETT

LOCATION: RENVILLE COUNTY,
NORTH DAKOTA

YEAR: 1958

A few thousand years ago, hunters on the Great Plains took failure a bit more seriously than we do today. The threat of death by starvation or exposure will do that to you. While we modern hunters *want* to bag game, it's really not a matter of life and death if we don't. We simply get back into the truck, turn on the heater and drive home to a well-stocked pantry and warm bed. The stakes clearly were higher for folks whose very existence depended on scrounging up enough meat, hides and sinew to get them through another difficult day.

Faced with such perils, early hunters used whatever tricks they could devise to keep the meat coming. That wasn't always easy. On plains devoid of tall vegetation, sneaking up on something could be a real chore so stalking frequently was abandoned in favor of other tactics. Commonly, animals were spooked into some sort of "trap." Sometimes, this was done by setting fire to the grasslands. In other cases, hunters on foot (and later horseback) pushed game, perhaps toward waiting bowmen or maybe over a cliff. These game drives proved highly effective, particularly on the huge herds of bison that then dotted the plains. Generation after generation, hunting parties used carefully orchestrated drives to stampede the shaggy beasts off cliffs to their deaths.

While neither the "buffalo jump" nor the intentionally set wildfire is a part of the Great Plains hunting scene today, the idea of using forced movement to drive game is still very much alive, and just as effective as ever. In fact, it's one of the most dependable ways to hunt prairie whitetails. Because these deer instinctively know that the lack of brush and timber makes them more visible to predators, they are by nature largely nocturnal. When hunted to any significant degree, they become even more so. Faced with the reality of this behavior pattern, Plains hunters often start driving deer in the early season rather than waiting to use it as a last resort, as is commonly the case elsewhere.

Back in 1958, the only North Dakota whitetail ever proclaimed a world record was taken in just this way…with a bow. The historic hunt occurred in Renville County, roughly 15 miles north of the town of Tolley at a spot on the Mouse River known locally as Swenson Bend. It was the opening day of bow season, and the four hunters involved—Bobby Triplett and his brother Darrell, along with Richard Neubeck and Martin Irgens—decided to use drives from the start. After all, since forced movement had always worked well for them in gun season, they might as well employ it for bowhunting as well.

Swenson Bend certainly seemed a prime location for trying such a tactic. It was a perfect bedding area for deer that fed in the surrounding crop fields each night. Much of the best whitetail cover in the area

Ross Triplett shows off his late father's 1958 buck from Renville County, North Dakota, winner of the second annual National Field Archery Association (NFAA) competition. The massive 12-point rack's typical score of 163 4/8 points pushed it well past George Ferber's 1957 New York trophy, making it a new NFAA "world record." Photo by Roger Selner and Don Stemler.

was in those Mouse River bottoms, where trees, brush and thick grass offered ample cover. With any luck, a short drive through the area would produce a shot for one of the hunters. Darrell and Martin agreed to be the "pushers." Bobby and Richard would do the "posting."

Once everyone was ready, the drive began. It didn't take long for the plan to show its merits. The pair of moving hunters quickly kicked out two big bucks. Both deer began heading straight toward Bobby and Richard, who were hiding close to each other. Hunters sometimes try for years to get a single trophy buck to go where they want him to go. Here were *two* that seemed to be following the game plan to the letter!

In just a few anxious moments, each hunter realized that he would have a shot. Both of their bows were drawn in nervous anticipation. As the two deer zipped past within 10 yards of the hunters, two homemade cedar arrows were released—one at each of the startled animals. Unfortunately, Richard's broadhead never cut a hair. But, Bobby's shot was picture-perfect, catching the massive buck right in his vitals. The deer went only 150 yards or so before piling up. Minutes later, the quartet of excited hunters were celebrating their success, even though they had missed out on a rare "double!"

If this hunt seems unlikely, you're right. But, the circumstances of the kill were remarkably normal in comparison to what Bobby did after field-dressing the deer: He threw away the head—antlers and all!

What might prompt a hunter to do such a preposterous thing? Darrell told me that all anyone in that area cared about at the time was meat, of which there was plenty on this buck. (He dressed out at 227 pounds.) As hard as it might be for us to imagine that a hunter could throw away a world-record rack, that's exactly what happened, without as much as a second thought.

Fortunately, it wasn't long afterwards that one of Bobby's acquaintances was reading about the National Field Archery Association (NFAA) records program for bowhunting trophies in an outdoor magazine. From that, he apparently came up with a description of the current world record—George Ferber's New York buck scoring 149 3/8 points (Chapter 11)—and realized that the North Dakota deer was at least that size. The guy persuaded Bobby to retrieve his buck's head and have the antlers officially measured. Thankfully, the rack had remained undamaged during its unceremonious stay out in the elements and was recovered intact.

Soon, the antlers were measured for entry into the NFAA big-game competition for that year. Based on the entry score, Bobby's rack looked to be a

In this photo, taken soon after the kill, Bobby looks mighty proud of his big 12-pointer. Because meat was far more of a priority than antlers, he chose not to keep the rack—at least not until someone suggested it might be a record! Fortunately, Bobby found the deer's head right where he had dumped it! Photo courtesy of Shirley Nore and Ross Triplett.

shoo-in as the world's biggest typical by bow! Verifying that would take another round of measurements, however. Bobby's widow, Shirley Nore, has graciously provided copies of her husband's correspondence from this time, and these letters offer fascinating insights into the certification process:

May 12, 1959

Mr. Bobby Triplett
Tolley, North Dakota

Dear Sir:

The measurements on your application indicate that you have set a new world record for whitetail deer by approximately 15 points. Before a rack can be accepted as a new world record it must be measured by a panel of official NFAA measurers. Therefore, so that your rack can take its rightful place as the new world record whitetail deer, please send it to Mr. Glenn St. Charles at the address indicated on the above letterhead. The rack will be returned to you as soon as the measurements and pictures have been taken. We would like to request that we be permitted to delay returning the rack until after the National Tournament in Bend, Oregon, the last of July. Please advise if we can display your trophy at the tournament.

Please note that your trophy rack will take the yearly award this year if it is sent in before June 1 of this year. So, please do not delay in sending it in. It is adequate to send your rack in a cardboard box.

Anxiously yours,
(Signed)
Mr. Audrey E. Bryan
Member, Bowhunter's Boone & Crockett Records
Committee

Following receipt of that letter, Bobby shipped the antlers to Glenn in Seattle. Shortly thereafter, the hunter received the following letter:

June 25, 1959

Bobby Triplett
Tolley, North Dakota

Dear Bobby:

Your Whitetail deer is the new World Record Bowhunter Trophy by a wide margin, with 163 4/8 Boone and Crockett points.

We would like to have this rack on display at the National Tournament at Bend, Oregon, July 27 through 30. Shall I keep this rack and take it there myself and then return it to you? Or, would you rather I send it back with the idea that perhaps you would ship it to Bend, Oregon. Possibly you will be there in person?

Please let me know what your plans are concerning your rack, but keep in mind that we would certainly appreciate having it for display. You will get a plaque award for this record Whitetail, and it will be available at the tournament. If you are not there, it will be mailed to you.

Thank you very much for your cooperation.

Yours truly,
(Signed)
Glenn St. Charles

Bobby decided to let them display the rack at the tournament, even though he couldn't attend himself. A few months after the event, he received in the mail both his antlers and his plaque from the NFAA, thus officially bringing the world-record award to North Dakota. Not bad for a rack that once had been thrown away!

One interesting side point. You can count on one hand the number of river systems that begin in Canada and then flow into the U.S. before heading back into Canada again. Yet, against all odds, two of these river valleys have produced world-record whitetails. Bobby's buck is one. Jim Brewster's buck from British Columbia (Chapter 8) is the other. The Mouse River, near which the Triplett buck was shot, flows into North Dakota from Saskatchewan, loops to the east and then heads north into Manitoba. Brewster's former No.1 B&C non-typical was shot on the Elk River in British Columbia, which flows into the Kootenay, which then runs down into Montana and Idaho (as the Kootenai) before heading back into British Columbia again.

While Bobby Triplett hoped to bag a deer during the 1958 bow season, the thought of setting a record clearly didn't cross his mind—even *after* he had shot the new No.1 typical. He had no idea there was a new program for ranking the racks of archery bucks. If he hadn't heard about it when he did, his big 12-point rack might have been dragged away by coyotes or chewed up by hungry rodents, wiping out North Dakota's greatest claim to whitetail fame in the process. Thank goodness this bowhunter remembered where he had dumped his "trash!"

BOBBY TRIPLETT, NORTH DAKOTA, 1958

Measurements	Right	Left	
No. of points	5	7	
Main beam	25 4/8	25 5/8	
Inside spread			18 0/8
Net typical score			163 4/8

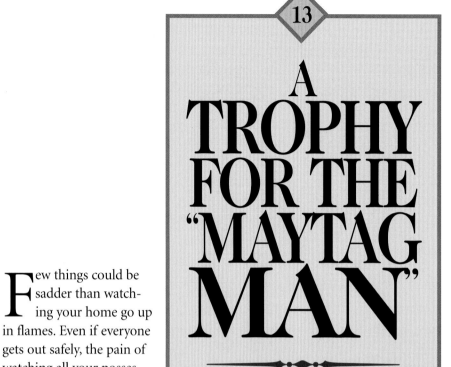

13

A TROPHY FOR THE "MAYTAG MAN"

What could an old washing machine and a world-record buck possibly have in common? You'll see!

TITLE: THIRD (TIE) P&Y TYPICAL WORLD RECORD
SCORE: 164 3/8
HUNTER: GILBERT GUTTORMSON
LOCATION: NORMAN COUNTY, MINNESSOTA
YEAR: 1953

Few things could be sadder than watching your home go up in flames. Even if everyone gets out safely, the pain of watching all your possessions being consumed by fire must be almost unbearable. While most homes are insured against the monetary value of such losses, the victims of a fire soon realize that some belongings simply can't be replaced.

Gilbert Guttormson knows this feeling all too well. In 1988, the then-80-year-old resident of Georgetown, Minnesota, found himself picking through the ashes of an electrical fire that had ravaged part of his residence. Besides all else the inferno consumed, it destroyed the rack of the former world-record buck he had arrowed 35 years earlier and the hunter's prized plaque that signified his whitetail as No.1 in the P&Y records. Since then, Gilbert has had only a handful of old photos to remind him of one of bowhunting's most significant deer. In fact, except for the account you're about to read, this great buck has never been featured in any other book or magazine.

Back in the 1950s, bowhunters had to learn things the hard way. There were no specialized magazines, videos, television shows or seminars to offer instruction. In that era, to pursue whitetails with bow and arrow was to suffer one frustration after another, often for years on end. Scant few experts were around to tell you what you were doing wrong. It helped to have a sense of humor, because you needed one to deal with the botched opportunities that were sure to come your way.

But even in 1953, when most whitetail hunters had never even thought of giving archery a try,

Gilbert was no new-comer to the sport. Way back in his childhood in the second decade of the 1900s, the northwest Minnesota native began experimenting with a bow, though not for deer hunting. "We'd cut an elm limb that had the right bend in it and use that for a bow," he told me. And in later years when his interest in archery did turn to deer, he would prove just as creative, building an innovative target system that undoubtedly helped him claim his world record.

Being a farmer by trade, Gilbert was a natural at "tinkering." When he and some friends began bowhunting for deer in the early 1950s, they realized they needed a realistic but safe way to practice on moving targets since their favored hunting method, deer drives, didn't offer many standing shots. Finally, Gilbert came up with a plan—one that involved, of all things, a washing machine.

"I had a Maytag washer that we rigged up to pull a line between two trees, with a riverbank for a safe

A 1953 deer drive in Minnesota's Red River bottoms pushed this huge-bodied 164 3/8-point typical right to Gilbert Guttormson, whose unique archery practice regimen had prepared him for a running shot. The rack turned out to be a record-breaker, but unfortunately, it was lost in a fire at Gilbert's home. Photo courtesy of Gilbert Guttormson.

backstop," he recalled. "We'd put a piece of cardboard shaped like a deer on that line. With the washing machine, we could crank the deer from one end to the other, then back the other way. We spent a lot of time shooting at those moving targets, because that's the only way you can hope to have much chance of killing a running deer with a bow. After a while, we got to be pretty good at hitting where we wanted. I actually still have the remains of that old washer in my junk pile somewhere."

In those days, hunting bows were either of "straight" or recurve design (the latter was considered pretty fancy by Gilbert and some other practitioners of the sport in those days). Gilbert's own weapon was a 52-inch-long, fiberglass, takedown "straight" bow with the enormous draw weight of 80 pounds at 28 inches. "It had a pretty heavy pull," he noted, "but I didn't draw it all the way to 28 inches. My draw length was around 26 to 27 inches." Armed with this bow and fiberglass shafts tipped with double-edged Ben Pearson broadheads, Gilbert entered the 1953 season with hopes that he would finally arrow his first deer after several seasons of failure.

His hunting party varied in size each day, depending on how many guys could shake loose from their obligations. Among those who frequently joined Gilbert for a hunt were Harold Anderson, Francis and Harold Wambaugh, Jim Herman and Arnold Anderson and his son, Jewell. All were locals who knew the country well. Because there were virtually no other bowhunters around in those days, they had free rein to hunt a lot of country. On this particular October morning, five of the guys met up with Gilbert for a day of deer drives on the Red River bottoms between Georgetown and Perley near the North Dakota border.

The Red is highly unusual for a North American river—it runs almost directly northward for its entire 310-mile length before flowing into Manitoba's gigantic Lake Winnipeg. Most of the watershed offers scant cover—huge fields stretch for miles to the virtually flat horizon—but right along the river there's a strip of brush and timber in which wildlife thrives. It was in this slender band of riparian habitat that Gilbert and friends hoped to find deer.

Gilbert's buck had such a big body—270 pounds field dressed! – that local folks didn't notice the antlers very much at first. The rack's significance hit home only after the deer became a world record by bow more than six years after the hunt. Photo courtesy of Gilbert Guttormson.

Deer drives are most productive when conducted by hunters who know both the land and their quarry well. Fortunately, the hunters in this group were all experienced—even Jewell, who in his early 20s was the youngest member of the bunch. As the day progressed, the guys conducted drive after drive, hoping that someone would get to test those well-honed shooting skills.

In mid-afternoon, the party approached one of the largest bends in that stretch of riverbottom. The bend, located in the southwestern corner of Norman County, contained a large brushy area. The men had been taking turns posting and driving, and by chance, it was Gilbert and Jewell's turn to wait in ambush while the other hunters pushed. With several drives already behind them, the standers were dragging a bit by the time they walked the half-mile to get into position. Still, the great amount of cover in this broad stretch of riverbottom sparked thoughts that this could be the lucky spot. Eventually, everyone was in place and the push began.

"I set up along the river in a draw," Gilbert remembered. "I'd been there for a little while when I heard a deer coming my way, following the river's edge. I couldn't see anything, though, because I was down below the riverbank near the bend. Finally, I saw him. It was a big buck. He was coming right past me, running from my left to my right. He was close, maybe only 20 feet away, when I shot."

All of those hours spent practicing on cardboard deer "running" down that rope between the trees had given Gilbert confidence that he could make such a shot, especially at close range. But as is so often the case under real-world hunting conditions, something went awry. Instead of hitting the buck in the chest cavity as intended, the arrow struck a shade too far back, catching the buck in the paunch. As the massive deer whirled into the brush and bounded out of sight, the hunter could see the broadhead sticking out one side of the body and the fletching out the other. Not good.

When the guys met up at the end of the drive, Gilbert told them what had happened. Fortunately, they decided to hold tight for a couple of hours before going after the buck. By the time that nervous waiting period had passed, there was only enough daylight for one more push through the area. With luck, one of the drivers would either find the buck dead, pick up his trail or push him out in front of another hunter, who might put the deer down for good. Gilbert, of course, was again one of the posters, and as he waited in ambush, all he could do was hope for the best.

We'll never know exactly how the deer would have been listed in the record book had he selected a different route of escape on that second drive. Perhaps he would be listed with two hunters' names alongside him rather than just one. It's a moot question anyway, for when the wounded animal once again started moving, he headed right to the

guy who had already put an arrow into him.

"I heard him coming," Gilbert told me, "but the brush was so thick I couldn't see anything. Finally, I jumped up onto a log and pretty soon I spotted him. Just like the first time, he was coming past me at a slow gallop from left to right. That was good because it's easier to follow a target from left to right than right to left. He was maybe 20 to 25 feet from me, and I aimed for his chest again. This time, I made a much better hit. I luckily caught him with his right front leg forward, and my arrow hit him in the heart. He went down in just a few yards. Had I caught him with that front leg back, I don't know if it would have been as good a hit."

Two hours after the buck had first been hit, Gilbert had finished the job. When the hunters examined the huge-bodied 15-pointer, they discovered that the initial arrow was gone, apparently knocked out or pulled out by the buck. A trip to the sporting-goods store in Fargo would replenish his arrow supply. All Gilbert or any of his friends cared about at the moment was that they had teamed up to shoot a really big deer, one that would provide plenty of welcome venison for the long winter ahead.

Even though this prime agricultural region regularly produces hefty bucks, Gilbert's trophy was something special. "We hung him in a tree that night, and the next evening, we took him into Georgetown to the grain scales to weigh him," the hunter noted. "Even after being field-dressed and hanging for a day, he still weighed 270 pounds! That was the biggest buck I ever saw. We all had to work way into the night to get the carcass cut up and ground into burger. We divided the meat among everybody in the hunting party, but we all still had a good bit to take home."

If the deer had chosen a different route of escape, perhaps he would be listed with two hunters' names instead of just one.

You might assume that news of this big buck's demise at the hands of a bowhunter would spread rapidly since archery hunting for deer was such a novelty at the time. But, Gilbert told me there was no major publicity surrounding his kill, only some short mentions in a couple of local newspapers. He didn't even get a shoulder mount of the buck.

Instead, he simply sawed off the skull plate and hung the rack on his wall, a prized memento of a special day in the deer woods.

At the time, there wasn't much else for Gilbert to do with his buck, anyway. After all, the first big-game competition for bowhunters, conducted by the National Field Archery Association, was still several years away. Once the meat was in the freezer and the rack on the wall, as far as Gilbert was concerned the story was over. Over the next few years, he continued to bowhunt with his friends and arrowed a few more deer. Family and farming dominated his life, and the big deer became just a pleasant memory.

Finally, Gilbert read in a magazine (probably one published by the Minnesota Bow Hunters Association) that there was a new program designed to honor the top trophies taken with bow and arrow. Figuring his 1953 buck might be one of the better ones ever taken by an archer, he decided to enter the buck in this competition, which was being conducted by the fledgling Pope and Young Club. The hunter was informed that he should send his antlers to a Dr. Shepard in the Twin Cities, who was one of the very few official measurers then in the state.

Soon, the news came back that the effort had been worthwhile. According to those first measurements, the Guttormson typical was a potential No.1! However, there was no way of knowing if an even bigger rack might show up prior to the next awards ceremony scheduled for Grayling, Michigan, in 1960. There, the top trophies of every North American big-game species would be honored. Gilbert was invited to box up his rack and again submit it for scoring, this time to P&Y founder Glenn St. Charles in Seattle, Washington. There, several official measurers would render a final "panel" score on the deer.

When the banquet was held in Grayling that summer, Gilbert didn't attend but his rack was there. At 164 3/8 net points, it was named the official world record in the typical category. The only "bad" news, if you could call it that, was the fact that another buck (Chapter 14) had been measured at exactly the same net score by the panel, meaning world-record honors would have to be shared!

In effect, Gilbert's great 8x7 typical had been the

This is the only existing close-up photo of Gilbert's rack. Sadly, the antlers and the plaque signifying the deer as a P&Y record were lost in a fire at the hunter's home some years ago. Photo courtesy of the Pope and Young Club.

lone "world record" by bow for several years. But because of what can only be called unlucky timing, the Minnesota trophy never was recognized as the sole-holder of that honor. Had the deer been entered into either of the first two big-game competitions held by the National Field Archery Association in 1958 and 1959, he would have beaten out both the 149 3/8-point Ferber buck from New York (Chapter 11) and the 163 4/8-point Triplett buck from North Dakota (Chapter 12) for the record in the typical category.

GILBERT GUTTORMSON, MINNESOTA, 1953

Measurements	Right	Left	
No. of points	8	7	
Main beam	25 4/8	25 4/8	
Inside spread			19 6/8
Net typical score			164 3/8

The fire couldn't destroy his recollections of an autumn afternoon spent with good friends on an amazing hunt.

It's almost certain that Gilbert's deer would have netted higher if measured relatively soon after being harvested. During the eight years between the buck's death and the panel's measuring of the rack, the bone undoubtedly dried enough to lose an inch or more of score. This seems especially likely when we consider that Gilbert's trophy hung for all those years in a dry environment. Had this buck been officially measured soon after the kill, he almost certainly would have stood alone at the top for nearly a decade.

None of these "ifs" seem to bother the man who put Minnesota on the bowhunting map nearly a half-century ago. The sportsman is happy just to have been a part of whitetail history. What Gilbert told me he really wanted was to have the big rack back, but he knew that would never happen. Still, the fire couldn't destroy his recollections of an autumn afternoon spent with good friends on an amazing hunt. When all is said and done, such memories really are what matters most.

14

ONE SEPTEMBER TO REMEMBER

Quick thinking gave this prairie bowhunter the chance he had been hoping for, and quick shooting helped him capitalize on a fleeting opportunity.

TITLE: THIRD (TIE) P&Y TYPICAL WORLD RECORD

SCORE: 164 3/8

HUNTER: JERRY POLESKY

LOCATION: WIBAUX COUNTY, MONTANA

YEAR: 1959

If you close your eyes, take a deep breath and open your imagination, it's easy to see the scene in sharp detail. Somewhere out on the prairie, a hunter creeps along the edge of a winding ravine, his eyes constantly probing the landscape for any sign of game. Suddenly, there's a flicker of movement in the brush and a deer appears. The hunter instinctively scrambles into shooting position, draws his bow and releases, flicking the arrow toward its target. Minutes later, the triumphant archer and the rest of his hunting party gather around the fallen animal and give thanks for their hard-earned success.

A scene of Indian life on the Great Plains? That description might fit, but this was actually a far more modern event, one played out in the latter half of the 20th century by men whose ancestors had long since moved beyond the bow as a weapon of necessity. It was one of the earlier kills of the so-called "modern" era of bowhunting, in which hunters rediscovered both the allure and the frustration of trying to take wild game with stick and string. And, it was noteworthy in another way as well—the whitetail buck lying at the hunters' feet was destined to become a world record.

Jerry Polesky need not close his eyes to envision that scene. He was the leading man in this real-life drama. It happened back in 1959 during one of Montana's first modern bow seasons, when only a handful of sportsmen in the state had enough interest in archery hunting to give it a try. But, the passage of several decades has not obscured Jerry's memories of that fateful trophy hunt when he and his deer became a part of whitetail history.

Back then, as now, Jerry was a resident of the eastern Montana town of Glendive, which lies on the Missouri River in the middle of wide-open ranching country. He had been bowhunting for several years but hadn't filled a tag, despite the presence of plenty of whitetails and mule deer in the area. Some newcomers to the sport might have become discouraged by this lack of success but not Jerry. Instead, he found himself becoming more and more passionate about arrowing a deer. By the time the 1959 season opener arrived, he and his hunting partner, Keith Johnson, were shooting their recurves with greater accuracy than ever. This year, they believed one of them finally would break the ice.

The season began in early September. Sure enough, Keith got things going that first week with an 84-pound mule deer doe, which was taken with a single arrow through the lungs. Keith was eager to follow up this success with another kill, because state law then allowed bowhunters to take one

On September 19, 1959, a three-man drive in Wibaux County, Montana, gave bowhunter Jerry Polesky a chance to launch an arrow at this big 12-pointer and he made it count. The clean, symmetrical rack's net typical score of 164 3/8 points was recognized as a new world record at the Pope and Young Club's 1960 banquet in Grayling, Michigan. Photo by Roger Selner and Don Stemler.

mulie and one whitetail per season. Jerry, meanwhile, could only hope his first chance would come. He had not been able to get away to hunt at all during opening week and was anxiously counting the days until the following Saturday, September 19.

When Jerry picked up Keith that morning and they began the drive to a friend's ranch in neighboring Wibaux (WE-bo) County, their anticipation was at an all-time high.

As Jerry and Keith headed out, they discovered that a rare fog had settled over the land. About 20 miles into the trip and 10 miles from their destination, they hit a little-traveled gravel road just as legal shooting light came. The young men had permission to hunt the private land on either side of this road, so if they saw a deer they were free to go after it.

No more than a mile down the road, Keith yelled, "Hold it!" Jerry hit the brakes and spotted a group of four nice whitetail bucks about to cross the road 40 yards in front of the car. They weren't monster bucks, but that didn't matter to the two novice bowhunters, who were eager to get *any* whitetail. Jerry and Keith allowed the bucks, seemingly unconcerned, to ease across the road and into a nearby draw.

It was time to plot strategy. Jerry, they decided, would sneak around to the top end of the ravine and settle into a hiding spot. Keith would give him 15 minutes to do so and then would begin walking up the ravine at a slow pace, hoping to push at least one of the deer within range of Jerry's recurve. The wind would be in Jerry's favor. Perhaps they could pull it off.

After getting into position, Jerry waited for several minutes but saw nothing. He decided to move uphill a short distance to a point that would offer him a better view. That's just what he found—in the form of four deer walking quickly in single file toward him at a range of 50 yards! But, Jerry immediately realized the deer would pass on the far side of some brush. From where the archer sat, he knew he would have no chance of getting an arrow to the deer. He had to move again.

The plan was going well, and Jerry believes he would have pulled it off...except for the cock pheasant that flushed under his feet. When the big bird burst into the air with a cackle, the deer looked up, saw Jerry and crashed out the side of the draw. At a range of only 50 yards from either hunter, they were in archery hunting's "frustration zone"—close

Surprisingly, Jerry's record buck, which dressed out at 181 pounds, is one of very few No.1 whitetails ever photographed at the scene of the kill. In those days, Montana bowhunters were required to wear bright clothing even weeks prior to the start of gun season! A young Jerry looks justifiably proud. Photo courtesy of Jerry Polesky.

enough to offer their pursuers a tantalizing look but not close enough for a good shot. Neither Jerry nor Keith loosed an arrow.

The hunters were discouraged by how that encounter had turned out, but they didn't take time to bemoan their fate. They already were running late for a rendezvous with their friend, Zane Wood, at his family's farm down the road. They hopped back into the car and cruised on to the Woods' residence, arriving at 7 a.m.

Jerry and Keith recounted their close call with the four bucks in the draw to Zane, who, though a first-year bowhunter, was an experienced gun hunter. As the three discussed their plans for the morning, Zane said his sister had recently seen two big whitetail bucks while she was horseback riding on the property. The hunters decided to pursue those deer. If the two bucks were still in the area, Zane, who had grown up on this property and knew it well, said he had a good idea where they would be. So, the trio of young bowhunters gathered up their gear and headed out. By 7:30, they had arrived at the chosen spot roughly two miles from the farmhouse.

What a great-looking piece of deer habitat it was! The site included a long, winding draw with steep sides and plenty of brushy cover to make old bucks feel right at home. Zane dropped off into the bottom. Keith stayed up on one slope, and Jerry crossed over to the other. The two flankers were to walk as quietly as possible and try to stay about 40 yards ahead of Zane. If he did bump a buck, the animal might sneak out and pass close enough to one of them for a shot, though they all were well aware that big bucks have a habit of bedding tightly in such situations, only to explode up virtually when stepped upon.

The three bowhunters began their push. For roughly 90 minutes, they worked their way up the draw, which was growing progressively narrower, steeper and deeper. Only one deer was seen, a small doe that busted out several hundred yards ahead of the men. By now, the sky had grown much brighter, though a chill lingered in the air and the sun still was veiled by a thin layer of clouds. With sweaty palms, Jerry clutched his 52-pound bow and tried to watch every direction at once.

As so often happens on a deer drive, the scene went from quiet to chaotic in the blink of an eye. Suddenly, the sound of cracking brush erupted from the bottom. "Coming out! Coming out!" yelled Zane.

—◆—

They were all well aware that big bucks have a habit of bedding tightly in such situations, only to explode up virtually when stepped upon.

—◆—

Jerry's eyes frantically searched the brush below him for any sign of a deer. Despite the ruckus, he could see nothing. He quickly glanced across the gorge at Keith, who apparently had a much better view of the proceedings—because his bow was drawn and his eyes were the size of saucers!

Faced with such a situation, many hunters might have lost their composure and simply watched the proceedings. To Jerry's credit, he didn't. Instead, he glanced ahead and saw a small clearing. To escape the draw, he realized the deer would have to pass through that spot. Jerry started running as hard as he could, hoping to get there in time for a shot.

—◆—

There was no time to calculate the lead or think about the shot. Jerry simply drew his bow, picked out what looked to be the larger of the bucks and let the arrow fly.

—◆—

As he reached the opening, he saw two big bucks literally run into each other in their effort to scramble to safety. But, neither fell or even slowed appreciably. Regrouping, the two whitetails were now running hard, headed toward Jerry. In a moment, they would be within bow range—15 yards below him and 15 yards out.

There was no time to calculate the lead or think about the shot. Jerry simply drew his bow, picked out what looked to be the larger of the bucks and let the arrow fly. The 30-inch cedar shaft caught the buck near the spine but apparently didn't sever it. The deer kept going with perhaps six inches of arrow still protruding from his near side. Then, just as quickly as they had appeared, both bucks disappeared into the thick brush.

"He's hit! He's hit!" Jerry yelled. He then glanced at his wristwatch. It was 9 a.m. Wisely, the hunters suppressed their desire to begin trailing the deer immediately. Though excited, Jerry had a bad feeling about his shot, which had caught the buck high in the back. The three young hunters sat down and forced themselves to wait a full 50 minutes before starting on the animal's trail.

The plan was to continue up the draw in the same way the drive had been proceeding before the bucks were jumped. The only difference was that instead of simply walking along the bottom of the ravine, Zane now would be trying to follow fresh tracks and/or blood. As it turned out, he found no blood, which told the hunters that the buck's bleeding was strictly internal. This wasn't exactly a boost to Jerry's hopes of finding his prize, but at least the relatively thin strip of cover should narrow the search area considerably.

After moving about 100 yards up the deep draw and checking every speck of cover along the way, Zane spotted the back portion of Jerry's arrow lying on the ground. Perhaps 50 yards farther up the ravine, Keith suddenly dropped to his knees and silently pointed ahead to the buck, which was lying on Jerry's side of the draw and still very much alive.

The Polesky buck is not only big, but he is quite symmetrical, a rare combination. Today, the mount of the former world record proudly occupies a wall of Jerry's well-stocked trophy room. Photo by Roger Selner and Don Stemler.

Coming to full draw just as the buck made it to his feet, Jerry picked out an aiming point behind the left shoulder and let the bowstring slip from his adrenaline-charged fingers. The archer watched as the arrow leapt from his recurve and struck the target perfectly. Wheeling on impact, the big buck took off, making it perhaps 20 yards before falling.

As if on cue, the sun broke from the clouds and shined down brightly on the ecstatic trio of bowhunters, who immediately gathered around to admire the deer. The hunt had been a team effort, and so was the celebration. After field-dressing the huge, symmetrical 6x6, the men did something quite unusual for that era—they found a camera and shot an entire roll of film of their prize in the field.

On a set of scales in town, Jerry's pre-rut trophy would prove to weigh 181 pounds, quite respectable for that area. But ultimately, the buck's rack would draw far more attention than his body.

The National Field Archery Association (NFAA) had held its first two big-game awards for archery trophies in the summers of 1958 and 1959. The typical whitetail category at those two competitions had been won by the 149 3/8-point George Ferber buck from New York (Chapter 11) and the 163 4/8-point Bobby Triplett buck from North Dakota (Chapter 12), respectively. The entry score on Jerry's Montana buck suggested it might be a shade bigger than the Triplett buck, the world record at the time. But, Jerry would have to wait until the summer of 1960 to learn if he had indeed taken bowhunting's No. 1 typical.

That awards period ended April 1, 1960, after which Jerry's 12-pointer was one of the big-game trophies invited to be panel-measured by the club at Grayling, Michigan, in June 1960. There, the rack was awarded a final typical score of 164 3/8, high enough to claim the official world record by 7/8 inch over the Triplett buck. But, the Montana deer wouldn't have the stage to himself. Exactly the same net score had been given to Gilbert Guttormson's 13-pointer from Minnesota (Chapter 13), which had been taken in 1953 but not previously entered. So, Jerry and Gilbert's great bucks became co-holders of the P&Y world record in their category.

---◆---

Jerry's trophy remains Montana's only whitetail ever recognized as a world record.

---◆---

Today, Jerry remains an avid hunter. Indeed, after taking his historic whitetail, he went on to claim one of the state's best mulies by bow. There are now far more bowhunters in his area. That, along with the increased awareness of Montana as a hunting hotspot, has made it increasingly difficult to obtain access to prime ranches. Jerry now spends most of bow season on public land. "There aren't as many trophy deer there," he told me, "but I don't have to worry about getting permission to hunt."

There has been plenty of justified hype about Montana's monster whitetails in the past two decades, and you might assume the Treasure State has produced several world-record bucks. But, that's not the case. Jerry's trophy, taken in the early part of bowhunting's modern era, remains Montana's only whitetail ever officially recognized a world record. We might one day see another, but even if that happens, the "tag-team" buck from Wibaux County will always be the first.

JERRY POLESKY, MONTANA, 1959

Measurements	Right	Left	
No. of points	6	6	
Main beam	21 4/8	21 6/8	
Inside spread			16 5/8
Net typical score			164 3/8

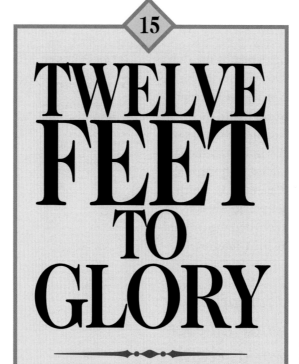

15

TWELVE FEET TO GLORY

When a young Maryland bowhunter decided to climb a tree, his chances of taking a world-record buck began to rise as well.

TITLE: FIFTH P&Y TYPICAL WORLD RECORD

SCORE: 165 4/8

HUNTER: KENT PRICE, JR.

LOCATION: KENT COUNTY, MARYLAND

YEAR: 1962

Historic moments often depend upon several seemingly unrelated factors coming together in just the right way. Kent Price, Jr.'s world-record archery typical is a perfect illustration. If ever a whitetail was destined to be recognized as No.1 in his category, this is the one.

Consider the evidence. Prior to taking his beautiful 10-point buck on Maryland's Eastern Shore, Kent had never shot a deer with either gun or bow. He had never even heard of the Pope and Young Club, the organization that ultimately would proclaim his buck a world record. And amazingly, by the time Kent's deer was recognized as No.1, an even larger typical had been arrowed by another bowhunter, though not yet verified as the record. The line between fame and anonymity can be incredibly thin, and perhaps nobody ever proved that fact more conclusively than Kent did back in 1962.

The story of Maryland's only world-record deer began in the late 1950s when Kent was still in his early 20s. He bought a 50-pound Ben Pearson Mustang recurve and some wooden arrows and began practicing whenever he could. Soon, he set out to shoot his first deer. In those days, the region harbored far fewer whitetails than it does today, but the hunting spot Kent had access to was one of the best. You see, the University of Delaware student was married to the daughter of Dr. Joe Linduska, then manager of Remington Farms.

While the name of this huge Kent County property has now been changed to Chesapeake Farms, it is still owned by DuPont, the parent company of Remington when Kent killed his buck. Back in the late 1950s and early 1960s, the gun and ammunition maker used the farm for entertaining corporate guests, including many outdoor writers. Joe, now deceased, had great expertise in managing land for wildlife and turned Remington Farms into a tremendous hunting spot. The combination of fertile soils, mild coastal climate and vast agricultural plantings made the place a haven for various game species, especially whitetails.

It was here, on one of the first intensively managed wildlife properties on the Atlantic Seaboard, that young Kent began his quest for his first deer. The situation could hardly have been better. Deer trails crisscrossed many of the woodlots on the farm, and there was no shortage of obvious feeding areas, including fields of soybeans and corn. In addition to the quality of the habitat, Kent practically had the place to himself during the early bow season. That may seem odd at first, but it makes perfect sense when you think about it.

The only world-record whitetail in Maryland history was arrowed by Kent Price, Jr. on November 6, 1962, on what was then Remington Farms in Kent County. A net typical score of 165 4/8 P&Y points pushed the 5x5 into first place, just 1 1/8 inches ahead of the Guttormson and Polesky bucks, which had been tied for the record. Photo courtesy of Kent Price, Jr.

The brass at Remington (pardon the pun) figured they had nothing to gain by entertaining bowhunters because the company didn't make archery gear! So, except for wingshooters and employees, Remington Farms was pretty much deserted in October and early November prior to the opening of gun season for deer.

Even so, Kent found his first three years of bowhunting the property to be a lesson in frustration…and futility. Like most archery hunters of that era, Kent relied on ground blinds, figuring that if he spent enough time in them (he had several scattered

around the area) sooner or later he and a buck would end up in the same place at the same moment. Then, he would get a good shot. In an effort to avoid being seen, Kent traded his everyday clothes for full camouflage, including a facemask. He even painted his bow olive drab and black to eliminate glare. Yet, even when the young hunter managed to avoid the prying eyes and ears of his quarry, a stray wind current always seemed to compromise his ambush. Kent was increasingly annoyed by his inability to get a buck within bow range. Desperate for a solution, he finally decided to listen to those stories about hunting from trees.

Opening morning of the 1962 bow season found Kent once more in a ground blind but not for long. Following that uneventful hunt, he decided it was time to start looking for an elevated ambush. (There was no such thing then as a commercially available portable stand. Besides, Kent was looking for a "natural" elevated stand, a rare commodity for bowhunters.) At first, he couldn't imagine how he was going to find one. It would take just the right tree to provide a safe, comfortable vantage point. Finally, as Kent was about to give up his search for a workable site, he found what he had been looking for—an oak tree, perhaps three feet in diameter, that had been sawed off some 12 feet above the ground. The level cut would provide a fairly comfortable seat, and there was even a back-rest of jagged wood that had been formed when the upper part of the tree sheared off before toppling. The sawed-off top part still leaned up against the standing "stump," giving Kent a convenient ramp up to his seat.

Of course, no matter how comfortable a stand might be or how good a view it might offer, none of that matters if there are not deer in the area. Fortunately, this particular ambush was in an ideal spot and Kent knew it. Before him lay a huge drained pond that had been planted to millet, and cornering into this area was a picked cornfield with plenty of scattered kernels remaining. Rounding out the whitetail smorgasbord was an adjacent woodlot with ample acorns. One big trail was 40 yards down the woods' edge from this tree. Another ran almost beneath it. In short, there was every reason to think this was a focal point for deer feeding activity. When the rut got underway, it also figured to be a great place to find a buck in search of female companionship.

For Kent, a major question still remained. How could he possibly keep from being seen atop this exposed 12-foot-high stump along the edge of the field? When he climbed onto this perch and surveyed his surroundings, he knew he would stand out like a lighthouse if he hunted from it. As the

When the big buck passed within spitting distance of Kent's makeshift stand in a broken tree, the young bowhunter drove his 26-inch arrow home and the buck piled up within 100 yards. Photo by Dr. Joe Linduska, courtesy of Kent Price, Jr.

young hunter was trying to decide whether or not to keep looking for that perfect stand, a doe walked into the field and began to feed at fairly close range, oblivious to the fact that a hunter was in plain view. She eventually moved out of sight without concern, convincing Kent that both his camo and the height of his elevated perch were good enough to let him hunt undetected by deer. Then and there, he decided that he would try hunting from the stump after all.

In the early weeks of bow season, Kent did indeed spend some time in his new tree stand. Though he bagged no deer, he remained convinced that hunting from this broken oak was far superior to being "land-locked." In fact, he actually got a crack at a 4-pointer from the tree, but a bad case of nerves prompted him to shoot before that deer was close enough. The shot missed. What the young hunter didn't know at the time was how lucky he had been that his single deer tag remained in his pocket rather than on the rack of that young buck.

On Tuesday morning, November 6, Kent gave the stump another try. Two does approached early on, but he had no intention of shooting them. After a while, they began to peer intently off into the distance across the huge millet patch. When Kent looked that way, he immediately saw what had caught their attention. Six bucks —every one of them big—had walked into view perhaps a half-mile away! Kent's blood pressure pegged out.

"My mind's eye registered *elk*," Kent later would recall, even though he knew full well that the animals before him were not wapiti but whitetails.

The bucks were in no particular hurry to go anywhere. They slowly fed along the edge where the millet and woodlot joined, coming closer to Kent with each step. For some hunters, this leisurely pace might have been a relief, offering a chance to get the nerves under control before a potential shot. In this case, however, the young archer found the wait to be torture. "Ten minutes of this, I thought, and I'll be too rattled to shoot even if they do come into range," he recalled.

Gradually, all the bucks began to fade back into the brush. Before Kent's hopes could be dashed yet again, however, a huge 10-pointer apparently decided he had rather carouse than browse. Turning his attention to the does, which were feeding on acorns perhaps 100 yards from the bowhunter's hideout, he began moving straight toward them, coming ever nearer the tree stand. As Kent watched, the thick-necked buck paused to check out the does and then walked right on past them, apparently convinced they weren't yet in heat.

Before Kent's eyes, his dream of getting a buck into bow range was coming true. The wide-racked 5x5 was practically on a collision course for the stump stand! But as the monster bore down on him at a steady walk, Kent soon realized that he was directly in the deer's line of sight, and thus unable to move. All the breathless bowhunter could do was hold steady and wait for a chance to draw his bow.

As the buck neared bow range, Kent could fully appreciate both his size and his keen awareness of

With a live weight of 236 pounds, Kent's buck was a chore to drag. The Eastern Shore of Maryland is a smorgasbord of agricultural plantings and ideal for growing bucks with big bodies and big racks. Photo by Dr. Joe Linduska, courtesy of Kent Price, Jr.

everything around him. The deer kept staring intently into the woods behind the stand and frequently tested the air currents for danger, but Kent's elevated position shielded him from detection by either sense. Then, the majestic whitetail veered slightly off his previous course and headed for the trail winding almost directly beneath the hunter's perch.

Kent eased his bow into position and drew back the string just as the deer passed below him at a range of scarcely more than five yards. Aiming for the liver, the hunter let the bowstring slip from his shaking right hand and watched as the 26-inch arrow buried itself nearly up to the fletchings in the upper part of the rib cage.

Instantly, the massive buck dug his big hooves into the soil, spun, snorted and took three huge leaps into the timber, but not before Kent had marked the shot placement in his mind. Even though he had never before even touched a deer with an arrow, the young hunter felt confident about his shot. From all indications, he had put the Bear Razorhead right where he had hoped. Now, 30 heart-pounding minutes after the pod of bucks had first appeared in the distance, the woods fell quiet once again.

Kent forced himself to wait 15 minutes before even beginning to look for blood…and then could not find any. All that remained to prove the buck had even existed was a bloody, snapped-off arrow shaft and some faint tracks marking his exit route down the sapling-lined trail. Because the relatively short arrow had been shot almost straight down into the buck, the broadhead hadn't punched an exit hole. The deer had vacated the scene without leaving even a drop of blood on the ground.

Fortunately, before Kent had time to begin doubting the accuracy of his shot, he looked ahead through the woods and saw his prize. The deer had gone little more than 100 yards in a straight line before falling over dead. The broadhead had indeed performed as intended, slicing through major arteries and blood vessels around the liver and causing the buck to die within seconds of being hit.

The beast lying at Kent's feet was far bigger than any hunter has a right to expect of a first deer, no matter what the weapon. With a live weight of 236 pounds, the deer's body was pretty impressive but it placed a distant second to the rack. "When I saw his antler spread, I really began to shake," Kent later would admit.

Today, for someone to arrow a big buck on Maryland's Eastern Shore is a fairly common happening since the region is well known for its trophy potential. But when such a deer was taken by bow back in the early 1960s, the event was especially noteworthy. The *Kent County News* eagerly photographed Kent with the buck and published the photo on the front page of the next week's edition, giving the young archer his first taste of publicity.

Despite this immediate local recognition, Kent told me he probably would never have become the world-record holder if not for the guidance of Bob Elliott, an active member of the Kent Archery Association and an official P&Y measurer. The deer would be an easy winner in the local club's annual

An inside spread of 21 inches adds to the impressiveness of the Price buck. The 10-pointer loses just 5 4/8 inches of his 171-point gross typical score to asymmetry deductions. Photo by Dr. Joe Linduska, courtesy of Kent Price, Jr.

buck contest, but Bob realized it potentially was far more than that—a world-record typical, to be precise. The rack's "green" score was 167 5/8 net points, according to measurements made by Bob and Tim Kohl. That was well above the 164 3/8-point scores of the two bucks then tied for the archery world record. (Those deer, taken by Gilbert Guttormson and Jerry Polesky, were profiled in chapters 13 and 14, respectively.)

Kent's rack naturally shrank a tad during the mandatory 60-day drying period, but when Bob later measured it for official P&Y entry, he still came up with a net of 167 3/8 points. Maryland looked to be inline to claim the outright world record by bow, assuming a panel of club measurers concurred that the buck scored higher than 164 3/8… and it did.

In the summer of 1963, Kent's buck received a panel score of 165 4/8, high enough to take over the top spot. But, here's the stunner: By the time this deer was proclaimed the world record, he was no longer the biggest known typical by bow. In fact, as profiled in Chapter 16, an Iowa buck that eventually would succeed Kent's as the world record had hit the ground less than a month after Kent's Maryland buck was taken!

Today, P&Y refuses to proclaim any animal a world record until the banquet following the end of the awards period in which that trophy is entered. In the case of the Maryland and Iowa bucks, that logically would have been the 4th Awards Banquet, which took place in 1964. So, how did Kent's deer ever reach the top of the list? On the surface, the answer is simple. The 4th Awards Period had an early cut-off date. While Kent got his buck entered before the deadline, the other hunter didn't. What's harder to answer is exactly why the entry period was shortened.

On January 21, 1962, the club had moved to have its awards periods include two years rather than one, effective immediately. That ostensibly should have given both guys until December 31, 1963, to get their deer entered. While it is difficult from club records to reconstruct the exact sequence of events surrounding this early closure, we do know that it happened. Kent's buck was panel-measured at 165 4/8 shortly after being entered in early 1963. A certificate proclaiming the buck as an official P&Y world record was dated June 30, 1963, and it bears the signature of club founder and president Glenn St. Charles. Whatever the reason for the early cut-off on entries, there can be no denying that six months prior to what normally would have been the end of the 4th Awards Period, the Price buck had already been signed, sealed and delivered as a new No.1 typical.

Does this suggest that Kent's deer was never a true world record? Hardly. For starters, Kent has the certificate to prove what he accomplished. Plus, at the moment his buck was panel-measured at 165 4/8 points, no other typical ever taken by bow had received as high a score. And if we wanted to go purely by when the Maryland and Iowa bucks were *shot*, Kent's kill occurred weeks earlier. Thanks largely to Bob Elliott's efforts in quickly getting the Maryland buck measured and entered, Kent's place in the annals of deer hunting was ensured.

His unlikely story reached its climax on February 5, 1964, with P&Y's 4th Awards Banquet at Chicago's McCormick Place. There, before a crowd that included many of the pioneers of modern archery, Kent proudly accepted his award for having taken a world-record buck. In fact, his mounted deer was part of a huge display of bowhunting trophies at the National Sporting Goods Association Show, which was also being held in Chicago at the time. All in all, it was the perfect ending to a real-life fairy tale.

Looking back on the sequence of events that took Kent Price from frustrated novice bowhunter to world-record holder, it's amazing how perfectly everything fell into place. But, let's not forget that three years of utter failure preceded that historic morning when a monster whitetail came from a half-mile away to pass within 20 feet of the waiting archer. Perhaps more than anything else, let's learn an important lesson from a young hunter who dared to experiment when his old approach just wasn't getting the job done. After all, had Kent been unwilling to try something as novel as hunting from atop a 12-foot-tall "stump," chances are that no one in the whitetail community today would even know his name.

KENT PRICE, JR., MARYLAND, 1962

Measurements	Right	Left	Difference
No. of points	5	5	
Main beam	25 6/8	25 1/8	5/8
1st point (G-1)	4 1/8	4 2/8	1/8
2nd point (G-2)	10 6/8	12 7/8	2 1/8
3rd point (G-3)	9 1/8	10 3/8	1 2/8
4th point (G-4)	7 4/8	6 4/8	1 0/8
5th point (G-5)	–	–	–
1st circ. (H-1)	4 4/8	4 4/8	–
2nd circ. (H-2)	4 3/8	4 2/8	1/8
3rd circ. (H-3)	4 0/8	4 0/8	–
4th circ. (H-4)	4 1/8	3 7/8	2/8
Total	74 2/8	75 6/8	5 4/8
Greatest spread		23 1/8	
Inside spread		21 0/8	
Gross typical score		171 0/8	
Assymetry deductions		-5 4/8	
Non-typical deductions		–	
Net typical score		165 4/8	

16

LAST-DAY HUNT, FIRST-PLACE BUCK

If it weren't for bad luck, Iowa's Lloyd Goad would have had no luck at all... until that day when, in the blink of an eye, his bowhunting career changed in a world-record way.

TITLE: SIXTH P&Y TYPICAL WORLD RECORD

SCORE: 197 6/8

HUNTER: LLOYD GOAD

LOCATION: MONROE COUNTY, IOWA

YEAR: 1962

A s a state, Iowa doesn't exactly jump off the map and scream to be noticed. It's smaller than any of the five states bordering it; in fact, it's the second-smallest state lying entirely west of the Mississippi River. There are no lofty mountains, no sprawling forests, no miles of pounding surf. The Hawkeye State is simply a patchwork of big agricultural fields and small woodlots stretching from one horizon to the other. If you are looking for picturesque natural wonders, you had best keep on driving.

But despite its unremarkable appearance, Iowa is indeed a magical place, one with a unique resource that simply dazzles those who know how to appreciate it. You see, what Iowa possesses, as much as any other place in the world, is world-class typical whitetails.

While that fact won't merit mention in the travel sections of major newspapers, it is definitely an item of note in the world of trophy hunting, especially trophy bowhunting. Indeed, as of this writing, fully half of P&Y's top 10 typicals were arrowed in Iowa, even though only a tiny percentage of North American archers hunt within the state's borders. Monsters continue to turn up there almost every season, leading many experts to pick Iowa as the most likely place to produce the next No.1 typical by bow.

That's a tall order. To do it, the deer will have to beat Illinois' current world record, a 204 4/8-point giant that will be profiled in Chapter 17. If it does happen, some Iowans will undoubtedly remind us that turnabout is fair play. After all, that Illinois buck snatched the title away from the only official world-record whitetail Iowa has ever produced. I'm speaking of the tremendous 14-pointer shot in 1962 by Lloyd Goad.

While Lloyd's buck is no longer the world record by bow, he remains the highest-scoring typical ever

Despite 12 7/8 inches of assymetry deductions, Lloyd Goad's enormous 1962 buck from Monroe County, Iowa, was a blow-away archery world record, netting 197 6/8 typical P&Y points. True 7x7 typicals such as this are exceedingly rare animals in the whitetail world. Photo by Larry Huffman, "Legendary Whitetails."

taken by bow in Iowa, which is saying plenty as the P&Y records attest. What's more, Lloyd's buck has held the state-record title for well over three decades, proving that he is just as impressive today as when he was proclaimed No.1 in the world.

The first-person account of the hunt comes to us from historical documents since Lloyd tragically passed away in December 1993, just as he was retiring from a 15-year career with the Knoxville Water Department. We're fortunate, however, that over the years he graciously told his story in the pages of more than one magazine. What follows is largely based upon his own account in a 1967 issue of *Archery World*.

Like most other states in the Midwest, Iowa suffered dramatic losses of deer in the early years of the 20th century. However, the Department of Natural Resources' restoration program proved highly successful, and by the early 1950s, the recovery was going well enough for the state to allow a hunting season. Lloyd and his brother-in-law began shotgun hunting at the first opportunity and filled a number of tags during their first few years of pursuing whitetails.

By today's standards, there weren't many hunters in the woods back then. But to Lloyd, it seemed people were everywhere during those early slug seasons. "It became a real rat race," he noted. Getting away from the crowds is what first intrigued him about the growing sport of bowhunting. When one of the area's most avid archery hunters brought in the biggest buck Lloyd had ever seen, that interest became an obsession. Midway through the 1961 season, Lloyd bought a 45-pound York Crescent

recurve with some cedar arrows and began practicing with them near the Champlin service station where he worked.

The final weeks of that 1961 bow season proved unsuccessful in terms of deer tagged, but there was no shortage of action. First, Lloyd missed a six-foot (!) shot at a button buck, sending an arrow several inches over the fawn's shoulder. A few days later, a 20-yard broadside chance at a forkhorn went awry. The arrow hit an oak limb just before reaching the deer, resulting in another clean miss. Even though Lloyd had downed nothing with either arrow, the short-range drama of the sport thrilled him. He was completely sold on bowhunting for whitetails.

Amazingly, before Lloyd's world-record typical came along, the young bowhunter had missed every deer he had ever tried to arrow! But, he kept at it, and his persistence was rewarded with what is still the all-time No.2 buck in the P&Y records. Photo courtesy of Jody Goad and Duncan Dobie.

During the early weeks of the 1962 bow season, two more close encounters with deer ended in missed shots. Before Lloyd knew it, the season was winding down and once more he still had an unfilled permit in his pocket. The last day of bow season was December 2, and Lloyd decided to spend the entire day in the woods if need be. Early that morning, he made the 18-mile drive out to his hunting area with the windows of his pickup rolled down to help air-out his camouflage suit. He still wasn't sure exactly where he should sit on this final day of the season but figured a plan would come to mind once he got to his familiar parking spot.

◆

Lloyd missed every deer he had ever shot at—four in all— but he was sold on the short- range drama of bowhunting.

◆

When Lloyd pulled in, he encountered one of his buddies, Bob DeMoss, who was heading afield with his gun in search of squirrels. Bob had decided to try the woods south of a nearby dirt road. Lloyd already knew that a couple of bowhunters would be searching to the north and west for a doe one of them had arrowed the previous evening. With all of this human activity, Lloyd concluded that watching a trail in the center of the area wasn't a bad idea. So, as daylight came to the mist-shrouded woods, he splashed some deer lure onto his clothing and started out.

Lloyd hunted on the ground in those days, as tree stands were just coming into use for bowhunting. Easing into a small woodlot near the intersection of two dirt roads, he found a major deer trail near a brushy fencerow. Only a few yards away was an elm tree wide enough for the hunter to hide behind while awaiting a deer's approach. It was here

that Lloyd decided to take his chances on the season's final morning.

It didn't take long for the wisdom of his choice to become evident. Only a few minutes after settling in, he heard the sounds of movement on the other side of the fencerow. Something was coming down that trail, and the hunter anxiously waited to see what it might be.

"I peeked around the elm tree and there he came, slipping through the wild plums and sumac bushes with his head down," Lloyd later recalled. "He had so many points I couldn't distinguish his antlers from the limbs. My heart started pounding so hard that I thought he must be deaf not to hear it."

The huge buck now stood scarcely 20 feet from Lloyd, but they were separated by a brushy fencerow that prevented a shot. Then, in a fluid leap, the deer hopped the wires and emerged in plain view of the archer, who already had his bow up and ready to draw. As Lloyd began pulling the arrow back to its anchor point, the great deer spotted the movement and swung his head around to face the hunter. Within moments, the buck had convinced himself that something was wrong and began to vacate the premises. But by then, the arrow was on its way.

◆

Before Lloyd knew it, the season was winding down and once more he still had an unfilled permit in his pocket.

◆

As the string slipped from Lloyd's shaking fingers, the shaft seemed to travel in slow motion. The buck, caught flat-footed in the open, whirled away in a desperate lunge for freedom…just as the arrow struck home. Lloyd couldn't tell if the entry was just in front of or just behind the right flank, but he knew it was certainly farther back than he had intended. In the blink of an eye, the deer bounded into the brush and out of sight.

◆

Where had the arrow hit? In the leg? In the gut? It all had happened so quickly, there was just no way to know.

◆

Lloyd stayed still and listened as the buck crashed away through the brush to his left. Then, all was quiet…and the doubts began to sweep over Lloyd. Where had the arrow hit? In the leg? In the gut? It all had happened so quickly, there just was no way to know. "I was in real agony," the hunter later recalled.

After a jittery half-hour of holding his position, Lloyd quietly slipped back to his vehicle and met up again with Bob, who had already returned from his squirrel hunt. Once Lloyd explained the situation, the two men decided the best move was to go to town for reinforcements. By the time Lloyd and several friends had made it back to the scene to search for the deer, a full four hours had passed.

The bowhunter's worries were for nothing. The Hill's Hornet broadhead had sliced through an artery in the buck's right rear leg, and he had traveled a mere 150 yards before falling dead from heavy blood loss. The animal almost certainly had been dead before Lloyd even left the woods that morning, but waiting several hours before taking up the blood trail still had been a prudent decision under the circumstances.

Though Lloyd didn't need much trailing help, his buddies came in handy when the time arrived to load the huge buck into the vehicle. Even though somewhat rundown from the rut, the bruiser field-dressed 224 pounds! Had he been taken a month earlier during the final days of the pre-rut, he certainly would have tipped the scales at better than 250.

Ah, but the rack! The mere fact that it was a 7x7 typical made the antlers extraordinary, but that by no means told the full story. The antlers were just plain huge, with a wall of hefty tines on each sweeping main beam. Though a substantial 12 7/8 inches in side-to-side deductions were taken from the 210 5/8-point gross score, the lack of abnormal points on the rack helped achieve a whopping net of 197 6/8 P&Y points. That was a full 20 percent higher than the then-No.1 bow bucks, a pair of 164 3/8-pointers taken by Gilbert Guttormson (Chapter 12) and Jerry Polesky (Chapter 13)! The Goad buck was far and away the world's top typical by bow, surpassing the previous mark by a margin never before or since accomplished by a typical whitetail in *any* of the major record books.

◆

The Goad buck eclipsed the previous world record by 20 percent—a margin never before or since accomplished by a typical whitetail.

◆

Yet, he wouldn't become the next P&Y record. As chronicled in Chapter 15, that honor instead would be bestowed upon Kent Price's 165 4/8-point buck from Maryland, a deer taken less than a month prior to the Iowa monster. Lloyd didn't even know about the P&Y record book at the time he shot his trophy, and the rack wasn't officially measured until January 1964, more than a year after the kill. By then, the Price buck had already been accepted as P&Y's No.1 bow typical. Fortunately, the Goad buck was awarded the world record following the next awards period. Thus, in the end, Iowa did get its turn in the limelight…as did Lloyd.

Although Lloyd never shot another world-class buck, he arrowed his share of deer before he passed away in 1993 just as he was retiring. Those who knew him said he had enjoyed every moment of his many days afield. Even if he had never again walked into the woods after that amazing first bow kill, he could have taken pride in knowing he was the only archer in history to turn a last-day hunt into a first-place whitetail!

LLOYD GOAD, IOWA, 1962

Measurements	Right	Left	Difference
No. of points	7	7	
Main beam	25 6/8	26 4/8	6/8
1st point (G-1)	5 0/8	3 3/8	1 5/8
2nd point (G-2)	6 3/8	9 0/8	2 5/8
3rd point (G-3)	11 2/8	10 0/8	1 2/8
4th point (G-4)	11 0/8	11 3/8	3/8
5th point (G-5)	9 6/8	10 1/8	3/8
6th point (G-6)	2 4/8	5 5/8	3 1/8
7th point (G-7)	–	–	–
1st circ. (H-1)	5 1/8	5 2/8	1/8
2nd circ. (H-2)	4 7/8	5 0/8	1/8
3rd circ. (H-3)	5 4/8	5 5/8	1/8
4th circ. (H-4)	5 2/8	7 5/8	2 3/8
Total	92 3/8	99 4/8	12 7/8
Greatest spread		21 2/8	
Inside spread		18 6/8	
Gross typical score		210 5/8	
Assymetry deductions		-12 7/8	
Non-typical deductions		–	
Net typical score		197 6/8	

17

MEL JOHNSON'S FIELD OF DREAMS

— ❖ —

No world-record buck would stroll across 300 yards of open ground to give you a broadside shot at close range, would he? Before you answer, read this story!

— ❖ —

TITLE: CURRENT P&Y TYPICAL WORLD RECORD

SCORE: 204 4/8

HUNTER: MEL JOHNSON

LOCATION: PEORIA COUNTY, ILLINOIS

YEAR: 1965

The lives of trophy whitetails frequently revolve around water. If you doubt it, just grab a map of North America and, using the whitetail record books as references, circle the places that have produced history's biggest bucks. You'll soon find yourself marking a string of localities up and down the continent's major river systems. The pattern is far too consistent to be a coincidence. The truth is that the combination of fertile soils, abundant moisture and heavy cover makes big riverbottoms among the best of all places to find trophy deer.

Perhaps nowhere else in North America is this winning combination so obvious as in the Midwest in general and Illinois in particular. Two of the greatest rivers on the continent—the Mississippi and Ohio—drain this state, as do a number of their major tributaries. Through the eons, floods along these waterways have deposited enough nutrient-rich silt to help produce some of the most fertile soil anywhere. That black dirt produces lush native browse plants as well as nutritious agricultural crops like corn and soybeans, all of which contribute greatly to the size of deer. Bucks get fat and heavy-racked by spending their nights feeding on this veritable "salad bar" provided by both man and nature. Nearby, brushy, untillable drainages allow those same deer to hide from danger during the day. Combine such favorable growing conditions with a short, restrictive gun season (no centerfire rifles allowed), and it's little wonder Illinois has developed such an enviable reputation for growing monster whitetails.

One of the first bucks to bring widespread attention to the Prairie State also confirmed the validity of the "big-water" theory. You see, he was arrowed near the Illinois River, one of the major tributaries of the Mississippi. The year was 1965, and the hunter was a young man named Mel Johnson.

He had begun bowhunting in the late 1950s. With the assistance of two Army buddies at Missouri's Fort Leonard Wood, Mel had enjoyed great success, taking several deer during his first six years of carrying a bow. Meanwhile, Illinois' whitetail herd had been growing rapidly, thanks to years of zealous protection by both wildlife officials and private landowners. Still, deer numbers were modest then by today's standards but some of the bucks were getting a chance to reach maximum size. When Mel's rapidly devel-

At 204 4/8 P&Y points, Mel Johnson's 1965 buck from Peoria County, Illinois, is easily the highest netting typical in bowhunting history. In three decades atop the list, he has seldom been challenged. Photo courtesy of Larry Huffman, "Legendary Whitetails."

oping bowhunting skills were combined with this prime trophy resource, the stage was set for an historic event.

In a way, the fateful hunt actually began a year before the buck was arrowed. During the 1964 season, Mel and bowhunting buddy Bill Kallister kept seeing big bucks on a piece of ground they did not have permission to hunt. Back then, it was far easier to gain free access to prime Illinois deer land than it is today, and when the two young hunters asked for permission to hunt the tract, it was granted. As the 1965 season approached, Mel and Bill were hopeful of running into one of the trophy whitetails they had seen previously.

During the early weeks of bow season, the hunters split up to hunt separate parts of the property. Mel focused his attention on an area containing a soybean field surrounded by expansive hard-

In "Monarch's Morning," Ron Van Gilder offers an intriguing look at how the great 204 4/8-point Mel Johnson buck looked and likely behaved as the rut kicked in during the fall of 1965, the year Mel set the all-time archery record—a mark which has seldom been challenged in all these years. Print courtesy of the artist and Wild Wings, Inc.

wood timber. The field seemed to be a hub of afternoon feeding activity, and one of the deer using it was a big buck—make that a *huge* buck. Twice, Mel had spotted the wide-racked typical, but each time the buck came into the field, he was faraway from the bowhunter's hideout.

◆

After watching this brute stroll nearly 300 yards across an open field, the deer was about to be too close for Mel to draw the bow undetected.

◆

Mel had been splitting his time between tree stands and makeshift ground blinds that offered him a good view of the beanfield. He had hoped

one of his set-ups would get him a shot at the monster while he stood in the open field, but the old deer seemed to prefer walking the edge of the bigger timber, well away from Mel's ambush locations. Finally, he decided it made more sense to go to the buck instead of waiting for the buck to come to him.

On Friday, October 29, Bill had to work late and couldn't hunt but Mel managed to slip away that afternoon. When he arrived at the property, he walked the edge of the beanfield and picked out what looked like a good spot in the tall grass and scrubby brush. From there, he had a commanding view of the field. With the wind blowing across the field squarely in his face, he hoped the buck, if he showed, would not detect him until it was too late. Mel rearranged some of the brush and grass to improve his concealment then settled in for what might be a long wait.

The vigil turned out to be much shorter than

expected. Almost before the bowhunter had crawled into his hiding spot, the buck walked out of the woods far across the field. Even though the distance between them was a good 300 yards, Mel had no trouble telling that this was the gigantic buck with a wide rack and long points he was looking for.

The young hunter watched and hoped as the huge-bodied animal cautiously tested the wind, took a few steps and scrutinized his surroundings. The monstrous buck was coming out into the upper end of the field, but he was doing so at his own slow pace. Watching the biggest typical whitetail in bowhunting history slowly angling toward you from 300 yards out, in full view nearly every step of the way, would be an almost unimaginable blend of anxiety and anticipation. Under the circumstances, all Mel could do was watch and try to

The minutes leading up to Mel's fateful shot were a test of nerves for the hunter, but he passed with flying colors. After watching this deer walk toward you for nearly 300 yards, would you even be able to draw your bow? Photo by Jack Ehresman.

remain calm as the massive animal moved ever closer, unalarmed yet wary about being so exposed in the light of day.

It soon became clear that if the deer didn't change course, he was indeed going to come close enough for a shot. That would have sent many archers into a fit of uncontrollable shakes, but Mel was so focused that he never really lost his composure, even as the buck approached within 30 yards of his brushy hideout. The southpaw archer gripped his 72-pound recurve tightly in his right hand and did what he could to remain hidden from the deer's prying eyes.

Mel knew he would need to stand up to get off a good shot. That led him to an ironic realization: After having watched this brute stroll nearly 300 yards across an open field, the deer was about to be too *close* for Mel to draw the bow undetected. Soon, the buck was only 10 yards from the hunter and staring straight at him, trying to determine what was in that brushpile that didn't seem quite right. Mel stared right back, fighting the combined effects of tension and a tightening leg cramp. Somehow, he had to find an opportunity to draw his bow.

That chance came when the buck, having decided everything was in order, finally turned his huge head away from Mel to scan the open field. When the deer began to walk again, the hunter sensed it was time for action, now or never. Springing to his feet as he drew the bow, Mel focused on an aiming point and let the arrow fly.

The buck jumped and took off for the center of the beanfield. Within seconds, the deer disappeared over a rise in the field and all was still. Mel nocked another arrow and tried to calm down. Then, inexplicably, here came the buck again, popping into view to scan the area as if trying to figure out what had happened! The deer stared at the hunter, and then he again wheeled and vanished from sight over the rise.

When he found his arrow in the field, Mel realized he had indeed connected. The shaft and fletchings were smeared with blood, indicating a pass-through hit. Continuing along the buck's route, he topped the slight rise and spotted him ahead in the field, down but not quite out. As the hunter approached his trophy, the deer died. One of bowhunting's great dramas had ended, right there in the same beanfield it had begun.

Mel was a strapping young fellow, and he had plenty of adrenaline to help him drag his deer out of the field. Even so, he soon discovered that it would take more than one man to move this brute, which had a live weight of around 340 pounds! Fortunately, the farmer was willing to help, and they eventually got the animal gutted and tied across the back of Mel's car. With the monster secured, the hunter headed home, though not without making some adjustments en route. The deer's head was hanging over the left side of the vehicle, dangling perilously close to oncoming traffic on the two-lane road. Mel finally pulled over and repositioned the carcass to alleviate the problem. He then made it home without incident. (How might whitetail history have been changed had some vehi-

The Sagamore Hill award is the highest honor the Boone and Crockett Club can present a hunter, and Mel won it for his whitetail. B&C felt the hunter deserved this award not only for the quality of his trophy but also for the quality of the hunt itself. Photo courtesy of the Boone and Crockett Club.

cle clipped this huge rack?)

Today, Illinois has a well-developed network of trophy measurers and news of monster racks travels with lightning speed. It wasn't that way in 1965, however, and while Mel's deer did get prominent coverage in the *Peoria Journal-Star* newspaper, months passed without notice from any measurer. Finally, Mel found mention of the B&C scoring system in a magazine. He wrote to the club in search of information on where and how to get his huge buck measured. The club responded that he should take the rack to the only official B&C measurer in Illinois at the time, a man who worked at the Field Museum of Natural History in Chicago. Soon, Mel hauled his trophy to the Windy City.

Under virtually any circumstance, a net typical score of 197-plus points would thrill a whitetail hunter, but when the measurer came up with a figure in that neighborhood, Mel wasn't exactly jubilant. That is because he had picked up a book on measuring before coming to Chicago, and his own rough figures had yielded a net score in the range of 207 points. That was higher than the new B&C world record of 206 1/8 for the just-discovered Jordan buck from Wisconsin! (Chapter 6) Had Mel made an obvious mistake in his figuring?

No, but the official measurer had. He had somehow omitted a circumference measurement in his calculations, thereby reducing the net score considerably. When the proper numbers were added back in, the Johnson buck tallied 204 4/8, slightly behind Jordan's B&C record but well ahead of the then-No. 2 typical, John Breen's 202-pointer from Minnesota (Chapter 5). But, it was a

Illinois ranks as one of North America's top producers of P&Y typicals. Even so, there has never been another Prairie State typical that has come close to the score of Mel's, which says a lot about just how great this white-tail is. Photo courtesy of Illinois Department of Conservation and Jack Ehresman.

different story when Mel checked the Pope and Young Club's all-time list of bowhunting trophies. Among those records, his buck would be No.1 by a considerable margin, easily surpassing the 197 6/8-point Lloyd Goad buck from Iowa (Chapter 16).

The Illinois giant eventually was named P&Y's official world record by bow. In addition, Mel was presented with the Ishi Award, the highest honor P&Y can bestow upon a bowhunter. (As noted in Chapter 19, Nebraska's Del Austin had received the first Ishi Award in 1964 for taking the world-record non-typical by bow. To this day, Del and Mel remain the only archers whose whitetail-hunting achievements have been acknowledged with this most prestigious award.)

But, Mel's honors didn't end there. From B&C, he also received the Sagamore Hill Award, given for a truly exceptional animal taken under undisputed fair-chase conditions. The prestigious award is named for the Long Island home of Boone & Crockett Club founder Theodore Roosevelt and is given by the Roosevelt family in memory of Mr. Roosevelt and his sons. Mel has the singular distinction of being the only person ever to receive both the Ishi and Sagamore Hill awards.

At this writing, Mel remains an active bowhunter. He has even been an official trophy measurer himself for many years. He has never seen another typical whitetail to match the one he got back in 1965, but there's always the chance it will happen. One thing is for sure—considering Illinois' legacy of giant riverbottom bucks, no whitetail expert would bet against it!

MEL JOHNSON, ILLINOIS, 1965

Measurements	Right	Left	Difference
No. of points	7	6	
Main beam	27 5/8	26 6/8	7/8
1st point (G-1)	5 4/8	7 2/8	1 6/8
2nd point (G-2)	11 3/8	12 0/8	5/8
3rd point (G-3)	12 6/8	12 0/8	6/8
4th point (G-4)	10 1/8	9 7/8	2/8
5th point (G-5)	5 7/8	4 4/8	1 3/8
1st circ. (H-1)	6 1/8	6 2/8	1/8
2nd circ. (H-2)	5 0/8	5 0/8	–
3rd circ. (H-3)	5 1/8	5 1/8	–
4th circ. (H-4)	4 6/8	5 1/8	3/8
Total	**94 2/8**	**93 7/8**	**6 1/8**
Greatest spread		26 1/8	
Inside spread		23 5/8	
Gross typical score		**211 6/8**	
Assymetry deductions		-6 1/8	
Non-typical deductions		-1 1/8	
Net typical score		**204 4/8**	

18

EASY HUNT, TOUGH TRAIL

Sometimes, a bowhunter's biggest challenge comes *after* the arrow is turned loose.

TITLE: FIRST P&Y NON-TYPICAL
WORLD RECORD
SCORE: 186 2/8
HUNTER: DON VRASPIR
LOCATION: OTTER TAIL COUNTY,
MINNESOTA
YEAR: 1959

Perhaps the most common hunting cliché is the one that describes a hunter as being "in the right place at the right time." Of course, that phrase has become a cliché because it is often a valid description of the situation. It's funny, though, that you almost never read about a deer being "in the wrong place at the wrong time," although most of the time that observation is equally valid.

Either phrase would paint a pretty accurate picture of the events that unfolded 20 miles northeast of Fergus Falls, Minnesota, on October 27, 1959. The hunter, Don Vraspir, clearly had everything going his way; the deer, a 21-point buck, clearly didn't. But, to credit what Don did only to good luck would be to diminish his accomplishment on that autumn afternoon. Don was no novice. He was a veteran hunter who strongly suspected a big buck was living in those woods. While he admittedly didn't know exactly how big the deer was or how he was going to get him, he had solved the more important half of the trophy equation—he was in the "right place."

How Don came to be in that spot on that afternoon bears telling. At the time, he was 35 years old and living in Fergus Falls, a small town roughly 30 miles east of the North Dakota border that has changed little over the years. The landscape there, then as now, consisted of broken farm country with assorted crop fields and meadows intermingled with scattered wetlands and patches of hardwoods. Thanks to marvelous genetics, rich soils and abundant crops, an old buck in this region is invariably a big buck. Today, the trick is for a buck to stay hidden from the multitude of hunters long enough to become an old buck, but during the time of Don's fateful hunt, there weren't enough other hunters around to be a concern.

He and friend Russ Shol were among the very few devotees of bowhunting in that part of the state.

Don Vraspir's 1959 trophy from Otter Tail County, Minnesota, is one of the more massive non-typicals taken in the early days of modern bowhunting. His eight circumference measurements total 45 7/8 inches, or right at 5 4/8 inches each! He netted 186 2/8 points to become P&Y's first-ever official world record in the category. He held the title from 1960 to 1964. Photo courtesy of Don Vraspir.

During the early archery season, they had vast expanses of land to themselves, except for the odd shotgunner in pursuit of upland game. Yet, as it would turn out, hunting pressure was to play a direct role in making Don a record-holder, though that pressure came into play totally by accident!

Neither Don nor Russ had been successful in the first few weeks of archery season that fall, but typical of hardcore bowhunters, they were determined to stay at it, hunting every chance they could. Undoubtedly, the fact that they were in a prime deer area made it easier to keep plugging along. The 160 acres of woods they were hunting consisted of large oaks, ash, "popple" (aspens) and what's locally known as "buckbrush." Don and Russ had been hunting the area for several years but hadn't shot anything there, despite numerous deer sightings and close calls.

An incident earlier in the 1959 season had given the men hope of eventually shooting a trophy in this spot, even though no big buck had been seen.

"One day we heard a deer charge off through the woods, and it sounded huge," Don explained. "But, we could never get a look at it."

In those days, the Minnesota bow season was shorter than it is today. As the final week of October arrived, the hunting partners knew they were running out of time. On the afternoon of October 27, Don decided to drive up to the woods for a few hours, hoping somehow to get a shot—heck, even a look—at the big deer the guys knew was hanging around. He checked with Russ to see if he could join him, but other obligations stood in his way. Oh well, Don thought, a solo hunt was better than nothing.

The cedar arrow buried itself in the bouncing deer, but it caught him higher and much farther back than Don had hoped.

Once he reached the hunting area, he gathered his gear and put the finishing touches on his camouflage. Just acquiring the materials needed for concealment had been a chore. Don wore a mail-order camo suit since no such garments were available locally. The camo paint he applied to his face and hands was World War II surplus. A few more smears of the stuff were applied to the limbs of Don's short, fast, 50-pound Mamba recurve. As a final touch, the hunter added a bit of deer scent to his garments, giving him added confidence that he might escape detection by a buck's nose. Then, it was off to the woods for a hunt that, to be honest, figured to be just another fruitless effort.

Whenever Don and Russ bowhunted together in this area, they liked to still-hunt on parallel paths some distance apart in hopes that one of them would bump a deer toward the other. Since Russ wasn't there to help on this occasion, Don decided his best bet was to use a solo version of the same strategy. He would creep forward a few steps, survey his surroundings and then take a few more cautious steps, repeating the routine until shooting light was gone.

For the first 100 yards on that pleasant afternoon, nothing happened. Then, Don suddenly realized he was no longer alone. The thud of pounding hooves and the snaps of breaking brush told the hunter something big was heading his way! The bowhunter froze in place, holding his breath. Turning his eyes to the left, he spotted the cause of that "terrible racket" he had heard. A running buck, with a huge body and a massive rack, was barreling almost straight at him!

The bruiser apparently hadn't seen Don, and if the deer didn't change his line of travel, within moments he would be only a few paces in front of the startled archer. With virtually no time to become nervous or even consider his options, Don raised the recurve, drew, swung with the animal and let go of his arrow as the buck zipped past at a range of only 11 yards!

The cedar arrow buried itself in the bouncing deer, but it caught him higher and much farther back than Don had hoped. The buck never even broke stride as the hand-sharpened Ace broadhead sliced into his loin. Within moments, he was gone from sight. Still in shock, all Don could do for the moment was to try to collect his frazzled thoughts. *"That's the largest deer I've ever seen, and I've hit it!"* his brain screamed, as if to reassure him that the beast really had been more than just an apparition.

What had prompted the buck to practically jump into the hunter's lap? As Don walked over to the buck's trail and found the first drops of blood, that question answered itself in stunning fashion. Russ was walking toward him from the same direction the big buck had come!

Don couldn't believe his eyes. He had never

expected his partner to make it to the woods that afternoon. As it turned out, Russ had shaken free at the last minute and decided to go hunting after all. He had parked a bit farther west than Don had, and purely by coincidence, he had entered the same woods at almost exactly the same time as his friend. The bedded buck had heard Russ coming and had vacated the premises in a hurry. Don—through what could only be called incredibly good luck— had been smack in the middle of his escape route!

The two friends briefly discussed the events and decided to follow the buck's trail for a bit, hoping to confirm the nature of the wound. They hadn't covered more than 30 yards before coming upon the back half of Don's arrow. With only 15 minutes now passed since the deer had been hit, the men didn't want to take any chances by pushing him too hard. They marked the spot with white tissue paper then retreated from the area for a half-hour before taking up the trail in earnest.

As every veteran bowhunter knows, the time between releasing an arrow at a deer and recovering the animal seems to be measured not in minutes or hours, but in years. Even when you know the hit is good, there is no greater mixture of joy and relief than walking up to your dead quarry and confirming that you really did come through under pressure. But when you've made a marginal hit and the animal in question is a world-class whitetail…well, you can be sure Don was anything but confident as he and Russ started down that buck's trail in the fading daylight.

This was no easy trailing job. "There was blood, but it took some real patience, care and concentration on the part of both of us to make progress," Don told me. "We continued to mark blood spots with white tissue. A first, I was hopeful. Then as daylight began to fade, I became doubtful. Yet, it seemed to me the hit was lethal, if we could only stay on the trail."

When it grew too dark to see blood, Don and Russ drove back home to get lights for the search.

Don retrieved a gas lantern he owned and borrowed another from friend Jack Maurin. The hunters then returned to the last marked spot and resumed their search. Having used gas lanterns to find a deer under similar circumstances in Montana, Don and Russ were hopeful that the technique would work again. As these experienced hunters knew, the white light of a gas lantern makes blood stand out vividly at night. But, would there be enough of a trail to follow?

———◆———

As every veteran bowhunter knows, the time between releasing an arrow and recovering the animal seems to be measured not in minutes or hours, but in years.

———◆———

After another 90 minutes of agonizingly slow trailing with the lanterns, there still was no buck in sight. By this time, the weary hunters had covered perhaps a quarter-mile in a generally northward direction. Finally, Don and Russ followed the sign up onto a small hill perhaps 20 feet high. There, their spirits soared. Blood was everywhere in the brush and grass!

Expecting to find the deer any moment, the hunters looked all over the hilltop but came up empty. Where was that buck? Though no evidence indicated that he had left the small hill, Don and Russ desperately began moving slowly down the slope, shining their lights through the darkness. Suddenly, the lanterns revealed a massive buck lying stone dead only 15 yards below the hill's crest.

Don's Ace broadhead, manufactured by good friend John Schwenk, proved its merit that day. The welded-steel blade had sliced through a major artery lying alongside the spine, causing the deer to die from blood loss. The high location of the entry wound had resulted in relatively little external bleeding, making trailing a nightmare. Of course, all that frustration was forgotten as soon as they saw the dead buck.

Just as Don had told Russ, he had arrowed a giant! The deer's body was enormous, and his wide, dark, heavy rack had points jabbing out in every direction. The men spent several breathless minutes gawking at the unlikely trophy before field-dressing him for the long drag out.

Getting the 230-pound beast from that brushy hillside to the nearest road turned out to be yet another trying process. The hunters didn't drag him far before they decided to hike back to the vehicle for another trip into Fergus Falls, this time to round up muscle power. Jim Crowe, Don's business partner and a big man, joined them for the last 300 to 400 yards of the drag to the pickup. Jim's wife, B.J., and one of their kids provided welcome encouragement throughout the ordeal. Eventually, the crew got the prize to town.

Nobody in the area could recall a bowhunter

Don now lives just outside St. Paul and has long since stopped bowhunting due in part to a bad shoulder. But, he still has his buck, his archery gear and plenty of happy memories. Photo courtesy of Don Vraspir. (Note: Don's record whitetail also appears in the P&Y meeting photo in Chapter 1.)

having taken such a big-racked whitetail. There was, of course, a good reason—in the short history of modern bowhunting, the record book showed no archer *anywhere* had shot a whitetail with antlers that big! Don didn't realize this at the time, though. All he knew was that he stood a great chance of winning the annual contest held by the Minnesota Bow Hunters Association. He really wasn't considering anything on a grander scale. Fortunately, though, his friend Jack Maurin was.

———◆———

Nobody in the area could recall a bowhunter having taken such a big-racked whitetail.

———◆———

As secretary of the state association, Jack knew the National Field Archery Association (NFAA) was having a competition for North American big-game trophies taken by bow. He urged Don to check into it. He did and found out that the deadline for the next round of entries was rapidly approaching.

—◆—

The record book showed no archer anywhere had shot a whitetail with antlers that big!

—◆—

In early December, Jack measured the rack officially and came up with a choice of two net scores—192 4/8 non-typical or 143 2/8 typical. The men had no doubt as to the category the deer should be entered. While a typical rack scoring in the 140s would be one of the better bow kills on record, a non-typical in the 190s would easily be the biggest ever! In fact, during the NFAA's first-ever competition in 1958, there had been *no* non-typical whitetail entries at all. And, no one had heard of any this time, either.

Thanks to Don's meticulous efforts to keep track of everything involving his historic deer, we can replay the certification process as it unfolded in the months after his fateful hunt. The following letters between the hunter and NFAA officials offer a unique glimpse into how the first world record in the non-typical whitetail category was certified:

December 31, 1959

Mr. Donald F. Vraspir
604 W. Vasa Avenue
Fergus Falls, Minnesota

Dear Sir:

We have received at this office the forms concerning your Whitetail deer. It appears by these forms that
it will do better as an entry in the non-typical class. This is the first non-typical entry that we have had so far. Because of this, it will be a bowhunter record.

To officially declare this a record, it should be measured by a panel of measurers at this office. Would it be possible for you to ship the rack to us either by parcel post or express? We are very interested in this entry and would appreciate any cooperation you can give us along this line.

Thank you very much for your entry and for submitting this trophy.

Yours very truly,
(Signed)
Glenn St. Charles

This must have been pretty heady stuff for Don. Scarcely two months earlier, the "phantom" buck of Otter Tail County was no more than a loud crash in the brush. Now, Don was being invited to submit the deer's rack for consideration as a new archery world record! It didn't take him long to build a crate, stick the huge rack inside and ship it straight to Glenn in Seattle, Washington. There, the NFAA panel of measurers put their tapes to the massive rack on January 23, 1960 and came up with an official net score of 186 2/8 non-typical. Just over three weeks later, Don found the following letter in his mailbox:

Dear Donald:

Enclosed find a copy of our measurement for your non-typical Whitetail deer. It is now an established World Record for bowhunters, and if this record holds up until the competition's close April 1, 1960, we would like very much to display this trophy at the National Field Archery Tournament at Grayling, Michigan, the latter part of June. Before that time, however, we would like a picture of the mount taken on a contrasting plain background. This picture will appear in the tournament program.

Please let me know what your thoughts on this are

*and if you will cooperate with us. Thanks very much
for your interest in making this entry. It is truly a fine
one. Incidentally, the awards will be made at the
Grayling Tournament and the program that we
plan there would make it well worthwhile to attend
the awards.*

Yours truly,
(Signed)
Glenn St. Charles

Don didn't need to be asked twice. Before long,
he had the deer mounted, photographed and sent to
Grayling for the tournament and awards program,
where it would soon be proclaimed the world-
record non-typical by bow, assuming no larger
whitetail showed up. None did. The second-best
non-typical entered before the April 1 deadline
ended up being a 156 1/8-pointer shot in southwestern Minnesota by Joe Earl of Worthington.

◆

"A lot of guys argued that if you were going to put a sight on your bow, then you might as well just use a rifle!"

◆

The gathering in Grayling turned out to be an
historic event featuring nine new world records by
bow, as well as some of the more legendary names
in the history of modern bowhunting. (See photo in
Chapter 1.) Foremost were Glenn St. Charles, the
first-ever holder of the archery world record for typical mule deer (182 6/8 points) and founder of the
Pope and Young Club, and famed Grayling resident
Fred Bear. Fred already held the bow record for elk
at 311 points, and now, the great bowhunter was to
receive an award for his new No.1 barren ground
caribou, a giant scoring 417 points.

Given the presence of such famous figures and
exotic bowhunting trophies (including a world-
record polar bear taken by recurve), the whitetails
on display at that event might not have seemed to
be real headline-makers. But in retrospect, it was
indeed a special moment in whitetail history. That
ceremony is the only one in history that featured
not one, not two, but *three* new whitetail world
records. In addition to Don's non-typical, Jerry
Polesky's 164 3/8-point typical from Wibaux
County, Montana, and Gilbert Guttormson's 164
3/8-point typical from Norman County, Minnesota,
were also on display, having tied for the record in
their category. Because there are just two categories
in the whitetail record books, it is highly unlikely
that we'll ever again see three simultaneous record-
holders, much less three being certified at the same
event!

After downing his great non-typical, Don continued to bowhunt for another 15 years. Then, he
had two problems that hampered his further
involvement in the sport. First, a career change cut
into his practice time, causing him to lose confidence in his ability to shoot accurately. Plus, Don
developed severe bursitis in his right shoulder, making it difficult to draw and hold a bow. Faced with
these realities, he gave up the sport that had been so
good to him. Fortunately, the man still has his
memories of bowhunting's formative years. He also
has some interesting observations about how the
sport has changed since then—and, for that matter,
how it hasn't.

"Back when some guys were starting to put
sights on their recurves and longbows, before anyone was even shooting compounds," Don recalled,
"there was quite a bit of controversy about whether
or not using sights was really even bowhunting.
Everyone had been shooting instinctively up to that
point, and a lot of guys argued that if you were
going to put a sight on your bow, then you might as
well just use a rifle! Another squabble of the times
was cedar shafts versus fiberglass and aluminum,

which were just appearing. Even back then, we had a lot of debate about what should be allowed and what shouldn't, just like today." Yes, as this bowhunting pioneer confirmed, the debate over archery technology is nothing new!

To claim that Don Vraspir had his record deer completely figured out and the outcome all planned would be stretching the facts. Three hundred pounds of world-class Minnesota whitetail converged with that arrow partly because the hunter was in a good spot, partly because he was hunting as much as possible and, finally, because a friend intervened—albeit unintentionally—on his behalf. We'll never know just what would have taken place that fall afternoon had Russ *not* been able to slip away from work. Maybe Don would have shot the deer anyway a few minutes later or on a subsequent hunt that season or even the next. These dramas always seem replete with "ifs" and "buts." The fact is that trophy whitetail hunting doesn't follow a script. Every time we head into the woods, we and the deer must write our own scenes.

DON VRASPIR, MINNESOTA, 1959

Measurements	Right	Left	Difference
No. of points	9	9	
Main beam	23 1/8	22 5/8	4/8
1st point (G-1)	6 7/8	6 2/8	5/8
2nd point (G-2)	8 3/8	8 3/8	–
3rd point (G-3)	9 0/8	8 0/8	1 0/8
4th point (G-4)	6 6/8	4 6/8	2 0/8
5th point (G-5)	5 2/8	–	5 2/8
1st circ. (H-1)	6 4/8	6 4/8	–
2nd circ. (H-2)	6 4/8	5 1/8	1 3/8
3rd circ. (H-3)	6 0/8	5 2/8	6/8
4th circ. (H-4)	5 0/8	5 0/8	–
Total	83 3/8	71 7/8	11 4/8
Greatest spread		25 7/8	
Inside spread		18 6/8	
Gross typical score		174 0/8	
Assymetry deductions		-11 4/8	
Non-typical additions		+23 6/8	
Net non-typical score		186 2/8	

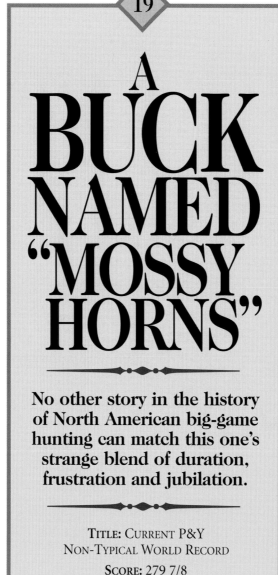

19

A BUCK NAMED "MOSSY HORNS"

No other story in the history of North American big-game hunting can match this one's strange blend of duration, frustration and jubilation.

TITLE: CURRENT P&Y
NON-TYPICAL WORLD RECORD
SCORE: 279 7/8
HUNTER: DEL AUSTIN
LOCATION: HALL COUNTY,
NEBRASKA
YEAR: 1962

Al Dawson's brain wasn't buying what his eyes were selling. In the open field in front of him, Al could see a buck and several does. But, the size and shape of the buck's rack were mind-boggling! The antlers were incredibly massive, with odd points poking in every direction. Strangest of all were the long points extending off each antler burr. They projected downward and outward, creating the impression that the deer possessed a set of bony "ears" to go with his real ones.

Not only had Al never seen such a bizarre buck, he had never even imagined one. For several seconds, all he could do was stare, trying to convince himself that what he saw in the field was genuine. Suddenly, reality hit home. If the buck were merely a mirage, it was the only one in history with sound effects and the ability to run!

This dreamlike scene unfolded one morning in October 1958 on Dan Thomas' farm near Shelton, Nebraska. Al Dawson, a young bowhunter who lived 30 miles away in Hastings, had been scanning an alfalfa field along the timbered Platte River when five or six deer broke cover and ran straight toward him. Leading the pack was the odd-racked whitetail spectacular enough to make any hunter wonder if he was hallucinating.

Years later, in the August 1963 issue of *Outdoor Life,* Al would recall his memory of that moment. "I knew I was looking at a dream trophy, a non-typical whitetail big enough to go well up on the record list, with antlers the likes of which I could never hope to see again," he wrote. "At that, I didn't realize how good he really was."

On that fateful morning, Al was jarred from his trance-like amazement by the realization that the buck was running in his direction, perhaps to offer a shot. Al was standing in the open near where a deer trail crossed a field fence. Figuring he would be spotted for sure if he didn't hide, Al cautiously took a couple of steps back into a clump of weeds and dropped to one knee, his recurve "loaded" with a waiting arrow.

By this time, the huge buck was within 100 yards of Al and still coming. Suddenly, something went wrong. Even though the wind direction favored Al, the buck abruptly veered off course, perhaps sensing something wasn't quite right about those weeds. The bowhunter watched in frustration and shock as the non-typical jumped the fence some 70 yards away then stopped and looked right at him, as if daring him to shoot. Unable to contain his adrenaline, the archer quickly obliged, releasing an arrow that fell short of its target. The buck and his lady friends immediately bolted back toward the riverbottom from which they had come.

Al simply walked over and picked up his arrow, trudged back to his vehicle and drove home. He hadn't been looking for a trophy of this caliber, but now that he had seen the magnificent buck, it was going to be very difficult to get enthused about any other deer. Like most high-scoring whitetails, the giant that Al spotted that morning is best-known today by his nickname. But unlike most of those other deer, "Mossy Horns" earned his nickname while he was still very much alive. In fact, Al decided Mossy Horns was the perfect moniker the moment he saw the beast. "I know it sounds corny," the hunter wrote, "but with that irregular rack and those two long tines on each side of his face, it fitted him."

Coming up with a nickname for the buck wasn't the only decision Al made that day. Figuring he would probably never again encounter such an animal, he promised himself to hunt that deer only.

While some trophy bucks are named after their death, "Mossy Horns" received that honor while still very much alive. Those long, drooping burr points and other characteristics give him a unique look and helped push his net non-typical score to a stunning 279 7/8 P&Y points. He has now been the P&Y record for more than 30 years and remains a fitting king. Photo by Tom Evans.

But, the odds were squarely against him. To begin with, it is always tough to single out a mature buck and kill him. Besides, this one had already proven his ability to sense a trap. Plus, Al wasn't the first local hunter to have spotted the odd-looking deer. He had heard other hunters talk of such a buck in the area but had dismissed those stories as pure fiction. Now, he realized he would have to compete with other hunters for that bizarre rack. Finally, as if he needed any more of a challenge, Al had sworn off gun-hunting several years earlier. If this dedicated hunter was going to outwit Mossy Horns, it would be with bow and arrow or not at all.

It didn't take long for the difficulty of Al's quest to become apparent. He never got another look at Mossy Horns that season, even though he hunted hard right to the end. Smaller deer came and went, but Al's bow remained undrawn, even though he never had taken a deer of any kind with archery gear.

That 1958 season turned out to be the last one in which Al had sole access to Dan's farm. In the fall of 1959, two other local archers, Gene Halloran and Charley Marlowe, became part of the hunting party. Gene was a retired farmer. Charley, an advertising executive from Hastings, was the only member of the local Oregon Trail Bowhunters Club who had ever arrowed a deer.

Dan, meanwhile, had witnessed firsthand just how belligerent this buck could be. Back in 1957, he had planted 50 small spruce trees to form a windbreak just 30 yards from his farmhouse. Over the

This earlier set of Mossy Horns' sheds, found by farmer Max Wilkie, now are on display at the Fred Bear Museum in Gainesville, Florida. Photo courtesy of Frank Scott.

course of several weeks before the 1959 bow season, the deer slipped in under the cover of darkness and destroyed every one of the young trees. According to Al, the tracks were so big that they only could have been made by Mossy Horns.

Although commercially made tree stands had not yet come into vogue in 1959, all three archers knew that an elevated location was most likely to yield a close shot at the big buck. So, they built a half-dozen permanent tree stands in strategic spots around Dan's property, hoping to catch Mossy Horns moving into or out of the dense riverbottom islands where he lived. The elevation of their platforms varied from 10 to 20 feet, depending on the height and thickness of the surrounding cover.

Despite these efforts, the bowhunters saw nothing of the big buck during the early season. Naturally, they began to question if the old deer was still around. Charley finally got a doe and quit hunting for the year, but Al and Gene kept at it. Then, one November afternoon, Al spotted Mossy Horns as he sneaked down a slough perhaps 150 yards from where the archer waited. Though happy to see the deer up and moving during legal shooting hours, Al wasn't pleased to see him headed in the wrong direction. This was before the advent of grunt calls or decoys, and rattling hadn't yet come onto the scene in Nebraska, so the hunter had no way to lure the buck within range. For a shot, the hunter would have to go to the deer.

While that figured to be a tough task, Al did have one advantage—a strong wind. Mossy Horns was heading into it, smelling for danger as well as

The huge buck knew every inch of the Platte River bottoms he called home, and that familiarity helped him reach old age despite heavy hunting pressure all around. Ron Van Gilder's print, "Old Mossy Horns," shows the legendary whitetail as he looked in early fall 1962, the year Del Austin finally arrowed the great deer. Many think this is a record that will stand for years to come. Print courtesy of the artist and Wild Wings, Inc.

for does. If the hunter played his cards right, he could flank the deer for a distance in hopes of getting a shot before shooting light faded. As soon as the buck moved behind a screen of brush, Al climbed down from his stand and struck out across the bottomland.

Amazingly, the old buck never caught on as the hunter shadowed him for perhaps a half-mile. Three times Mossy Horns stopped to rub his massive rack, and on each occasion, Al took the opportunity to close the gap. Twice, in fact, he had the deer within reasonable shooting range, but in each case, there was too much brush between them for a good shot. Rather than risk spooking or possibly crippling him, Al waited.

When Mossy Horns finally stopped again on the edge of a thicket and began to thrash the brush with his antlers, it appeared Al's patience finally would be

rewarded. The bowhunter's every sense was on full alert as he crept closer and closer, finally inching to within 25 yards of the buck of his dreams. A couple more feet around the edge of a willow clump and that long-awaited shot would be his.

As Al took that final step, his foot came down on a stick. When the twig snapped, Mossy Horns instinctively bounded out of sight in a blur. Stunned, Al was left to ponder what might have been. Though frustrated, all he could do was give a tip of the hat to his adversary, who had won yet another round.

That was the only real opportunity anyone had to get the buck that year. He wasn't even seen again until after shooting hours on the last evening of the season, when Al spied him at a distance standing out in the open. As the bowhunter watched the giant whitetail slip out of his life again, he felt a mixture of frustration and resolve. *Ok, Mossy,* he said to himself as the buck disappeared from the far end of the field, *next year will be different.*

While going about his daily chores in the summer of 1960, Dan saw Mossy Horns several times. In each case, the buck was down in the riverbottom. Al was keeping track of the buck's pattern, and in the course of his summer scouting, he found what seemed to be an ideal stand site. It was a cottonwood tree near the bottom end of a cornfield that abutted the thick riverbottom. The huge tracks regularly seen there convinced Al that this was one of Mossy Horns' regular crossings.

When the September 10 bow-opener arrived, Al, Gene and Charley were more confident than ever that somebody would get the deer. By now, their hunting party had grown to four. The new guy was a Hastings warehouse manager named Del Austin. He had recently taken up bowhunting and had really been bitten by the "bug," so he was a welcome addition to the chase for Mossy Horns.

Despite their optimism, the four bowhunters came up empty-handed. In fact, during seven long weeks, no one even caught a glimpse of the deer. But, the four persisted, hoping that the approaching

The author provides some size perspective to Mossy Horns' actual rack (right) and his largest known set of sheds, which was grown two years prior to the deer's death. Although aged at 9 1/2 years when taken, the buck's antler growth was still phenomenal thanks in part to the abundance of lush crops along that stretch of the Platte River. Few record bucks have such a rich story as this one. Photo by Tom Evans.

rut would cause the big buck to step within range of someone.

One afternoon in late October, it almost happened. Al was sitting in his cottonwood tree when two big bucks entered the standing corn 200 yards down the field fence. Neither was Mossy Horns, but neither was exactly small, either. Al weighed the situation and, frankly, did what most other bowhunters would have done. He decided that no matter how badly he wanted the big non-typical, two good bucks in the corn were worth one monster in the bush. When the two deer stepped into the stalks, Al eased out of his tree stand and began sneaking in their direction, a decision that took only minutes to regret.

After he had covered perhaps 70 yards, some inner voice told him to turn around. When he did, he got an eyeful. Mossy Horns was standing beneath his just-vacated tree stand! Before Al could react, the buck got a whiff of the hunter and disappeared into the brush.

The year's only other sighting of this phantom came roughly a week later. Charley shot a young buck from a tree stand, and in the process of gathering his gear, Mossy Horns walked out of the cover at 30 yards! It almost seemed the old buck somehow realized Charley had no more tags!

Al was growing more frustrated, of course, but he kept plugging away, hoping Mossy Horns would somehow slip up and walk beneath his stand while it was occupied. And one afternoon late in the season, that's just what happened. Al was sitting in the cottonwood. His wife, Velma, was perched in another tree stand some 50 yards away. Not much happened until just before dark. Then, Al heard a twig snap. Mossy Horns was heading his way, every sense on red alert.

The deer finally made his way just past Al's tree, and when he did, the archer went into action. Slowly drawing his recurve, he aimed at the shoulder and let the string slip from his fingers. The sound of the impact suggested a solid hit, and the monster buck took off. In his wild dash to safety, the deer ran smack into a woven-wire fence nailed to Velma's tree. The force of the impact nearly knocked her to the ground! The huge animal quickly collected himself and kept going. Within seconds, everything was quiet again.

All the search party ever found was the backend of the cedar arrow, snapped like a toothpick. There was no blood, hair or other evidence to suggest what might have occurred. Al was distraught, not knowing if he had wounded the buck of a lifetime or merely missed on his long-awaited chance.

The smile says it all: a 39-pointer on the ground! Though only one person, Del Austin, released the arrow that fell the historic buck, Mossy Horns was literally a "team trophy." Photo courtesy of Del Austin.

Neither alternative was very comforting.

The season ended with Al taking his first bow buck, a 160-pound 6-pointer. Normally, the first deer is a proud moment for a bowhunter, but in this case, the elation was mixed with disappointment. No one had so much as glimpsed Mossy Horns since the afternoon he had been hit. The question of whether he was dead or alive still tormented Al.

Those nagging doubts continued through the summer of 1961 when, for the first time in three years, Dan failed to see the buck in velvet. Had Al's arrow indeed proved fatal? Had Mossy Horns simply died of old age? Had he relocated his core area? No one had a clue. All Al knew was that the upcoming bow season lacked the excitement and anticipation of the previous two years. With the non-typical gone from the scene, the fun of deer hunting had been taken from him—perhaps by his own hand.

Then, one frigid afternoon late in the 1961 bow season, Al again found reason to smile. Sitting in the big cottonwood from which he had shot at the big deer the year before, the bowhunter detected a button buck heading his way. Right behind him was a bigger buck, and behind that deer came…Mossy Horns! Al's heart pounded as he watched the wary giant alertly pick his way through the willows, never stepping into the open. Amazingly, the rack looked even bigger than it had the year before!

A few minutes later, six does walked out and fed near Al's perch. As the hunter sat rock-still, two smaller bucks joined them. Finally, just before dark, Mossy Horns entered the cornfield but stayed well away from the tree stand from which that arrow had come a year earlier. It was the only time anyone on the farm saw the old deer that year, and Al ended yet another frustrating deer season by arrowing a consolation 8-pointer.

The next spring, Dan was working in an unharvested milo field when he came upon both of Mossy Horns' sheds. While some of the tips were gone, plenty of bone was left. One of the two huge, down-turned burr points was 11 inches long, the other 13. Some lingering velvet hung on near the tip of the longer one. Even without giving the deer credit for an inside spread, the rack still possessed way more than 200 inches of measurable antler, proving he was every bit the "world record on the hoof" Al had claimed he was. (The bow world record was then Don Vraspir's 186 2/8-point Minnesota buck profiled in Chapter 18.)

Some bucks possess huge racks and others huge bodies, but Mossy Horns had both. Despite being quite run down, he still field-dressed 240 pounds – and no one could question the size of his headgear! Photo courtesy of Del Austin.

By now, Mossy Horns had to be ancient. The fall of 1962 would be the hunters' fourth full season of pursuing him, and October would mark the fifth anniversary of Al's first sighting. Even if the buck had been just 3 1/2 years old when first seen, he would be 7 1/2 now, approaching "retirement age" for a wild whitetail. In all likelihood, he was even older, perhaps 9 1/2 or even 10 1/2, though he still seemed to be in decent physical condition and had a rack as magnificent as ever.

Desperate to find a way to get the deer within bow range, Al spent every free moment that summer landscaping the riverbottom. He cut trails through the thick brush, hoping that Mossy Horns would adopt them as his own. The bowhunter then constructed a number of platform-type tree stands in various spots overlooking those new runways. With those jobs finished, Al vacated the riverbottom a month prior to opening day, allowing deer patterns to return to normal.

By this time, the number of guys bowhunting Dan's farm had swelled to six, with local farmer Kenny Whitesel and Charley's 16-year-old son,

152

Chad, joining the group. Everyone in the party was talking about getting Mossy Horns, and so were a lot of local gun hunters. But, no one knew just how big the deer's rack was, or even if he was still alive since he had not been seen over the summer. When bow season finally came around, yet another challenge emerged. Because construction crews were building a stretch of Interstate 80 through Dan's farm, the Platte's north channel had been dammed temporarily, leaving dry land where there should have been a flowing river. Al didn't know what this would do to Mossy Horns' pattern, if the old buck was even still around.

Both questions were answered in encouraging fashion one October afternoon when the hunter discovered a set of huge, distinctive tracks in the dry riverbed. After studying the sign, Al deduced that his old nemesis was still bedding in the riverbottom and feeding on nearby crops. When he backtracked into the thick riverbottom, the bowhunter soon jumped his quarry from a willow-choked island. As the deer leaped from his bed and vanished, Al's hopes were confirmed. Mossy Horns was alive and his antlers were still gigantic!

———◆———

Closer and closer he came…until only 15 yards separated him from the archer. Finally, after five years… victory was at hand.

———◆———

Al had found the buck's hideout, but he realized it would be a mistake to try to hunt there. Instead, the archer began to play a guessing game with Mossy Horns, hastily building new platform tree stands near this core area but far enough away that he could enter and exit the stands without spooking his target. The strategy immediately proved sound.

The next week of hunting yielded two sightings for Al. The first was from a stand near a trail that crossed a slough. Several does and a 4x4 appeared as light was fading, and the buck stopped to rub his rack within just a few yards of the waiting hunter. Al ignored him, though, and soon spotted Mossy Horns passing through. Unfortunately, the big buck disappeared without ever coming into bow range. A few days later, Mossy Horns again teased Al by walking into view just beyond bow range. When the buck caught the hunter's scent, he wasted no time in easing off through the brush.

A week of frustration followed. The old buck totally disappeared, perhaps because Al had scented-up that area. Al figured it was time to do more scouting. Sure enough, when he began checking around, he discovered those huge tracks on a different trail, one Mossy Horns hadn't been using before. Once again, Al built a perch in a nearby tree and settled in for what seemed to be his millionth afternoon vigil.

Darkness was still an hour away when Mossy Horns suddenly emerged from a willow thicket and turned toward the new stand. Closer and closer he came…until only 15 yards separated him from the archer. The wind was right. There was plenty of shooting light left. Al even had sprinkled deer lure around the base of the stand tree. Every fiber in the hunter's body was attuned to the task at hand. Finally, after five years of pain and frustration, victory was at hand.

Then, instinctively, the old deer stopped in thick brush and waited…and waited…and waited. Ten minutes passed with neither hunter nor hunted daring to make the next move. Finally, Mossy Horns began to walk again, climbing a nearby bank and angling around Al's tree. Every step he took was in cover too thick for an arrow to penetrate. When the monster stopped again to assess his surroundings, he was *seven* yards from the stand! He stood there, still partially obscured by brush, for another 10 agonizing minutes before hopping over a fence and into an alfalfa field. When he finally cleared the brush, he was a full 45 yards from the hunter.

It wasn't the shot Al had wanted, but it would have to do. Drawing the arrow, he held well over the monster and let the string go. A moment later, the shaft passed right over Mossy Horns' back, leaving him unscathed for the umpteenth time in this long war of wits. In the blink of an eye, he bolted back into the thick brush…and Al's heart sank into his boots. There's only so much agony a hunter can stand, and this deer seemed bent on exceeding that limit!

Now, the clock was really working against the bowhunters. The nine-day gun season was about to open. During that span, it would be illegal to hunt with a bow. Mossy Horns' legend had grown to the point that every rifleman in the area was sure to be looking for him. Not only that, the old deer seemed to be more visible than ever. There was every reason for the guys on Dan's farm to believe that if they didn't get him before the gun-opener, they never would.

On Halloween afternoon, Al, Kenny and Gene headed out to the farm earlier than usual so they could get into their riverbottom stands well before dark. Charley and Del, however, had to work until

The Ishi Award, shown here to the right of Del's original mount, is the highest honor P&Y can bestow on a hunter. Del's award was the first ever presented by the club, and in bowhunting history, only one other person, Mel Johnson, has received the prestigious Ishi Award in honor of a whitetail trophy. Photo courtesy of Del Austin.

normal quitting time before making the drive from Hastings. Still, when the season has been whittled down to a precious few days, you hunt every possible minute.

Al had several good stands set up in the riverbottom, and he had offered one of them to Del for his abbreviated hunt. But, Del was afraid he would not be able to locate it very easily, and he certainly didn't want to mess up his friends' hunting by wandering around the area at prime time. Instead, he decided to tote with him something few other deer hunters had ever seen—a small, *portable* platform that could be attached to a tree trunk. Slipping into the riverbottom late that afternoon, he found a likely tree, hung the stand then climbed aboard, trimming a few nearby branches before settling in.

Due to the platform's diminutive size, Del was forced to stand in one soon-to-be-uncomfortable position. Before long, he was feeling the strain in his legs and wondered if he could hold out until dark. Finally, the pain became so severe that he realized he simply couldn't continue. Disappointed with his short hunt, Del stuck his arrow back into the bow quiver and pulled out a cigarette.

Then, all thoughts of nicotine were replaced by something even more addictive—the adrenaline surge of seeing a monster whitetail! Del heard brush breaking about 50 yards upwind of his stand. When he peered in that direction, an enormous buck materialized out of the thick cover and was headed in his direction!

With the light fading rapidly and the big buck running wide open, there was no way for Del to know if this was indeed Mossy Horns. All he could be certain of was that a trophy-class buck had just entered his life. The stunned hunter frantically shoved the cigarette lighter into his pocket, jerked that arrow back out of the quiver and nocked it…just as the brute came to a stop only 20 yards away. Moments later, the arrow was on a collision course with the broadside animal's rib cage. When the broadhead slammed into the buck, Del watched him disappear through the brush. From the sounds of it, the deer paused some 40 yards away then walked out of earshot.

When Del hadn't returned to his vehicle an hour after dark, the other guys became concerned and headed into the riverbottom to look for him. Halfway there, they encountered him on his way out to recruit help. Del hadn't found the deer, so he still couldn't be sure which buck he had shot. Al, however, had few doubts.

There was no shortage of blood to follow. Soon, the men found Del's arrow, snapped off some 10 inches or so behind the broadhead. There had been ample penetration to reach the vitals, so everyone

The Ishi Award

Bowhunting's highest honor, the Ishi Award, keeps alive the memory of a Yana Indian by the same name. The last member of his tribe, this lonely, starving "wild man" wandered into the corral of a slaughterhouse near Oroville, California, on the morning of August 29, 1911. Gradually, he was nursed back to health by T.T. Waterman and Alfred Kroeber, two professors of anthropology at the University of California.

In San Francisco, Ishi was befriended by Dr. Saxton Pope and his hunting companion, Art Young, for whom the Pope and Young Club later would be named. Ishi lived for only five years in the "modern" world before dying of tuberculosis, thus ending the history of the Yana tribe. During that span, however, he shared his knowledge of bowhunting with his new friends, both of whom already were intrigued by the idea of hunting with archery gear.

Perhaps it's ironic that during the fall of 1962, right about the time Del Austin was shooting Mossy Horns, P&Y's Dick Mauch was suggesting that the club name a new award in honor of the Indian who had inspired "the fathers of modern bowhunting." Dick's idea was enthusiastically accepted by the P&Y membership, and archery legends Fred Bear and Charlie Kroll soon began designing the special rosewood plaques. A spectacular obsidian spear point from the hand of master flintknapper Jim Ramsey then was mounted onto each one. The Ishi Award features the club's emblems and a small, engraved plate with the hunter's name and information about his trophy animal.

At this writing, Del Austin and Mel Johnson (Chapter 17) are the only bowhunters to have received this award in honor of whitetail kills. Perhaps that, as much as anything else, shows just how special their long-standing world records really are.

was confident the deer would be found soon. Three hours later, though, they weren't sure what to think. The trail was getting harder to see and the flashlights were fading. When no one could find any more blood to follow, the search was called off for the night.

Even though it wasn't Al's broadhead in the deer, he was back in the riverbottom at dawn the next morning. He found where Del had tied his handkerchief in a bush to mark the last blood found. In the gathering light, he soon picked up the trail again. After he had followed it perhaps 100 yards, Del and Dan arrived. The three then spread out to canvass the area, looking for more blood or the buck himself.

Finally, Del spotted something in the thick cover ahead. The deer was lying in a clump of willows, his rack entangled in the brush. Coming to full draw just in case the animal was still alive, Del watched him carefully. Then, he let the bow down and motioned for Al to approach. It was over.

A bizarre blend of elation and despair must have swept over Al as he walked up to the dead deer, for it was indeed Mossy Horns. The buck was every bit as impressive up close as he had looked from afar. He had a huge rack and a body to match. Even at his advanced age (later estimated by state biologists

Del isn't hard to recognize on the road; all you have to do is catch a glimpse of his license plate! When he first put this personalized tag on his vehicle, a woman in his hometown of Hasting, Nebraska, asked what it meant. Del told her about shooting "Mossy Horns" back in '62, and the woman began calling Del "Mossy!" He doesn't mind the title. Photo courtesy of Del Austin.

to be at least 9 1/2 years), the lean animal was enormous, tipping the scales at a field-dressed weight of 240 pounds. Al, who had seen him more times than everyone else combined, figured that in his prime he would have been perhaps 60 pounds heavier.

As they looked at the dead deer, there was no doubt that the P&Y record was about to be obliterated. Sure enough, when P&Y founder Glenn St. Charles measured the rack, he came up with 279 7/8 net points, beating the Vraspir world record by an unthinkable 93 5/8 inches. Del had raised the bar on bow-killed non-typicals by more than 50 percent! But, that's not the only staggering statistic. At the time Mossy Horns was entered into P&Y, the minimum entry score for non-typicals was only 120 points. In other words, he scored far more than *double* the minimum, making him the only whitetail in any record book to do so, before or since!

There's more. At the time Mossy Horns was shot, he might well have been the highest-scoring whitetail ever taken by a hunter using *any* type of weapon. The only buck then known to outscore him was the "Brady" buck from Texas (Chapter 9), which might not even have been a hunter kill. Since the Texas deer lived in the 1890s, Mossy Horns was at the time the biggest known buck in more than 60 years! Why, he even was 50 inches bigger than the then-No.1 non-typical *mule* deer, the 229 7/8-pointer Lee Lindley had arrowed in Utah in 1942!

In short, even among the deer world's top trophies, Mossy Horns stood out. Little wonder, then, that when P&Y's 4th Awards Banquet was held in Chicago on February 5, 1964, Del was presented not only with a certificate proclaiming his buck to be the archery world record, but he also received the first-ever Ishi Award, the highest honor P&Y can give a bowhunter. (See accompanying sidebar.)

———◆———

At the time Mossy Horns was shot, he might well have been the highest-scoring whitetail ever taken by a hunter using any type of weapon.

———◆———

Mossy Horns and the sheds picked up by Dan are now part of Larry Huffman's "Legendary Whitetails" collection and have been seen by tens of thousands of trophy enthusiasts. Another pair of Mossy Horns' sheds were found by local farmer Max Wilkie and are on display at the Fred Bear Museum in Gainesville, Florida, under the watchful eye of curator Frank Scott. All of this has added to the fame and mystique of what is still the indisputed king of bow-killed whitetails.

Del remains an avid bowhunter. He didn't hunt Dan's farm much after that watershed 1962 season. As he told me, "It just wasn't the same knowing Mossy Horns wasn't around any more. You'd think that with him having been there for so long we would eventually have seen some younger bucks with some of the same antler characteristics, but we never did. Also, the farm eventually was sold. Now, it's becoming hard to get access to farms along the Platte so I mainly bowhunt other private land."

Was there justice in the fact that Del got Mossy Horns after his good buddy, Al Dawson, had put so much time and effort into the quest and failed? It's hard not to feel for Al, who named the deer, hunted him longer and harder than anyone else and on several painful occasions fell just short of tagging him. But, both Al and Del have freely noted that the hunt for this world record was a group effort involving not only themselves but several other sportsmen, along with Dan, the farmer on whose property the men were allowed to pursue their dream. Maybe it's not totally fair that someone other than Al got the buck but…well hey, that's trophy hunting. A real hunter can accept that, and anyone who can't shouldn't play the game.

DEL AUSTIN, NEBRASKA, 1962

Measurements	Right	Left	Difference
No. of points	21	18	
Main beam	27 7/8	28 1/8	2/8
1st point (G-1)	7 2/8	6 5/8	5/8
2nd point (G-2)	11 0/8	11 3/8	3/8
3rd point (G-3)	6 6/8	9 6/8	3 0/8
4th point (G-4)	7 2/8	8 2/8	1 0/8
5th point (G-5)	–	–	–
1st circ. (H-1)	6 5/8	6 6/8	1/8
2nd circ. (H-2)	5 3/8	5 2/8	1/8
3rd circ. (H-3)	5 0/8	5 2/8	2/8
4th circ. (H-4)	6 2/8	5 2/8	1 0/8
Total	83 3/8	86 5/8	6 6/8
Greatest spread		29 5/8	
Inside spread		21 3/8	
Gross typical score		191 3/8	
Assymetry deductions		-6 6/8	
Non-typical additions		+95 2/8	
Net non-typical score		279 7/8	

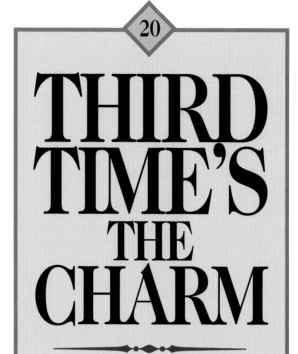

20

THIRD TIME'S THE CHARM

How many chances will a world-record whitetail give you to shoot him? This one just wouldn't give up!

TITLE: FIRST BLACKPOWDER TYPICAL WORLD RECORD

SCORE: 184 4/8

HUNTER: TOM MOSHER

LOCATION: CHASE COUNTY, KANSAS

YEAR: 1984

On the night of December 6, 1984, Tom Mosher lay tortured in his own bed. Hour after hour, he desperately tried to escape the visions that haunted him. But, the horror wouldn't go away. To make matters worse, Tom knew he had no one to blame but himself.

His pain was self-inflicted, the result of a gunshot—make that *two* gunshots—that had turned his once-pleasant world upside down. You see, that morning the Kansas hunter had missed a "gimme" shot at the biggest buck of his life. Then, only hours later, he had done it all over again! Same spot, same gun, same deer, same wretched results! No wonder that as Tom tried to fall asleep that night he found it impossible to stop reliving the agony of those two blown opportunities.

The episode had begun innocently enough, with no foreshadowing of the misery to come. In fact, until the moment things started to unravel, Tom's hunt had all the earmarks of a textbook success story, one far less lengthy —and, to be honest, far less interesting—han it eventually would become.

Kansas is a legendary producer of trophy bucks. Outstanding genetics, plenty of high-quality feed and light gun-hunting pressure, nearly all of which comes well after the peak of the rut, combine to grow big whitetails. Pressure is held in-check by tightly regulating the number of sportsmen allowed to participate in rifle season. Thus, even though much of Kansas features wide-open habitat that makes deer vulnerable to long-range weapons, a surprising number of bucks manage to reach maturity.

In eastern Kansas' Chase County, where Tom has

hunted for years, rifle-season permits have long been almost as elusive as the bucks themselves. Tom moved to Kansas from Massachusetts in the 1970s, taking a job as a fisheries biologist for the Kansas Department of Wildlife and Parks (KDWP). He had done his share of gun hunting for deer, so when he moved to Emporia, he was eager to sample the whitetail action around his new home. But in Kansas, as opposed to "Back East," Tom first would have to draw a permit to hunt with a firearm.

A frequently overlooked aspect of being a good deer hunter is knowing how to create opportunities. A big part of that is simply being able to find the right piece of land to hunt. But in places where hunting privileges are tightly regulated, a more immediate challenge is discovering how to maximize your chances of getting a permit. In that category, Tom had an advantage, one of his own making. After

Tom Mosher's 1984 basic 12-pointer was taken with a muzzleloader in Chase County, Kansas, and is so big that he could have become either the top typical or non-typical in the blackpowder records! Despite 17 6/8 inches of deductions for abnormal points, the hunter opted to place his great whitetail in the typical category at a net score of 184 4/8 points. Photo by Gordon Whittington.

carefully studying the permit system, he realized that it was far easier to draw a muzzleloader permit than a rifle permit. So, he purchased a .50-caliber Hawken and applied to hunt with that weapon.

Even though the annual allocation of muzzleloader permits was minuscule in comparison to the number of rifle permits, Tom's chances of getting one were good. Over the years, he got one regularly. These permits allowed him to hunt with a muzzleloader during the designated blackpowder season and during the December rifle season.

Early in his Kansas deer-hunting career, Tom befriended a landowner whose property was bisected by a river that had gouged out a path through the rolling prairie. Some of the best deer cover in the area lined this waterway, and nearby fields provided ideal food sources. Tom immediately recognized this bottom as a potential hotspot, and he began to hunt there as much as possible.

In 1984, he drew a muzzleloader permit but didn't shoot anything during the early season. When the eight-day rifle season got underway, he remained eager to find a big buck. He had no idea just how fully that wish was about to be granted.

Tom hunted several spots during the first few days of the season but saw no sizable bucks. By mid-week, he knew time was running out. When the hunter awoke well before dawn on Thursday, December 6, he thought long and hard about where to hunt that day. He decided on a stretch of riverbottom where two brushy draws filtered down from the surrounding prairie and linked up with the main part of the timbered bottom, forming a classic funnel for whitetail activity. A nearby cornfield no doubt was being visited by plenty of deer each night, and the animals had to be using the adjacent bottom to travel back and forth to that feeding area. A storm had dumped several inches of snow on Tuesday, and with the temperature still holding below freezing, plenty of the white stuff was still around to aid in visibility and sign reading.

At dawn, Tom began slinking through the bot-

Tom might have needed three chances at the suicidal buck, but in the end, he bagged one of history's most symmetrical world-class whitetails. Only two corresponding measurements between one antler and the other vary by more than 2/8-inch! Photo by Gordon Whittington.

tom in search of the best place to sit. As he eased along, scanning for both deer and their sign, he came upon a couple of does, which, unfortunately, had seen him first. Hopeful that they would not start blowing and alert every nearby creature, Tom patiently waited for them to move off. Once they were out of sight, he cautiously worked his way over to a nearby hackberry tree big enough to shield him from the prying eyes of any other deer that might be in the vicinity. It seemed as good a spot as any for a morning stand.

Even though the hunter was wearing heavy clothing and was somewhat protected from the chilling wind in the riverbottom, the conditions were pretty raw for sitting on a stand all day. Fortunately, relief wasn't long in coming. Around 9 a.m., Tom looked to his left and spotted a doe moving along the base of a steep wall of rock. Right behind her, almost as if his nose were surgically attached to her tail, walked a stunning buck.

The two deer already were within range, and their route was bringing them closer and closer to where Tom waited. He quickly raised his rifle in preparation for the shot of a lifetime but then noticed that the set-trigger wasn't in proper position to fire. As the buck and doe approached within 30 yards, seemingly oblivious to the world around them, the hunter frantically got the trigger set and placed the iron sights on the buck's chest.

Almost before the percussion cap had ignited the powder charge and sent the ball on its way, Tom knew he had erred. In his rush to make the gun operational, he had not noticed that the two deer were approaching a depression. At the moment the trigger was squeezed, the buck was stepping down into that low spot, dropping him out of the line of fire. The ball slammed harmlessly into the ground over the giant's back.

Hurriedly, Tom began to reload, hoping against hope that the buck was still around. When the rifle was ready to shoot again, the hunter poked his head around the tree and looked for the two deer. They were gone. Tom walked over to check the trail the buck and doe had been walking and found exactly what he feared—no hair, no blood, no evidence of a hit.

Disgust set in. Tom had waited a long time for a chance like this at a world-class whitetail. Now, through a combination of seemingly minor missteps, the opportunity had vanished before his eyes. Figuring the spot was ruined for at least the rest of the morning, he grabbed his gear, headed back to his vehicle and went for lunch.

After pondering the morning's events, Tom finally decided to return to that same spot in the bottom, even though he figured there was little chance of seeing the tall-tined buck again. It seemed to be a hub of deer activity, so perhaps another good buck would show up, even if this monster and his lady friend were now long gone. With only 3 1/2 days left in the season, he knew his time needed to be spent in the best possible location.

Tom returned to the base of the same big hackberry tree and settled in for the afternoon watch. Late in the day, a "shooter" 5x5 came picking his way along the top of the same rocky bank the two

deer had passed under that morning. Tom started to ease his Hawken into position, but then, off to the left, something caught his eye. Only 20 yards away stood a buck—the *same* giant Tom had missed that morning!

Scarcely believing his good fortune, but not taking any time to question it, the hunter immediately forgot about the 10-pointer and swung his rifle toward the bigger buck. *You're not leaving here this time,* Tom thought, as he drew a bead on his best available target, the spot where the base of the neck connects to the front of the shoulder. When the smoke cloud erupted, Tom was far more confident of success than he had been that morning. But, where was the buck? Not seeing him, Tom grabbed his powder, patch, ball and ramrod and scurried to get the rifle reloaded, just in case a follow-up shot was needed.

Imagine the bewilderment that flooded the hunter's mind when he eased his head around that tree and saw the huge buck still standing there, just looking around. Apparently, both the deer and his pursuer were equally puzzled over what had transpired! Tom could have (and, in retrospect, *should* have) shot again, but he was certain the deer was hit and about to fall. He held off…and watched the buck of a lifetime just walk away. No limping, no staggering, nothing. He just walked out of sight through the trees and brush.

As Tom stood at the base of the tree, he still believed the deer was fatally struck. So, he waited a few nervous minutes then cautiously began to follow the big tracks. After about 100 yards, he found where the buck had bedded briefly. Fully expecting to see blood or hair where the animal had been lying in the snow, Tom was shocked to find neither. Once more, it appeared that the buck had managed to escape without a scratch!

Whether you're a rookie in the woods or have taken 100 deer, failing to kill a buck standing within rock-throwing distance can leave you a broken, babbling shell of a hunter. Tom had shot a number of deer in his career, most under far more challenging circumstances than this buck had presented, and he had no idea what to think. Sure, the morning's miss had been due to human error, but what could possibly explain his missing a 20-yard shot at a buck standing in the open, doing everything possible to get itself killed?

All through a long, restless night, the hunter searched for an answer to that question. In his mind, there just wasn't any way to reconcile what had happened. Tom kept trying to tell himself he had killed the buck, despite no sign of a hit. Slowly, he began to convince himself that, against all odds, he had flat-out missed the deer. You can bet Tom was back in the same

From above, it is especially easy to see the wrap-around configuration of the beams and their extreme length. One spans 30 4/8 inches and the other 30 3/8, making them among the longest main beams of any whitetail from the Great Plains. Photo by Gordon Whittington.

spot on Friday morning in hopes that this suicidal buck was still around. Although some does and small bucks passed the hunter's hideout at the base of that big hackberry tree, there was no sign of the monster.

Friday night, as Tom began to prepare for the season's final weekend, he knew there might be another obstacle to overcome. The landowner was sure to go hunting the next morning, but exactly where on his property would he be heading? A phone call to the landowner brought a discouraging

answer. "I believe I'll go down and hunt that bottom below the cornfield," the man said.

Tom was in a serious bind. He desperately wanted to return to that spot himself, even though common sense told him the chances of getting yet another crack at the huge whitetail were poor. The landowner hadn't seen this deer and wasn't an avid trophy hunter, so Tom decided to go for broke. "I was hoping to go back down there myself," he told the landowner. "I missed a really big buck in there yesterday, and I'd like to have one more chance at him."

"Well," the landowner said, "do you think there's room for two of us to hunt down in there at the same time?"

Tom swallowed hard and explained, "I think there's a good chance it would just foul up the area if we did."

Whitetail history hung in the balance. Then, the landowner finally spoke. "Okay, you go ahead and hunt there."

Tom thanked the man for his generosity and felt a wave of relief flow over him. He might not see the monster that was hanging out in that bottom, but at least, he would get another try.

Dawn found Tom once more at the base of that hackberry tree, watching intently for any sign of a deer. The snow had melted some, but patches were still scattered about. The crisp air brought promise of another good day to hunt. Then, as light began to filter down through the timber, Tom's worst nightmare became reality – he heard a trespasser crossing the stream behind him.

"Somebody's walking in on me!" Tom's brain screamed, not wanting to believe what was happening. Listening to the noisy footsteps sloshing through the water, he turned to look in that direction, silently cursing his misfortune. Then, in the blink of an eye, all thoughts of bad luck were dismissed and replaced by an atomic blast of adrenaline. Coming almost straight at the hunter through the trees and brush was a deer rack, bobbing with every step of the animal's massive body. It was the same bruiser Tom had missed twice only two days before!

Tom's first thought was one of relief, realizing that he apparently hadn't wounded the deer on Thursday. But, that relief almost instantly was replaced by a good case of buck fever. Against all odds, everything seemed to be falling into place for Tom to get the deer after all…if he could do his part.

The buck kept angling in Tom's direction, closing to the gap. Tom tried not to think of his two earlier misses. Instead, he attempted to focus on the shot yet to come, which presented itself when the deer walked behind a white-barked sycamore tree. He brought the Hawken snugly to his shoulder. When the buck conveniently stopped at 30 yards, with his front half protruding from behind the cover, Tom anxiously drew a bead on the left shoulder and fired.

This time, no agonizing self-analysis was needed. Hit squarely in the shoulder, the buck went down instantly and stayed down. With trembling hands, Tom hurriedly reloaded. But, there was no need. The buck of his dreams was dead.

Though certainly the same deer he had shot at on Thursday, there was no evidence of an earlier hit.

(To this day, Tom can't explain that second miss, unless the ball struck an unseen twig and deflected.) Of course, as the hunter knelt beside his heart-stopping trophy and admired the sweeping antlers, Thursday seemed like a long, long time ago.

After calming down enough to field-dress his prize, Tom grabbed one of the antlers and began to drag the carcass up toward the road. He had gone perhaps 100 yards when the landowner, who had heard the shot, arrived on the scene.

"Did you shoot him up here?" the man asked.

"No, down there in the bottom," Tom replied.

"No way. You couldn't have dragged that big a deer up here by yourself."

Tom assured the landowner that he really *had* pulled the buck up the slope, and to prove it, he grabbed one of the antlers and pulled. The carcass wouldn't budge! Tom had burned up all his adrenaline rush on the initial drag. Now, it was all he and the landowner together could do to get the massive animal loaded into the truck! (With a field-dressed weight of 230 pounds, the carcass outweighed Tom by a considerable amount.)

Once the hunter got his deer home, he had more time to study the trophy. Although the buck was only 4 1/2 years old, his antlers were huge, with more than enough bone to make the 170-point B&C minimum. Tom—who, coincidentally, had been certified as a B&C measurer only a few months prior to deer season—knew the net score would be hurt greatly because of a huge fork on each G-2 tine. When he measured the sweeping main beams at a bit over 30 inches, he went to the B&C record book to see just how many Kansas bucks in those pages could make the same claim. None could. Tom had known his whitetail was something special, but this revelation sealed it.

Fellow KDWP biologist Keith Sexson did the official measuring of the rack and came up with a net score of 184 4/8, the highest ever recorded for a Kansas muzzleloader typical. In fact, it was the highest score for any muzzleloader typical from anywhere. Tom's third-chance giant was a new world record!

At the time, there was a move afoot to compile a new muzzleloader record book to be known as the Carson and Glass listings. (See Chapter 1.) Tom submitted his buck for inclusion, but that record book never got beyond the concept stage. Then, in 1988, the National Muzzle Loading Rifle Association (NMLRA) finally got its Longhunter Society record book off the ground and began ranking whitetails and other North American big-game species taken by blackpowder. Old Carson and Glass entries were merged with Longhunter entries to compile this list.

Only a glove kept Mosher from possibly being the only two-time record-holder in whitetail history.

Unfortunately for Tom, his Kansas buck had slipped to No.3 by that time, having been usurped by Larry Lawson's huge Indiana typical (Chapter 21). So, in no book prior to the one you're holding has Tom's fabulous trophy ever been listed as a No.1 muzzleloader typical. Of course, that's neither the hunter's nor the deer's fault, just a matter of unfortunate timing. The Mosher buck can legitimately be called a former world record, even though there was never an official proclamation to that effect.

There are plenty of amazing aspects to this trophy, including the immensity and balance of the rack itself. As great as a net score of 184 4/8 is, it does not reflect just how awesome these antlers really are. A slight rearranging of tines would allow this deer to remain the world record by muzzleloader even today, as well as a Top 10 qualifier for B&C! The problem is not antler size, just conformation.

The gross typical score for the deer's 6x6 main-frame is 204 5/8, clearly world-class. Just think what the gross score would be if those two "mule deer" forks on the G-2s had grown off the main beams as typical tines instead. If they were matched typical tines, the buck's gross typical score would shoot up to 222 3/8, one of the highest such numbers ever seen on a whitetail. What's more, the net typical score would have been 217 2/8, a number that even today would make the Mosher buck the top typical of all time, bar none! (Milo Hanson's current No.1 nets 213 5/8.)

Of course, this speculation is all moot since the Mosher buck *didn't* grow those forks as typical tines. But, such lofty numbers are only possible even when "what-ifing" because the buck is both huge and unbelievably well balanced. Few other world-class typicals in any category can match this deer's symmetry. For example, the Jordan buck, universally considered history's most symmetrical top-end typical, has a gross typical score of 209 3/8 and a net of 206 1/8, a difference of just under 1.5 percent. Tom's deer, though, loses just 2 3/8 inches of his 204 5/8 gross typical score, a difference of only 1.2 percent!

And, let's not overlook what this deer would have been if Tom had chosen to enter him as a non-typical rather than as a typical, as was his prerogative. *Adding* the 17 6/8 inches for those gigantic forks would hike the non-typical score to an even 220. So what, you say? Well, at the time the buck was shot, the largest muzzleloader non-typical on record was the 185 3/8-pointer taken in 1983 by Tennessee's Terry Burns (Chapter 23). In other words, Tom's buck was easily big enough to hold *both* records simultaneously, though such double listings are not allowed in any record book.

All of this makes the Mosher buck one of the most fascinating deer in blackpowder history, but the story doesn't end there. As unbelievable as it seems, only a year after shooting his world-record whitetail, the hunter very nearly took an even higher-scoring typical by muzzleloader! It happened in the same bottom that had been so kind to Tom in 1984. This time, as he waited in ambush, a friend made a one-man drive through the brush, hoping to push something in Tom's direction. Soon, nine does came trotting past, followed by a massive buck. They passed Tom's position at only 40 yards, but the hunter didn't like the shot opportunity and decided to pass.

A few minutes later, Tom's friend made his way back into the bottom. The two men were discussing what had transpired when a lone doe appeared on top of a nearby ridge and immediately bedded down in a small thicket. Tom wasn't interested in shooting the doe but was curious to see how close he could get to her. He moved around to the downwind side of the ridge and began a slow stalk to the bedding cover. Finally, he saw the doe ahead of him. But as he was watching her, something big was watching *him*.

Suddenly, at a range 10 yards, that same huge buck rose from his bed and scrambled to make his getaway. Tom once again had gun problems. His gloved trigger finger wouldn't fit into the trigger guard of his Hawken. By the time he had ripped the glove off his hand, the old buck was out of range and heading for the horizon.

We don't have to speculate whether this buck would have outscored the one Tom got in 1984. A few months later, the biologist himself verified it. He received a call from a woman asking him to measure a large buck she had shot on the neighboring property, the very property the buck had escaped to when Tom jumped him. Sure enough, Tom recognized the deer as the same one he had encountered! And, the tag indicated the trophy had been taken later that same day! The typical rack netted 186 points!

Unfortunately, the woman's story about having shot the great deer proved to be false. Her husband, who had been unsuccessful in drawing a permit that year, had actually shot the buck and put her tag on it. The couple might have pulled off the ruse, but when the woman let a comment slip about not having shot the buck herself, game wardens investigated. Sure enough, the truth came out upon questioning. The rack was confiscated by KDWP.

Although Tom had a legitimate chance to harvest that deer, you won't hear him complaining about having missed out on becoming the only two-time record-holder in whitetail history. Instead, he just keeps going back to that riverbottom every year he draws a permit, hoping that yet another monster will pass within muzzleloader range of the big hackberry tree. The old tree now has a hollowed-out trunk that grows more rotten by the year, and Tom fears that before much longer he just might lose his old friend. But if it happens, he can take comfort in knowing there are more big trees in that bottom…and maybe a few more record bucks as well.

TOM MOSHER, KANSAS, 1984

Measurements	Right	Left	Difference
No. of points	7	7	
Main beam	30 3/8	30 4/8	1/8
1st point (G-1)	4 5/8	4 7/8	2/8
2nd point (G-2)	14 1/8	13 5/8	4/8
3rd point (G-3)	12 5/8	12 3/8	2/8
4th point (G-4)	7 5/8	7 7/8	2/8
5th point (G-5)	4 1/8	3 2/8	7/8
1st circ. (H-1)	5 0/8	5 1/8	1/8
2nd circ. (H-2)	4 6/8	4 6/8	–
3rd circ. (H-3)	4 6/8	4 6/8	–
4th circ. (H-4)	4 4/8	4 4/8	–
Total	92 4/8	91 5/8	2 3/8
Greatest spread		25 0/8	
Inside spread		20 4/8	
Gross typical score		204 5/8	
Assymetry deductions		-2 3/8	
Non-typical deductions		-17 6/8	
Net typical score		184 4/8	

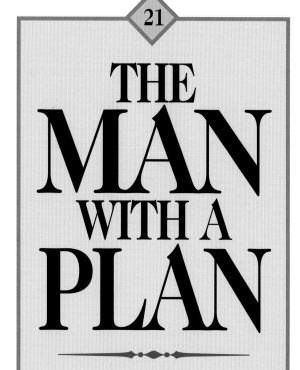

21

THE MAN WITH A PLAN

Many hunters believe that taking a record buck is purely a matter of luck. But, Larry Lawson bagged his top-ranked whitetail the old-fahsioned way—he earned it!

TITLE: SECOND BLACKPOWDER TYPICAL WORLD RECORD

SCORE: 187 1/8

HUNTER: LARRY LAWSON

LOCATION: MONTGOMERY COUNTY, INDIANA

YEAR: 1988

There are ways to prepare for that happy day when, if all goes according to your dreams, you finally get a crack at a world-record whitetail. First, you can practice your shooting, so you won't have to wonder if you and your gear are physically up to the challenge. Then, you can rehearse the many possible scenarios leading up to the shot, so you'll be mentally prepared to deal with what's often referred to as the "moment of truth." And finally, you can practice smiling for the cameras that are sure to immortalize your accomplishment.

Larry Lawson has a smile so broad that you would figure he has spent all his time working on that final part of the equation. But when his historic whitetail moment came along during the 1987 season, this serious trophy hunter also had done all the things necessary to be physically and mentally ready. In fact, he had even stacked the deck in his favor that such an opportunity would come his way.

Like no one else, Larry is and long has been a student of Indiana trophy hunting. Even before his fateful day in 1987, he had become an official measurer of big-game trophies and, as such, had driven thousands of miles along Indiana's highways and byways to measure other hunters' racks. An advantage, to be sure, but it does stop there. In the early 1980s, Larry authored and self-published one of the earliest state-specific whitetail record books, *Trophy Bucks of Indiana*. While engaged in the exhausting research needed to compile his first record book, he discovered that some Indiana counties were consistently good producers of big deer and others weren't. Eventually, Larry gained an intimate knowledge of where big bucks lived…and where he should hunt them!

The one undeniable truth in trophy whitetail hunting is that to bag big bucks you must hunt where they are. Once Larry's work had given him an idea of where that was, he decided he no longer wanted to shoot small deer himself, even though he had been hunting whitetails only a few years. Yet, even when Larry released his first volume of *Trophy Bucks of Indiana* back in the early '80s, there was no way he could have known that just a few years later he would put one of Indiana's most noteworthy deer on his own wall.

From his research, Jefferson County in southern Indiana immediately struck Larry as one of the better places in the state for trophies, and that's where he started spending a lot of time every hunting season. Larry's hunting areas were at least two hours from his home northeast of Indianapolis, but travel has never really bothered him—he has been known to "commute" several hundred miles for a single day of hunting in a great spot! So, private land in Jefferson County soon became his home base for deer hunting and remained that way for several productive years.

In 1979, the first season he hunted in southern Indiana, Larry arrowed a 127-point P&Y typical. Two years later, he got another P&Y trophy, this one netting 129 3/8 points. Then, during the 1983 slug season, he made the Hoosier Record Buck Program with a beautiful buck scoring 152 7/8 B&C points. Yes, hunting away from home was a lot of trouble, but it also was paying off. This success only inspired Larry to keep looking for more potential trophy pockets around the state.

He continued to find them, too, but not always in areas well known for big bucks. Indiana's herd was changing. While many of the traditional trophy counties still produced good deer, new hotspots were emerging, including the broken farm country of west-central Indiana. Counties such as Parke and Montgomery were no closer to Larry's home than

With long hours of research and fieldwork, Indiana's Larry Lawson paid his dues before taking his 187 1/8-point blackpowder world-record typical on December 11, 1988. Photo courtesy of Larry Lawson.

Jefferson County was, but as we've seen, he wasn't one to let a long stretch of highway keep him away from a hot hunting area. As Larry's interest shifted toward ever-bigger bucks, he made yet another move calculated to boost his chances of taking a top-end whitetail. He shifted his hunting emphasis to the farm country of west-central Indiana.

In his new area, getting permission to hunt proved easier than finding a cooperative trophy buck. For several frustrating seasons, Larry's quest for his best-ever buck was denied. Finally, in 1988, things started looking up again. During bow season that year, both Larry and his 13-year-old son, Roman, shot nice typical bucks netting in the mid-130s. (Roman's netted 135 4/8; Larry's 135 2/8.) That naturally lifted Larry's spirits. Perhaps, he thought, the drought was over. With renewed vigor, he prepared for the mid-November slug season. But once again, he was disappointed, as neither he nor his son saw anything of note during that hunt. Oh well, he realized, he could still hunt the late blackpowder season.

Larry knew his muzzleloader was up to the task of felling a trophy deer. He had the .58-caliber weapon spitting one-inch groups at 50 yards. Now, the challenge was to get a decent shot at one of those big deer he knew lived on the private proper-

Larry's son, Roman, examines one of several impressive rubs in their hunting area. By researching out where Indiana's best bucks had been killed, the Lawsons were able to zero in on prime trophy locations, which paid "big" dividends for them. Photo by Larry Lawson.

ties he hunted. That didn't figure to be a snap. The combination of hunting pressure and post-rut conditions had prompted the bucks to lead even more reclusive lives than usual. Still, buoyed by his success earlier in the year, Larry remained hopeful that another trophy was in his future.

By noon of the December 3 blackpowder-opener, that optimism had waned a bit. Larry, friend Dave Boaz and two other coworkers had spent the morning on private land in Parke County, but with piles of litter everywhere, their hunting spot looked more like a public dump than a prime hunting area. So, that afternoon, he and Dave drove over to neighboring Montgomery County, hoping to find a better spot on a private tract Larry knew about but hadn't visited in several years.

On the way, they came across a farmer having problems with a broken-down combine. Larry and Dave could have gone on by and kept hunting, but instead, they offered to help the landowner get his equipment running again. That task successfully completed, the farmer made the two hunters an offer they couldn't refuse – he gave them permission to hunt his entire 640-acre tract, something no one had been granted in several years.

Because of the time spent helping out with the

equipment repair, precious little shooting light remained that Saturday evening. The hunters took to the woods anyway and liked what they found. Big rubs were all over the place, and the area seemed to be undisturbed and free of littering trespassers. Larry even grunted in a decent 8-pointer before dark but decided not to burn his tag. Somewhere on the property, he figured there were bound to be bigger bucks.

The next Saturday afternoon, after a week of dreaming about getting into those woods again, Larry and Dave returned to the farm. They never saw a single deer. That had to be discouraging with all the big-buck sign scattered throughout the woods. Larry, ever the optimist, wasn't thinking about giving up. He called home to ask his wife, Debbie, if she would let him skip a scheduled Sunday shopping trip. She gave the green light, a gracious gesture with Christmas coming on and gifts to be bought. So, instead of heading home after their Saturday hunt, the two hunters checked into a local motel, determined to give the farm another shot on Sunday.

It was a bitterly cold night—so frigid, in fact, that when Larry and Dave awoke the next morning, they opted to begin the day with a couple of hours

Although the Lawson buck has a gnarly-looking rack, the total deduction for asymmetry is a minuscule 1 4/8 inches. But, had a hunter earlier that fall varied his aim just a bit, there would have been far less balance between the antlers. That's because halfway up the right G-2, a slug had blown a chunk out of the tine but hadn't snapped it off. A lucky non-break! Photo by Larry Lawson.

of still-hunting. After all, whitetail movement in the area had been extremely light on Saturday. Perhaps it made more sense for the hunters to go to the deer, rather than the other way around.

When the two friends rendezvoused at the farmhouse at 9:30 a.m., they still hadn't seen any deer. Unfortunately, Dave had developed such bad blisters on one foot that he had no desire to continue walking. The hunters weighed their options and decided it would be a good idea for Larry to still-hunt through one more section of thick woods, coming out at a bridge on the far end of the timber. Dave, meanwhile, would drive the truck around to pick up his partner after this final still-hunt of the weekend.

When Larry reached the pickup point an hour later, after yet another deerless trip through the woods, he expected Dave to be waiting there. But, his partner was nowhere in sight. Standing there at the bridge, wondering where his buddy was, Larry didn't know exactly what to do next. Should he hang around, hoping Dave would show up eventually? Or, should he just hunt his way back to the farmhouse, knowing he and his friend would catch up with each other eventually? Larry opted for the latter, which turned out to be the most pivotal decision of his hunting career. On the return route back to his starting point, Larry finally saw a buck big enough to have made all that impressive sign.

As Larry was sneaking along the edge of a stand of mature oaks, a sudden flash of white in an adjacent thicket caught his attention. The hunter stopped, hoping it was a deer but seeing nothing to confirm that notion. Finally, he decided to use his 4X scope to help him see through the tangle of briars, branches and tall grass. The image centered in the scope was one that every trophy hunter hopes to see at some point in his life – the rack of a world-class whitetail!

At a field-dressed weight of 171 pounds, the buck's body wasn't particularly noteworthy, making the rack look even larger. Larry knew the antlers were big when he saw the bedded deer, and after a masterful but tense backwards stalk, he kept his composure long enough to connect with a long, offhand shot with his .58-caliber smokepole. Photo by Larry Lawson.

Larry had a very different idea in mind, one that only the most confident and daring of hunters might try.

Unfortunately, the rack was just about the only part of the deer he could make out. All sorts of obstructions stood between the hunter and the hunted. The buck, based on the rack's square-on position to Larry, had undoubtedly seen his pursuer. The distance was roughly 90 yards, close enough for a shot but not until Larry had a better target than a set of antlers.

Larry didn't even consider attempting a "brush" shot. Nor did he give in to the temptation of trying to get closer to the buck, which probably would have sent the big guy crashing deeper into the "jungle" in which he was hiding. Instead, Larry had a very different idea in mind, one that only the most confident and daring of hunters might try—he was going to turn and walk away from the deer of his dreams.

He had his reasons. First, by appearing to be "leaving," the buck might hold his position for a few more critical seconds without fleeing. Just as importantly, Larry might be able to reach a small opening that would give him a chance to put that .58-caliber ball into the deer's kill zone. So, the hunter cautiously angled away from his quarry, keeping his gun pointed toward the buck as he moved slowly along. Anxiety running high, Larry occasionally looked back to check on the deer. Each time, he was relieved to find the buck still standing there, eyeing his retreat. Step by step, Larry got farther from the buck…and closer to the possibility of a clear shot.

Finally, the hunter was in position to make his move. As Larry eased into an opening, turning slowly he smoothly raised the rifle and faced the alert buck. Thankfully, the deer was still standing there and somewhat more exposed than he had

THE MAN WITH A PLAN

been, with his entire head and neck visible through the vegetation. There was no time to marvel at the huge rack. Larry had to get the scope centered on its target and squeeze the trigger before the buck bolted. When the crosshairs locked onto the buck's throat patch, the anxious hunter squeezed the trigger.

Instantly, the buck was running hard, angling toward Larry! Had the shot missed? Was the buck of a lifetime escaping back into those dreams from which he had appeared? The huge deer soon disappeared from sight in the oak woods, taking the answers with him.

---◆---

The antlers have a twisted, gnarly appearance that belies the numbers on the score sheet.

---◆---

With his heart racing, Larry reloaded his muzzleloader and then began to look along the buck's escape trail for some indication of a hit. Fortunately, that was easy to find. Bright-red blood was spattered on the fallen leaves. The shot hadn't missed after all! Looking ahead through the woods, Larry saw the buck. The round ball, fired from a distance of 127 yards, had done plenty of damage, clipping the deer's aorta and passing through both lungs. It had been nothing short of a great shot at what was nothing short of a great whitetail.

From the moment he first saw that rack in the brush, Larry knew he was looking at a world-class deer. Now, the smoke just drifting away through the December woods, he realized just how big the antlers really were. What lay before him was one of the biggest-racked bucks ever taken in Indiana! (The rutted-down buck field-dressed just 171 pounds.)

On March 3, 1989, Amy Davies of the National Muzzleloading Rifle Association gave the rack an official net score of 187 1/8 typical, edging out Tom

Mosher's 184 4/8-point Kansas blackpowder world record (Chapter 20). Larry's buck is one of the most symmetrical giant typicals of all time. The Indiana buck's typical 6x6 frame has only 1 4/8 inches of side-to-side deductions, a mere 0.8 percent of his 191 7/8-point gross typical score! In other words, he gets net credit for an unimaginably high 99.2 percent of his gross typical score!

It is hard to believe any magnum buck's typical frame could be this balanced. When you consider how uneven the rack looks at first glance, it's even tougher to swallow. The antlers have a twisted, gnarly appearance that belies the numbers on the score sheet. Without the 3 2/8 inches of deductions for abnormal points, the buck would have netted 190 3/8! World class anyway you look at it. It's only fitting that a sportsman who has done so much for the appreciation of Indiana's trophy bucks has given us yet another one to admire!

LARRY LAWSON, INDIANA, 1988

Measurements	Right	Left	Difference
No. of points	8	6	
Main beam	27 2/8	27 6/8	4/8
1st point (G-1)	5 5/8	5 4/8	1/8
2nd point (G-2)	12 4/8	12 4/8	–
3rd point (G-3)	11 1/8	11 5/8	4/8
4th point (G-4)	9 1/8	9 0/8	1/8
5th point (G-5)	3 4/8	3 4/8	–
1st circ. (H-1)	5 0/8	5 0/8	–
2nd circ. (H-2)	4 1/8	4 1/8	–
3rd circ. (H-3)	4 3/8	4 2/8	1/8
4th circ. (H-4)	4 0/8	4 1/8	1/8
Total	86 5/8	87 3/8	1 4/8
Greatest spread		19 7/8	
Inside spread		17 7/8	
Gross typical score		191 7/8	
Assymetry deductions		-1 4/8	
Non-typical deductions		-3 2/8	
Net typical score		**187 1/8**	

22

RISKING IT ALL FOR A RECORD

Dave Wilson literally went the extra mile—make that 2,000 miles—in pursuit of his trophy dreams. Ask him if it was worth it!

TITLE: CURRENT BLACKPOWDER TYPICAL WORLD RECORD

SCORE: 193 2/8

HUNTER: DAVE WILSON

LOCATION: CHITEK LAKE, SASKATCHEWAN

YEAR: 1992

When it comes to pursuing trophy whitetails, plenty of sportsmen claim to be serious about their sport. But even among hardcore hunters, Dave Wilson would have to be regarded as something special. After all, how many guys would walk away from a good job and move to another country, without any guarantee of employment, purely in search of better opportunities to hunt monster deer?

Prior to the 1990 hunting season, that's exactly what Dave did! Packing up everything, he moved from the East Coast of the U.S. to Saskatchewan, with every intention of becoming a Canadian resident. At the time, his friends and family must have thought he had lost his mind, that his obsession with trophy whitetails had finally gone too far. But, Dave got the last

laugh. Only a couple of years after making his bold move to the North Country, he was rewarded in a very big way—namely, with the largest typical buck ever taken by muzzleloader.

Shooting a world-record buck wasn't specifically what lured the young hunter northward. He just wanted to hunt trophy deer, and he knew his home area wasn't the best place to kill record-class whitetails consistently. Having hunted western Canada before, Dave realized it offered him far better odds of finding great trophies on a regular basis. Still, he could never have predicted just how well his move would turn out.

The 2,000-mile road to his No.1 buck might not have taken all that long to travel, but figuratively speaking, there were plenty of potholes along the way. Just finding work proved to be one of them. Even though Dave's engineering skills were quite marketable, very soon after arriving in Saskatchewan he discovered that the jobs he applied for kept going to residents instead. Finally, Dave decided to take whatever work he could get that would allow him to trade labor for hunting privileges.

Not surprisingly, he started out working for a whitetail outfitter. Unfortunately, it didn't pay many dividends in the short-term. He didn't even hunt during the early bow season because he could not find a buck that interested him. Yes, he scouted a lot and found some whitetails up to the 150-class, which are big by most standards. But, Dave had already taken deer of that size. He wanted something considerably better. He would just keep looking until he found one, which is exactly what he did one day in October. Unfortunately, it did him no good.

While scouting some land adjacent to the farm where he was working, Dave jumped an enormous

It's a long way from the East Coast to Saskatchewan, but Dave Wilson's 1992 pilgrimage was worth it. That September during the early muzzleloader season, he downed this 193 2/8-point typical, still the world's best by blackpowder. The beautiful buck is a basic 11-pointer and has a 24 6/8-inch inside spread. Photo by Joe Byers.

typical. He was carrying his deer rifle in hopes of encountering one of the wolves that had been causing problems in the area, but since the general gun season for whitetails wasn't yet open, all Dave could do was stare.

Though he didn't realize it at the time, he could have shot the buck had he been carrying a muzzleloader because the primitive-weapons season was open. How might whitetail history have been altered had Dave known that? Well, he told me that he believes that deer would have been a strong contender for the B&C world record! (At the time, that mark was held by Jim Jordan's 206 1/8-pointer from Wisconsin.)

Naturally, Dave was eager to scout that area thoroughly in hopes of figuring out the monster's pattern for the regular gun season soon to open. But as it turned out, he wasn't allowed to hunt the deer, even though the buck was in an area legal for Dave to hunt. (As an American, Dave could only hunt in certain zones and under the control of an outfitter.) You see, when Dave told his outfitter (who was his employer) just how big the animal was, he was denied permission to hunt there. The outfitter decided such a deer should be hunted by "paying" clients instead. Frustrated in his first autumn in Saskatchewan, Dave headed back to the States to weigh his options.

Fortunately, he was able to find work at home again. But when August rolled around once more, Dave traveled back to Saskatchewan, hoping to find a better situation. He quickly found work with a farmer who was also an outfitter but soon found that the area lacked big whitetails.

As amazing as it might seen, Dave wasn't in a hurry to shoot when this monster strolled out into an alfalfa field. The deer's body was so huge that it diminished the apparent size of the rack, and Dave thought the antlers looked "spindly." Fortunately, the hunter took a closer look and dropped the brute in his tracks with one well-placed shot. Photo courtesy of Dave Wilson.

them atop the wood stove. He then went over to the nearby farmhouse for breakfast. He had done this many times before with no problem, but today was different. A chunk of wood lying atop the smoldering coals in the stove caught-fire. When Dave got back minutes later, black smoke filled the cabin and his boots were ruined! So much for hunting. The rest of the hunter's day was spent cleaning the cabin's interior, as well as his gear, of the black gunk from the fire.

What a dreadful way to waste a precious day during the rut in one of North

Dave once again found himself growing frustrated at his inability to find the right hunting situation.

His luck finally improved in late November. With the rifle season coming to a close, Dave received a hunting invitation from Larry Prefontaine, an outfitter in the Chitek Lake area of northern Saskatchewan. Dave eagerly accepted the invitation and readied himself for the 120-mile drive to Larry's place. Before he departed, however, he decided to hunt where he was one last day—a day that, in retrospect, would turn out to be one of the worst of Dave's life.

It even started out badly. Due to the bitterly cold conditions he knew he would be facing that day, Dave decided to warm up his pac boots by setting

America's most famous trophy areas, but wait till you hear how the *night* went!

Late that afternoon, Dave threw his gear into his pickup and headed for Larry's camp. With a storm blowing in, the hunter took his time, hoping to avoid any problems. Unfortunately, Dave lost control of his vehicle on an unmarked curve. His truck slid off the road and rolled over onto its roof. In the grim moments that followed, as he hung upside down in his seat belt, unable to see anything in the darkness and thinking about the 35-degrees-below-zero temperature outside, the American was hardly having the sort of fun he had come to Canada to find.

In what seemed longer than it really took, Dave

dug himself out of the snow-buried truck and was on his feet again. Looking down the road, he noticed a light and began walking in that direction. It was a house and—miracle of miracles—the man living there was a mechanic! Returning to the scene with a tractor, they got the truck upright and began working on it, despite the frigid conditions. Before long, they had the engine running and the broken windows covered with cardboard. Dave was on his way again, keeping an even closer eye on the road.

By now, he knew there was no use trying to get to Larry's that night. So, he drove into the town of Meadow Lake and, at around 1 a.m., checked into a motel. That wasn't exactly a pleasant experience, either. The room was so cold that water in the sink was frozen. Dave had to wear half his hunting clothes to bed in order to get any sleep!

Things started looking up the next day, however, when he reached Larry's place. The outfitter said that he would be needing someone next summer to help him get ready for hunting season. The American, needing a place to hunt, struck a deal to provide that help.

Dave got in a few days of hunting in the Chitek Lake area during the waning 1991 season but didn't see anything big. He did, however, like the looks of the area. He went back to the States in early December with far more optimism than he would have thought possible while lying in that wrecked truck only a few days earlier.

Up to this point, Dave's primary focus had been on hunting during the rut, which falls squarely within the November rifle season. But, Saskatchewan had only recently implemented a lengthy blackpowder season, one that opened in September and ran for several weeks. Dave began to think about just how much this season could expand his hunting opportunities. He was going to be in the woods in early fall anyway scouting for rifle season. Why not hunt at the same time? If he could locate a trophy deer then, he might have a chance to shoot the buck before the rut sent him off

for parts unknown. So, before heading back north that next summer, the hunter invested in a new Gonic muzzleloader and 3x10-power Leupold scope, a rig capable of shooting groups tighter than six inches at 200 yards. If the right deer presented itself within that range, Dave knew he could get the job done.

The Chitek Lake area is truly on the edge of Canada's whitetail frontier. Few roads penetrate the "big bush" wilderness to the north. Deer densities are fairly low here, but crop fields in the area help concentrate feeding activity, making the animals much more huntable than they otherwise would be. As it turned out, the presence of agriculture was a major factor in Dave's amazing success that fall.

Wayne Tallmadge owned a ranch in the area that Larry had permission to hunt. On September 21, Larry and Dave hopped onto a pair of ATVs and began scouting the ranch's field edges in search of buck sign. It didn't take long to uncover what Dave was looking for – an alfalfa field corner and adjacent fenceline that contained a number of fresh rubs. Clumps of brush were snapped off a foot above the ground by a bullish buck's antlers, and big tracks and droppings littered the spot, leaving no doubt in Dave's mind that this was a regular pre-rut feeding spot for at least one good buck. The rubbing sign told him the deer had long tines. In fact, Dave was so certain of this that he "guaranteed" Larry that such a buck was using the spot. He even told the outfitter they didn't need to watch that field to find out if the deer was worth hunting.

They elected to glass other local fields that afternoon, hoping to spot something big in a location they hadn't had time to check for sign. However, before they did, Dave set up a Cam-Trakker, an infrared-triggered, all-weather camera, in hopes of getting a snapshot of the big buck using the alfalfa field.

A few days later on September 28, Dave and Larry showed up at Wayne's ranch again. Although the early muzzleloader season was open, their plan called for more scouting, not hunting. Dave headed north to glass some fields they hadn't scouted earlier. Larry sneaked down to the "hot" corner of the alfalfa field, hoping to catch a glimpse of whatever was leaving those impressive rubs and tracks. Based purely on sign, it was the best spot the duo had found so far.

Perhaps a dozen deer came into the alfalfa field before dark, but Larry's relatively poor set of binoculars prevented him from identifying several bucks back in the far corner. The following afternoon, he took advantage of a favorable wind to sneak down the fenceline for a better vantage point. Shortly before dark, a big, wide buck and several smaller ones sauntered into the opening only 75 yards from the outfitter. All Larry's stealth was needed for him to ease out without spooking any of them.

Infrared-triggered cameras are now widely used by hunters to pattern deer and identify individual bucks in their areas. When Dave tried one of these camera setups along the edge of the alfalfa field, he got the rarest of deer photos – a shot of a legitimate world-record buck strolling past in the darkness! Curiously, though, the hunter didn't know this photo existed until after he had already shot the animal. Photo courtesy of Dave Wilson.

With some very big bucks already to his credit, Dave hadn't gone to this much trouble just to shoot the first decent deer that came along. His goal was a buck that would stand out as "big," regardless of whether the antlers were big enough to make the B&C record book or not. Based on sign alone, Dave already had decided he was going to hunt the buck in the alfalfa field. Larry's sighting of the wide deer—which the outfitter said would score in the 160s—simply made the idea even more appealing. So, after lunch the next day, the men picked a spot about 180 yards up the fenceline from the hot corner and built a well-camouflaged ground blind. Although Dave couldn't quite see all the field corner from his blind, any buck that came out there would soon appear within range of his muzzleloader.

While setting up, Dave saw that the film counter on his nearby Cam-Trakker indicated that several photos had been snapped by the camera since it was set up six days earlier. He removed the roll of film and, upon returning to the farmhouse, gave it to Wayne's wife, Irene. She was about to head into town on her weekly grocery run and offered to drop off the film for processing.

It was a bluebird day with a warm wind out of the south, meaning conditions were good for hunting the stand that afternoon. Three hours before dark, Dave settled into his newly constructed ground blind to begin his vigil. He had confidence that bucks would show up in the alfalfa field that day, but when and which ones remained to be seen.

The first two hours passed without incident.

Then, a so-so buck walked into the alfalfa from the hidden corner. Before long, several more joined him for dinner. One of them was a huge typical matching Larry's description of the one he had seen there the day before. Dave, who knew he had plenty of time to hunt that year, was not quick to decide that this animal was for him. Feeding along, the buck had his head down for much of the time and was angling toward the blind, offering a less-than-perfect view of his rack. Dave could tell the antlers were wide and tall, but on the other hand, they appeared "kind of spindly." He could also see that there was no G-5 tine on the left side to match the long one on the right. But when he took a broader view and saw just how big the rack was in relation to the buck's 300-plus-pound body, he realized the antlers were bigger than he had originally estimated. A full 15 minutes after the buck had walked into the field, Dave realized he would be "nuts" to pass up such an animal. He moved into action.

Hoping for a broadside shot, he waited for the opportunity to present itself. However, as the minutes dragged on and shooting light began to fade, Dave saw the situation wasn't improving. All the bucks still were feeding without concern, but the biggest one never once turned broadside to the blind. Finally, the hunter decided to make the best of what he had. With the huge buck still feeding toward him, he put the crosshairs of his scope in the ample space between the deer's long back tines and centered the crosshairs on the base of the neck. When the sight picture felt right, Dave squeezed the trigger of his muzzleloader, sending the bullet on its way in a belch of acrid smoke.

At the speed of sound came confirmation of a hit. The solid *smack* removed any doubt his shot had found its mark. Even so, the hunter scrambled

Dave had done it in reverse… he shot the buck before realizing he had already captured the trophy on film.

to reload his firearm just in case he needed a follow-up shot. He didn't. When the smoke cleared, Dave saw the huge buck on the ground right where he had been feeding at the moment of the shot. Surprisingly, just one of the other deer in the field had bothered to stop munching on the sweet alfalfa! Only when Dave walked out into the field did they vacate the scene, leaving the hunter alone with his magnificent trophy in the fading light.

The closer Dave got to the buck, the bigger he looked. The hunter's mind was a swirling jumble of thoughts as he knelt beside the monster 11-pointer. Not even the tears welling up in Dave's eyes could keep him from seeing that the antlers were as big as any he had ever dreamed of putting a tag on. Offering a prayer of thanks, Dave knew he had been incredibly fortunate to take such an animal, particularly given the obstacles he had faced throughout his wild journey from the East Coast to this spot in the North Woods. But then, he thought back on all of those years of doing everything legally possible to give himself such an opportunity. True, this was the "easiest" mature buck he had ever taken, but the hundreds of miles of scouting and the close calls with frostbite he had endured over the years helped balance out the ledger.

Dave knew as soon as he walked up to the dead deer that he had finally achieved his goal of taking a B&C buck. What he didn't realize right away was that the rack might be world-record size. That thought came to mind only after the hunter's preliminary measurements showed a potential net score in the low 190s. Dave couldn't immediately recall the exact score of the then-No.1 blackpowder typical, but he thought it was in the 180s. He was right. At that time, the world record in the Longhunter Society rankings was Larry Lawson's

187 1/8-point Indiana trophy (Chapter 21), which had then been No.1 for four years. When Dave's buck received an official net score of 193 2/8, he became the hands-down world record, and remains so as of this writing.

Dave's buck could have easily scored even higher had he grown a G-5 tine on his left antler to match the 6 6/8-incher on the right. That would have raised his final score to 206 6/8 points! That would have made him the over-all world-record typical at the time.

It is doubt-ful that any other place in North Amer-ica can match Saskatchewan's staggering production of world-class deer during the past half-century, even though the Wilson and Hanson bucks are its only two official world-record bucks ever. What's ironic is that both of these giants share an unlikely antler feature for trophy deer from that province. Mention Saskatchewan to a whitetail hunter, and his first thought is likely to be of phenomenal antler mass. Yet, the Wilson and Hanson bucks both strike many observers as being relatively thin-antlered. Since the rules for scoring typicals by the B&C system are intended to reward tine length, beam length and symmetry more than sheer antler volume, the net score of these huge, balanced racks is not greatly penalized by their comparative lack of mass.

Dave's stepson, Ryan, holds the buck's left-side shed against the mounted rack for comparison. The antler was picked up after Dave had shot the deer. A G-5 tine can be seen on the shed, but the huge typical didn't grown one on that side the next year to match the long G-5 on his right side. Photo by Dave Wilson.

Numerous Saskatchewan whitetails have had enough antler on their heads to be world-record typicals, but in almost every case, they "wasted" too much of that bone in thick tines (a non-factor in B&C scoring) and abnormal points (a liability in B&C typical scoring). Of course, heavy tines and interesting non-typical points are among the favorite antler traits of most serious trophy hunters. So, the "problem" with such deer lies in our means of measuring them, not with the deer themselves.

You might figure that the story of Dave's hunt ended when he squeezed the trigger that late-September afternoon, but that was hardly the case. In fact, a couple of the interesting twists regarding this super buck were yet to materialize. For starters, when it came time to take photos of the dead deer on the day of the kill, Dave realized his regular 35mm camera was back at Larry's camp. So, Larry, who had joined Dave soon after the shot, went up to Wayne and Irene's to see if they had a camera handy. They didn't, but what they *did* have was the developed prints from Dave's Cam-Trakker. Amazingly, one of those photos showed Dave's huge deer strutting past the monitor site a few evenings earlier!

Infrared monitors, of course, are widely used for "observing" whitetails, both by laymen and deer researchers. It's fairly common for a hunter to get a shot of a buck walking around his area and then use that information to help him figure out the deer's habits. But, Dave had done it in reverse—he shot the buck *before* realizing he had already captured the trophy on film. Strange indeed.

And, that wasn't all. The Chitek Lake area had a two-buck season limit, so Dave continued to hunt in the area. A few weeks after shooting his great whitetail, he was scouting the nearby woods when he stumbled upon a shed. It was the left antler of the same buck he had just claimed, dropped the previous spring! As with infrared photos, sheds are often used for finding and identifying bucks—but again, it usually happens *before* a given deer is killed, not afterwards! Doubling the shed's score and giving the deer a 20-inch inside spread yielded a score of 167. He had really grown in the course of a single year!

Dave ended up his historic year by taking another trophy, a heavy-beamed buck grossing 164 typical, right at the end of the regular rifle season. And get this—earlier, he had passed up three bucks that were bigger!

At this writing, the hunter's dream of becoming a Saskatchewan resident, thus being able to hunt anywhere in the province without an outfitter, has been put on hold. Finding good work remains the problem. But, that's done nothing to douse his desire to hunt there, and every fall, you're likely to find him in his favorite stomping grounds in the northwestern part of the province, where he is now accepted as "one of the guys."

He still hunts with his blackpowder rifle, though he no longer holds out much hope for world-class success during that special September season. "It took me several years to realize how unique '92 was," he told me. "Years of hunting in Saskatchewan since then have shown me that the bucks don't generally get into such a heavy, predictable feeding pattern in the fields as early as they did that year. In '92, the area had some freakish weather, actually getting

snow in August. The cold had killed most of the weeds and other forage back in the forest, pushing the deer onto the agriculture far earlier than normal. A lot of things came together to make that an unusual year."

Looking back on Dave's pilgrimage to a world-record whitetail, we can see this devoted hunter invested far more of himself than most others would, could or perhaps even should. He risked virtually everything on a roll of the dice but came up a winner. It's easy now to say all his sacrifice was worthwhile. After all, he put the buck of several million lifetimes on his wall. But, how many of us would have committed ourselves so fully to the quest without the guarantee of that happy ending?

DAVE WILSON, SASKATCHEWAN, 1992

Measurements	Right	Left	Difference
No. of points	7	5	
Main beam	29 4/8	29 1/8	3/8
1st point (G-1)	5 7/8	5 2/8	5/8
2nd point (G-2)	12 5/8	11 4/8	1 1/8
3rd point (G-3)	12 1/8	11 7/8	2/8
4th point (G-4)	10 2/8	9 2/8	1 0/8
5th point (G-5)	6 6/8	–	6 6/8
1st circ. (H-1)	5 2/8	5 2/8	–
2nd circ. (H-2)	4 2/8	4 1/8	1/8
3rd circ. (H-3)	4 7/8	4 4/8	3/8
4th circ. (H-4)	4 5/8	4 1/8	4/8
Total	96 1/8	85 0/8	11 1/8
Greatest spread		27 5/8	
Inside spread		24 6/8	
Gross typical score		205 7/8	
Assymetry deductions		-11 1/8	
Non-typical deductions		-1 4/8	
Net typical score		193 2/8	

23

SHEDDING LIGHT ON A TROPHY

When a buck's antler reaches out and grabs your boot, it's telling you one thing: "Hunt right here!"

TITLE: FIRST BLACKPOWDER
NON-TYPICAL WORLD RECORD
SCORE: 185 3/8
HUNTER: TERRY BURNS
LOCATION: HAWKINS COUNTY,
TENNESSEE
YEAR: 1983

Mother Nature was into "recycling" long before man coined the term. From the very beginning, raindrops have spilled from the sky, made their way to the oceans and then evaporated back into clouds, starting the process anew. Since prehistoric times, plants have been poking up through the soil, converting sunlight into fruit and then withering away, making room for the next generation to have its turn. And each winter for millennia, the antlers of whitetail bucks have fallen to the ground, slowly returning minerals to the earth from which they came. Ashes to ashes, dust to dust…

The person who finds one of these shed antlers before it can complete its transformation back into topsoil should consider himself lucky. Dropped antlers aren't everywhere, even in good deer country, nor are they easy to spot on the forest floor. Any shed is a trophy to the person who retrieves it from the woods, and a big one deserves a special place in a sportsman's collection of natural treasures.

All too often, holding a huge shed is as close to the buck that dropped it as you ever get, for seldom does the hunter who finds an antler end up putting his tag onto the animal. In fact, there is only one known case in which someone who picked up the antler of a world-record whitetail then went on to harvest that buck. The hunter who pulled it off was Terry Burns, and the circumstances were unlikely indeed.

In mid-December 1983, Terry was not looking for loose antlers, but rather for a pair of them still attached to the forehead of a living buck. The 27-year-old blackpowder hunter was creeping around in a nasty tangle of honeysuckle and briars near the Holston River in his native Hawkins County, Tennessee when something grabbed his boot. When Terry looked down, he was amazed to see that his "attacker" was a hefty shed! From the looks of it, the antler had been there since the previous spring, long enough for the local squirrels, mice and other varmints to have gnawed away a good bit of the bone. Regardless, the general size and shape of the original antler were still evident and signified that a trophy whitetail had once walked this way.

Terry had known for a long time that big bucks inhabited these rugged hills and bottoms.

Occasionally, he had heard of someone bagging a trophy buck. He had even taken a hefty 10-pointer two seasons earlier. But, the gnarly shed he now held in his hand provided proof that something even bigger was haunting his favorite hunting area along the river.

Once a big shed has been found, a savvy hunter will try to determine whether the buck in question is a "regular" in that vicinity or was merely passing through when the antler popped off. Distinguishing between these two scenarios isn't always easy, but coming up with the right answer is critical. If the hunter mistakenly believes the deer is a year-round resident of that vicinity, an entire autumn can be wasted trying to kill a deer that may be several miles away during the hunting season. In some areas, deer relocate during the winter to find food, and thus drop their racks far from their fall range. In any habitat, a buck could shed one or both antlers while being chased by predators or while merely on a long winter "walkabout."

In Terry's case, the area in which the big shed was found possesses several characteristics of classic

Terry's 185 3/8-point Tennessee trophy, the Longhunter Society's first world-record non-typical, has magnum drop tines of 10 2/8 and 11 3/8 inches and an impressive inside spread of 24 inches. Overall, the Volunteer State isn't known for huge deer, but the Holston River valley that produced this one has turned out several whoppers over the years. Photo by Bill Cooper.

trophy country. First, that portion of southwestern Hawkins County consists mostly of private land with restricted hunting access, allowing deer a decent chance to reach maturity. Also, the riverbottom has relatively fertile soil and enough flat acreage for the planting of scattered crop fields, providing whitetails with good nutrition and hunters with a real advantage in locating concentrations of deer. Even so, fields in the area are hardly guaranteed to produce action. Acorns, beechnuts and honeysuckle in the woods give deer a rich and varied menu from which to choose.

Terry was familiar with the stretch of riverbottom in which he had found the antler, and he knew it was capable of holding big bucks. Strangely, though, as he investigated the spot for fresh sign, he saw little evidence of routine buck use. The hunter noticed only two rubs, hardly enough to inspire confidence. Then, Terry ran into an older hunter in the area and asked if anyone had seen a big buck. The man said that a big one had been seen on several occasions, each time in or near a soybean field in the riverbottom. That field was across the road from where Terry had picked up the antler.

"Why should I hunt him out around that field if he's coming from back across the road?" Terry asked himself. When he couldn't come up with a good

answer, he decided to hunt around the thicket where he had found the shed – or where, to put it more accurately, the shed had found him!

The next day, Terry slipped into the area to watch a heavy trail beneath a thick ridge. Nothing showed. Thinking perhaps he had simply picked the wrong day, he went there again the next morning. The results were the same. Chilly temperatures and strong winds made the lack of action seem even worse. Seeing no reason to invest more time or shivering in an unproductive setup, the hunter went home to think about his next move.

Although rodents had gnawed away much of the shed, there was little doubt it belonged to Terry's trophy. Against all odds, the deer was shot within yards of where the hunter had found the antler just two days earlier! Photo by Leigh Ann Smith.

The big shed and the other hunters' sightings had confirmed that a big buck was indeed using the area, but with all of the activity surrounding muzzleloader season, had the deer vacated the spot? Had he simply become more nocturnal and stopped moving in daylight? As is usually the case when hunting a cagey buck, the truth was less than clear.

Cold, windy conditions kept Terry home that afternoon and the next morning. As he sat there, running his hands over that shed, he thought about how much he would like to see the deer that had left this unique calling card for him to find. And all the while, hunting conditions were growing more favorable. By midday, the winds had subsided and the dry air held promise of a pleasant afternoon in the woods. Terry decided to give the deer another try.

Only a few days earlier near the thicket in which the shed lay, he had found a good deer trail con-necting a riverbottom cornfield to an oak and hickory grove. That seemed as good a spot as any for an afternoon vigil. So, Terry eased into position to watch the trail, hoping against hope that a big buck would walk past him before day's end.

As light faded in the riverbottom, the hunter scanned the terrain for any sign of a whitetail. Peering into the darkening timber of a nearby hollow, he saw movement. Unfortunately, a honeysuckle-covered knoll blocked Terry's view of the spot. From where he sat, he could not identify the source of the movement. He needed to change position. Keeping the knoll between himself and the spot he had seen something move, Terry eased along the edge of the field, his eyes searching. The hunter had gone some distance when a small doe spooked from the honeysuckle and headed toward the nearby woods—with a huge buck in tow!

Terry shouldered his rifle and drew down on the buck, which was well within range. Unfortunately, in his excitement, he forgot to remove the glove from his shooting hand, making what was already a tricky shot even tougher. Jamming his gloved index finger into the trigger guard, the anxious hunter jerked, sending the round ball on its way. Through the smoke, Terry could see no indication of a hit as both deer continued to run for the safety of the woods. Then, miraculously, the doe wheeled to a stop and turned to look back. The buck, still very much alive and enamored with his lady friend, did the same.

A muzzleloader is by no means the world's

quickest or easiest weapon to load. It takes a certain amount of manual dexterity to pour the right amount of powder, ram a patch and ball down the barrel and then seat a percussion cap. When your hands are cold, it's even more difficult. So, imagine trying to accomplish these chores while a monster buck is standing within shooting range, watching your every move and ready to bolt any moment! The pressure must have been virtually unbearable as Terry scrambled to get his muzzleloader back into shooting order, one eye on the gun and the other on the trophy of a lifetime.

With his rifle finally ready for a second shot, Terry pushed it to his shoulder and zeroed in on the rut-crazed buck, which was still peering out at him from behind a nearby tree. Once again, the powder ignited and a ball went whizzing out of the barrel. When the smoke cleared this time, the scene was far more pleasant from the hunter's perspective. The massive buck was down and out!

As Terry walked up to the 14-pointer in the glow of that December dusk, he knew his most ambitious hunting dreams had come true. Unlike the shed, this monster featured a big drop tine on both beams. Still, the general shape of the chewed-up antler was quite similar to that of the actual rack. The kill, Terry now realized, had occurred within 100 yards of where he had found the shed antler only a few days earlier! There was little doubt in the happy hunter's mind that this deer had dropped that antler in the thicket months earlier.

The rack's record-book size was confirmed when official Longhunter Society measurer Bill Cooper later stretched his tape over the giant. Even though the typical points weren't exceptionally long and the deer didn't have that many scorable points for a non-typical, the rack had everything else needed to achieve an impressive score. The 24-inch inside spread and those huge, broomed-off drop tines combined with good mass and long main beams to push the score to 185 3/8 net points, easily enough to make him North America's best blackpowder

non-typical whitetail at that time.

You would assume that in East Tennessee, an area not famous for huge deer, Terry would never see another buck that could match this one. But he did, only one year later. "I saw an awesome buck in 1984, but didn't get him," he recalled. "A guy named Luther Fuller shot him later in the season. That deer ended up being the state-record non-typical, and he still is."

Luther's 223 4/8-point monster reinforced the notion that Hawkins County has major-league trophy potential. Knowing the area can produce huge deer has helped Terry become a patient hunter, and he has been rewarded with several more fine bucks in the years since. While none of them has approached the size or significance of his muzzleloader record, he still lives by the trophy hunter's mantra: Tomorrow's another day and that next buck just might be the biggest one of all!

TERRY BURNS, TENNESSEE, 1983

Measurements	Right	Left	Difference
No. of points	8	6	
Main beam	25 2/8	28 6/8	3 4/8
1st point (G-1)	6 4/8	6 1/8	3/8
2nd point (G-2)	8 2/8	7 5/8	5/8
3rd point (G-3)	7 0/8	7 0/8	–
4th point (G-4)	–	–	–
5th point (G-5)	–	–	–
1st circ. (H-1)	5 0/8	5 1/8	1/8
2nd circ. (H-2)	4 3/8	4 2/8	1/8
3rd circ. (H-3)	4 0/8	4 0/8	–
4th circ. (H-4)	3 5/8	3 5/8	–
Total	64 0/8	66 4/8	4 6/8
Greatest spread		26 4/8	
Inside spread		24 0/8	
Gross typical score		154 4/8	
Assymetry deductions		-4 6/8	
Non-typical additions		+35 5/8	
Net non-typical score		185 3/8	

24

IT AIN'T OVER TILL IT'S OVER!

Bob Bromm isn't your average deer hunter, and his reward for seven hard months of scouting and hunting was certainly no average deer.

TITLE: SECOND BLACKPOWDER NON-TYPICAL WORLD RECORD
SCORE: 226 3/8
HUNTER: ROBERT "BOB" BROMM, SR.
LOCATION: CLARK COUNTY, INDIANA
YEAR: 1985

In theory, patterning a trophy buck is simple. You see the deer and/or his sign, then use your experience to figure out where he's most likely to be at a given point in the future. But, just because the theory is simple doesn't mean that *doing* it is easy!

While many hunters boast of being able to pattern deer, surprisingly few of the trophy bucks on den walls today were bagged as a result of true patterning. Anytime a hunter finds big-buck sign and later shoots a trophy in that area, he or she is likely to claim that the deer had been "patterned." But in truth, the buck taken might not even have been the one that made the inspiring sign.

This certainly isn't to suggest big whitetails can't be patterned. On occasion, someone can figure out a buck's tendencies so completely that the hunter can predict the animal's movements and use that information to shoot him. When such a buck ends up with that hunter's tag on him, he's a fine trophy regardless of his size. And, should that well-patterned buck turn out to be a world record…well, it's truly among the greatest of all hunting accomplishments.

A deer matching that exact description was shot in southern Indiana in 1985, and Robert "Bob" Bromm, Sr. was the guy who made it happen. What's more, he accomplished it not during the peaceful days of early fall or during the frantic rut, but rather in the difficult days of late season, a time when few monster whitetails are bagged. Bob's hunt offers us a fascinating glimpse into the tactics—and the persistence—of a hunter who truly got what he deserved.

The hardwood hills and field-dotted valleys of southern Indiana have long been home to fine trophy hunting. Many of the Hoosier State's top bucks have been shot on the rough terrain that slopes toward the huge Ohio River. Granted, the region is heavily hunted, but since centerfire rifles are taboo during the short gun season, bucks have a better chance of maturing than would otherwise be the case. The tremendous buck that Bob patterned and finally killed was one of those oldtimers that had slipped through the cracks long enough to grow a world-class rack.

There are many levels of intensity when it comes

Bob Bromm's 226 3/8-point non-typical whitetail was taken during Indiana's 1985 muzzleloader season and surpassed Terry Burns' Tennessee trophy to become the Longhunter Society's new No. 1 non-typical. Photo courtesy of Bob Bromm, Sr.

to hunting trophy deer, from mild to maniacal. Bob's style leaned to the latter end of the range. Before his record buck even was born, the hunter had spent years sharpening his physical and mental skills for just such a challenge, taking a number of good bucks along the way. In fact, during the 1976 and 1977 seasons, he spent month after month trying to kill a specific buck. Success finally came late in 1977, and the fine buck scored 148 6/8.

Along with sons Bobby, Jr. and David, this avid sportsman seldom missed a chance to be in the woods of Clark County. Whether hunting or scouting, they always had their eyes open for sign of a trophy buck. As it turned out, though, the first "sign" of this particular buck was picked up not by their eyes, but by their ears. Specifically, while hunting turkeys in the spring of 1985, Bob was told by the landowner that a mighty big buck was running around on his property. The landowner, who was strictly a bird hunter, invited Bob to hunt the beast, which he claimed was bigger than anything Bob had ever seen.

How could Bob and his sons *not* go after a buck

described in such a way? Well, it wasn't as easy a decision as it might seem. None of the Bromms had ever hunted that particular tract for whitetails. Their favorite deer land some miles away had produced a number of deer for them over the previous few years, and all three guys knew that property well. Ultimately, however, the decision was made to hunt the new property in hopes of taking this huge deer. So, Bob and his sons leapt over the first hurdle standing between every hunter and the chance at a monster— they went to where a monster actually lived.

The Bromm buck's most notable feature is his huge typical frame. As a basic 5x5, the deer's gross typical score is 203 5/8 and the net is 199 1/8. His 27 2/8 total inches of abnormal points are very low for a world-record non-typical. A 22 7/8-inch inside spread adds to his wall appeal. Photo by Dave Foote.

Scouting began that spring with far less information to go on than the hunters would have liked. Yes, the landowner had seen the buck several times the previous year, but turning those sightings into a viable hunting plan for the 1985 season would be difficult without a better handle on the deer's seasonal movements on and around the property. The landowner hadn't been able to provide much of a description of the buck, other than to say he was huge, so with only that nebulous image in mind, the patterning process began in earnest.

Bob started spending as much of his spare time as possible looking for both the deer and his sign, though he still wasn't sure he would know either if he found it. While he did locate some impressive tracks, as a veteran hunter he knew that big tracks didn't necessarily indicate a trophy buck.

Late that summer, the guys began to see an impressive 8-pointer they figured would score around 150 B&C points. Even though he wasn't outrageously big for the area, the obvious question still came up: "Is that him?" Finally, Bob got a chance to go straight to where they had just seen the big 4x4 standing. Upon close examination of his fresh tracks, Bob found they clearly were smaller than the "big" ones scattered around, which led Bob to believe there really was a yet-unseen giant living somewhere on the property. But until one of the hunters saw this mystery buck with his own eyes and confirmed he really was a world-class trophy, hunting this property exclusively was going to be like wagering everything on a hand of face-down cards. Such is trophy hunting.

As summer gave way to fall, more sign finally began to appear. Some four-inch cedars showed evidence of rubbing, and those very big tracks were scattered around the bases of the rub trees, telling Bob that the signposts weren't the work of the 8-pointer they had spotted that summer. But, there was still no glimpse of the huge-footed buck. It became apparent that even outside of hunting season this buck was moving only at night.

Today, a hunter in such a situation might purchase an infrared-triggered camera and set it up to snap a photo of the buck, regardless of what time of day or night he might walk past. That would tell the hunter not only the size of the animal, but also the hour at which he came through the area. However, no such option existed in 1985 because infrared monitors then were still in the development stage. No, Bob and his boys would have to figure things out the old-fashioned way, with their own eyes and minds.

By late September, with bow season just days away, the notion of giving up on this invisible buck and returning to the Bromms' familiar stomping grounds was starting to sound better all the time, even though a known 150-class 8-pointer was on this new property. Fortunately for Bob, he decided not to leave before checking with the landowner one more time. When he did, he got good news. The man had recently seen the monster again, in daylight. In that moment, Bob decided that, for better or for worse, the Bromms would continue their quest for this dream trophy.

Little happened in October to convince the guys that they had made the right choice. Bow season stretched into week upon week of frustrations. That big 8-pointer was still around—in fact, the guys passed up more than one good shot at him—but the big-footed mystery buck refused to show himself. The Bromms knew he hadn't vacated the area because those cedars were still being worked over and the huge tracks were still showing up. But, that wasn't much consolation to the hunters if the buck

only moved under cover of darkness.

What's more, as the end of the early bow season arrived, other hunters in the area began to report having spotted the monster a mile or more away in every direction. It was almost as if Bob and his sons, the three hunters who had devoted the most time and effort to this buck, were the only ones around who *hadn't* seen him. With the 16-day November firearms season set to open and run through the heart of the rut, the old deer would be increasingly vulnerable to the hunters on surrounding property. And to make matters worse, Bob's wife had made plans for them to be out of town on vacation for the first 10 days of gun season. Seemingly, everything was conspiring against the veteran hunter and his dream of shooting a world-class whitetail.

…the notion of giving up on this invisible buck and returning to the Bromms' familiar stomping grounds was starting to sound better.

A vacation normally seems to pass in a flash, but for Bob, this one dragged on and on. The rut was underway, offering him his best chance to take the big deer, but he couldn't hunt! In Bob's absence, David and Bobby, Jr. had decided to return to their old hunting area for gun season. The deer of his dreams now figured to end up with a stranger's tag on its rack.

When Bob returned home from vacation, he immediately began to check around to find out if anyone had taken the big buck. To his unexpected delight, no one had! Bobby, Jr. had shot a nice deer over on the old property, though. In hopes of making something positive out of what had thus far been a failed season, Bob decided that he, too, would give in to the temptation of hunting there. That effort went just as his earlier ones had, and nothing was shot during the remainder of regular firearms season.

Doubt is one of the more insidious "diseases" that can afflict a trophy whitetail hunter, and its effects are relentless. If you confirm the presence of a big deer but then don't get him or even see him, the natural tendency is to start questioning everything about your approach, from your choice of stand sites to your hunting skills. As a result, you soon come to a critical crossroads: Should you simply be patient, keeping the faith in your original game plan, or scrap it for a new one? As shotgun season wound down, a frustrated Bob Bromm found himself standing at that crossroads, wondering which way to go.

The dream of every trophy whitetail hunter. This is the stunning view Bob had as he walked up to his world-record blackpowder buck. Even though the buck appeared very early in the morning, the light-colored rack still stood out. Photo courtesy of Bob Bromm.

A welcome one-week break between the end of November's firearms season and the start of December's short muzzleloader season gave Bob time to rethink his approach. Nobody had showed up with a gigantic buck, so it seemed safe to assume the deer was in hiding now that the rut was over. Perhaps patience alone would be enough to get this deer…along with more information. Bob decided

to do some more scouting to see if the deer was holding to his old pattern.

On the way out to the farm, he stopped to check with the owner of a tract bordering the one on which the Bromms had been pursuing the monster whitetail. The man was indeed familiar with the buck, and he presumed the animal was still alive. When the farmer held his hands far apart to indicate the spread of this buck's rack, Bob knew he had to give the area another try. He decided to play a hunch.

Bob had wondered if he and his sons might have been alerting the old buck to their presence by coming into the area from the wrong direction. So, he asked for and received permission to cross this farmer's property in order to access the farm he had hunted earlier in the year. This new approach would require him to walk three-quarters of a mile and then cross a small, foot-deep creek to reach a thick weed patch he felt the old buck might be holding up in as he recuperated from a long, hard rut.

You might assume that, after having devoted so much time and energy to this big deer, Bob would have put his new plan into action on opening morning of the December blackpowder season. Instead, he was back in his old, familiar hunting spot. However, when he saw nothing of note and the hours wore on, he naturally began to wonder if he had erred in not trying his new strategy to get the mystery buck.

When the alarm forced Bob awake at 4:30 a.m. on December 8, the second day of muzzleloader season, the hunter had yet another choice to make. Wearied by this grueling season, he realized that the prospects of walking the better part of a mile in the darkness, especially while carrying a portable tree stand that would grow heavier with every step, had kept him from executing his sneaky strategy for the big buck during the opener. Now, it was decision time. Should he take the easy way out by hunting familiar ground again or lay it all on the line by investing even more effort on a buck he still had not seen?

Sightings by other landowners were all that kept Bob on the trail. Until right before the fateful shot was fired, he had never even laid eyes on his quarry! Photo courtesy of Bob Bromm.

"You're lazy, Bob," he realized. "You know that deer is out there. Now go get him."

Bob's portable stand was lying near the back door, and he kept looking at it as he pondered his next move. Finally, his thoughts crystallized. *You're lazy, Bob,* he realized. *You know that deer is out there. Now go get him. You can do it.* And so, out the door he went, heading for his newly arranged parking spot on the neighbor's property. But as a concession to his tired body, he left his tree stand behind.

Fortunately, the spot Bob planned to hunt offered a good alternative to hunting from a tree. The buck's suspected bedding spot was just within muzzleloader range of a vine-draped blowdown that would serve as a great ground blind. In the darkness, the hunter made the long walk in, crossed the small creek and slipped into his hillside hideout with minimal disturbance. If the buck really was using that nearby weed patch as a bedding spot, perhaps he wouldn't return to it before legal shooting time.

After you've suffered one frustration after another and have just trudged three-quarters of a mile to a new stand in the darkness, the last thing you want to deal with is another hunter walking in on you just after daybreak. So, when Bob heard crunching steps in the dead leaves, his heart sank. But, as his eyes zeroed in on the movement, a wave of adrenaline drowned out that disappointment – the intruder wasn't a person, but a buck! The deer was no more than 50 yards from Bob and heading for the weed patch, walking steadily along the backside of a small ridgeline. Although little more than the rack was clearly visible from where the hunter sat, it was the biggest whitetail rack Bob had ever seen, just as the landowner had promised him seven months before! This had to be the mystery buck. All thoughts of how much time and effort had been "wasted" on this deer suddenly vanished, never to return.

That surge of excitement hunters feel when they see a monster buck is a big part of the allure of trophy hunting. Yet, it also can be a curse when trying to shoot a great deer. There's no room for anything but clear thinking and a steady shooting hand when the critical moment finally arrives. Balancing the thrill of a big-buck sighting with the necessity of making all the right moves in the next few moments is what separates happy memories from sob stories. Bob, a veteran hunter, knew it.

This buck wasn't dawdling. His pace was a steady walk, as though he realized he was a few minutes behind schedule in reaching the security of his daytime lair. Bob anxiously scanned the thick brush, looking for an opening along the deer's route. He found one some 25 yards ahead of the steadily moving animal. When the big buck stepped into that hole in the cover, nothing would be between the hunter and his dream but 45 yards of thin air. Bob cocked his .54-caliber smokepole,

pointed it toward the opening and tried to get his heart back down out of his throat.

The gun had been sighted-in to hit dead-on at 100 yards, meaning it would be a few inches high at 45 yards. Fortunately, Bob had the presence of mind to compensate for that. When the deer stepped into the opening, the sights settled low on the shoulder. *Ker-pow!*

A huge plume of gray smoke instantly obscured Bob's view of the target, but there was no need to worry. The bullet had smacked into the spine, putting the animal down for good. After reloading, Bob hurriedly made his way across the small valley to get an "up close and personal" view of the deer that was no longer a mere rumor. Moments later, as the hunter knelt to admire his prize, he knew he had taken a world-class whitetail. In fact, he had just shot the highest-scoring blackpowder buck on record!

When officially measured, the wide-racked brute would yield the astonishing score of 226 3/8 non-typical points, wiping out the 185 3/8-point record established by Terry Burns' drop-tined Tennessee buck (Chapter 23) two seasons prior. Amazingly, Bob's trophy had shattered the mark despite having only 27 2/8 total inches of abnormal points. That's a

Few other record-holders have devoted the time and effort to one deer that Bob did in the months leading up to his historic kill. Who wouldn't be smiling after downing a buck of this class? It topped its predecessor by 41 points! Photo courtesy of Bob Bromm.

testament to a high, wide and heavy rack that, had it sprouted no non-typical points at all, easily would have become the No.1 blackpowder *typical* at 199 1/8!

The better part of a year of anticipation, frustration and exhaustion finally had ended with Bob Bromm taking one of the most impressive deer ever to come out of the Ohio River Valley. It happened according to a plan and without the hunter resorting to forced movement. Although Bob needed more time than he had hoped to bag the buck—or even to see him, for that matter—he had continued to try new ideas until something good finally happened. In his victory, this veteran sportsman proved a critical point about hunting trophy whitetails: To take full advantage of a buck's pattern, sometimes you have to change your own.

ROBERT BROMM, SR., INDIANA, 1985

Measurements	Right	Left	Difference
No. of points	8	10	
Main beam	27 2/8	26 2/8	1 0/8
1st point (G-1)	9 4/8	9 4/8	–
2nd point (G-2)	12 7/8	11 2/8	1 5/8
3rd point (G-3)	13 0/8	11 6/8	1 2/8
4th point (G-4)	9 2/8	9 3/8	1/8
5th point (G-5)	–	–	–
1st circ. (H-1)	n/a	n/a	n/a
2nd circ. (H-2)	n/a	n/a	n/a
3rd circ. (H-3)	n/a	n/a	n/a
4th circ. (H-4)	n/a	n/a	n/a
Total	92 3/8	88 3/8	4 4/8
Greatest spread		25 1/8	
Inside spread		22 7/8	
Gross typical score		203 5/8	
Assymetry deductions		-4 4/8	
Non-typical additions		+27 2/8	
Net non-typical score		226 3/8	

25

DODGING THE BULLET

Wayne Lindemans and his world-record buck were made for each other. What else could possibly explain their story?

TITLE: THIRD BLACKPOWDER NON-TYPICAL WORLD RECORD

SCORE: 232 0/8

HUNTER: WAYNE LINDEMANS

LOCATION: BARRON COUNTY, WISCONSIN

YEAR: 1988

Wisconsin is one of those magical places in the whitetail world. It is a state where deer hunting isn't just tolerated, but celebrated. From big cities to tiny crossroads, from opening day in late summer to season's end in early winter, hundreds of thousands of men, women and kids are consumed with the traditions of this age-old pursuit. Big bucks are held in such esteem that the National Basketball Association team in Milwaukee even features one as its mascot.

With such a huge throng of avid hunters probing Wisconsin's woods, swamps and fields every year, you might think that only the most hardcore among them would have a decent chance of taking a world-class buck. But when you're talking about the "biggest of the big" in the deer world, odds and logic often count for nothing. Consider the case of Wayne Lindemans, whose 1988 Wisconsin hunting season proved the power of providence.

Most world-record bucks go to great lengths to avoid being shot by hunters. If they didn't, they would never get to be so big in the first place. But occasionally, you'll find a giant that seems to have a death wish, as though he knows just how nice his mounted head would look on somebody's wall and wants to do whatever he can to help a hunter put it there. Nearly every whitetail hunter dreams of having one of these suicidal brutes come his way. For Wayne, it wasn't just a dream. You see, in the two-year span ending in November 1988, he bumped into just such a deer four times—all during open season!

The first time Wayne encountered this buck was during the November firearms season in 1986, just outside the town of Rice Lake in northwestern Wisconsin's Barron County. Centerfire rifles are the preferred weapon during northern Wisconsin's gun season, but Wayne wasn't carrying one that day. Instead, he was armed with a new muzzleloader.

When the buck appeared within range that day, Wayne cocked his open-sighted smokepole, took aim, squeezed the trigger…and nothing happened! At first, he couldn't figure out why the rifle had failed to fire, but eventually, the answer came to

At 208 4/8 gross and 203 7/8 net, the Wayne Lindemans buck, taken during Wisconsin's regular gun season in 1988, has the highest-scoring typical frame of any muzzleloader buck, typical or non-typical. Here, Don Schaufler of Rocky Mountain Antler Museum shows off the tremendous main beams and tines that pushed the 232-point non-typical to the top of the Longhunter Society record book. The buck has over 21 net inches of mass per side. Photo by Dick Idol.

light. The weather had been cold that day, and the hunter had gone back to his truck a number of times in an effort to keep warm. Because Wayne was new to black-powder hunting, he didn't know he should be leaving the weapon outside the heated truck cab. After several of these warm-up sessions, so much condensation had formed within the gun barrel that the powder wouldn't ignite.

At the time, Wayne no doubt was upset that an avoidable mistake had kept him from taking a trophy buck. But, he would later realize that his luck on that frigid day actually had been good, not bad. For had his powder charge gone off, he would not have made history two years later when the same buck —then considerably bigger—crossed his path again!

The "good" bad luck he had experienced in 1986

carried over to the following season, too. That year while bowhunting in the same area, Wayne got another crack at the buck but once again failed to connect. This time, the hunter's arrow sailed harmlessly over the deer's back. While Wayne didn't see the deer again in 1987, neither did he hear of anyone else harvesting a buck of that class. There weren't many hunters in those particular woods, so Wayne realized the buck must have survived the season.

By November 1988, Wayne was ready for his hunting luck to start getting better. This time, he and his wife, June, would be hunting together. Thoughts of the buck must have passed through their minds as they prepared for the season, but according to Wayne, getting that buck really wasn't a big deal. A freezer full of tasty venison was what the Lindemans needed more than a wall mount.

When Wayne entered the giant whitetail into the famed Staples Lake buck contest, local hunters were stunned to learn such a deer had been taken in the area. They were even more amazed to hear that Wayne and his wife had missed the monster one morning, only to have him walk down that same trail again the next day, something unheard of for a mature whitetail! Photo courtesy of James Kittleson.

Before dawn on Saturday, November 19, he and his wife were in that same woods off Tom Barr Road, anxiously awaiting legal shooting light. Once daylight came, they didn't have to sit around for long. At 7:15, that same buck—now a full-blown monster—walked down the trail June and Wayne were watching!

The story might have ended right there, without a world record being broken, because June was hunting with a centerfire rifle and got off the first shot. It missed. Now, it was Wayne's turn to make up for his two previous failures. He aimed his muzzleloader, pulled the trigger…and missed. This whitetail truly seemed to be leading a charmed life!

Later that day, Wayne tried to figure out how he had botched yet another golden opportunity to fill his tag. That's when he realized the lead ball he had loaded up that morning had been the wrong weight. He had sighted-in his muzzleloader with a much heavier ball, and switching ammo apparently had cost him dearly.

Early Sunday morning, Wayne headed back to hunt the same trail the big deer had traveled the day before. It seemed beyond reason to hope that this bold buck would show up yet again, but with the lack of hunting pressure, maybe the deer felt safe enough to show himself in daylight one more time. Before dawn, Wayne settled into his hideout overlooking the trail.

Nothing showed for a while. But at 7:45, the hunter's eye caught movement. Wayne could hardly believe what was happening: That same huge buck was walking down that same trail once again! "He just kept coming toward me," Wayne later told the *Rice Lake Chronotype,* the hometown newspaper. "I was on the ground, but he didn't smell me. He just didn't know I was there."

As the unconcerned buck stood a mere 25 yards from the hunter, Wayne steadied his rifle and touched the trigger. This time, his powder was dry and his aim true. The musket ball hit the deer squarely in the brisket, knocking him back on his haunches. A few seconds later, the giant was dead.

The benchmark by which trophy whitetails are measured in this part of Wisconsin is the Staples Lake big-buck contest. If your buck can win this annual competition, he is a tremendous deer. Well, Wayne's 19-pointer not only won the contest but left other local hunters astonished. Even by the lofty standards of this well-known trophy area, the rack was huge.

Few other bucks in the record books have longer main beams than this one (30 7/8 and 30 1/8 inches), and no other whitetail ever taken by blackpowder has a bigger typical frame (208 4/8 gross; 203 7/8 net). At 232 non-typical points, Wayne's great deer became the world's top muzzleloader buck, edging out Bob Bromm's 226 3/8-point Indiana trophy from 1986 (Chapter 24).

This new record was set by a hunter who, despite his perennial encounters with this buck, claimed he wasn't picky about which deer he shot. "If it would've been a doe, I would have shot it," Wayne noted. "I had a Hunter's Choice (either-sex) permit. I would have been happy just to get any deer."

We'll never know what this mighty buck was thinking (or even *if* he was thinking) when he decided to travel once more through an area where he had encountered gunfire from two hunters only 24 1/2 hours earlier. Whatever it was that led him back there, Wayne is mighty glad both he and the deer were willing to try that trail just one more time.

WAYNE LINDEMANS, WISCONSIN, 1988

Measurements	Right	Left	Difference
No. of points	11	8	
Main beam	30 1/8	30 7/8	6/8
1st point (G-1)	6 1/8	6 2/8	1/8
2nd point (G-2)	10 5/8	11 2/8	5/8
3rd point (G-3)	11 6/8	13 1/8	1 3/8
4th point (G-4)	9 5/8	10 5/8	1 0/8
5th point (G-5)	3 3/8	3 0/8	3/8
1st circ. (H-1)	5 4/8	5 3/8	1/8
2nd circ. (H-2)	5 1/8	5 1/8	–
3rd circ. (H-3)	5 6/8	5 6/8	–
4th circ. (H-4)	5 0/8	5 2/8	2/8
Total	93 0/8	96 5/8	4 5/8
Greatest spread		22 3/8	
Inside spread		18 7/8	
Gross typical score		208 4/8	
Assymetry deductions		-4 5/8	
Non-typical additions		+28 1/8	
Net non-typical score		232 0/8	

26

CURIOSITY KILLS THE BUCK

Every once in a while, just when you least expect it, a big buck will show he's only "human," too. Delmar Hounshell has the proof hanging on his wall!

TITLE: FOURTH BLACKPOWDER NON-TYPICAL WORLD RECORD

SCORE: 232 3/8

HUNTER: DELMAR HOUNSHELL

LOCATION: BREATHITT COUNTY, KENTUCKY

YEAR: 1990

If you think whitetail hunting is easy, you've probably never tried it in the higher elevations of the eastern United States. From the rolling ridges of northern Alabama and Georgia to the windswept peaks of New Hampshire and Maine, the rugged Appalachian Mountains may offer deer hunters as many challenges as any other place on the continent.

First of all, whitetail densities tend to be low in the mountains of the East. What's more, just trying to negotiate the rugged terrain to get to your stand, especially on a cloud-shrouded ridge, can present logistical problems never confronted by "flatlanders." Then too, these mountains are notorious for swirling winds that frequently carry your scent in every direction at once. In other words, this is a place where even very good deer hunters can go home empty-handed.

In this setting, bagging *any* deer can be a real accomplishment. So, imagine how tough it is to match wits with a cagey buck that's been running the ridges for several years. Such trophies certainly exist. Mountain hunting lore is filled with tales of monsters glimpsed time and again that almost never end up on the game pole. From the way some hunters talk, you would swear these "ghosts" were too elusive for any mortal man to place in his sights. But, let's not get carried away. True, a mountain buck that has survived into the prime of life is indeed a challenge, but he is still flesh and blood and, therefore, capable of error. Every so often, whether because of sex drive or simple carelessness, even the wisest of these old whitetails slip up. When that happens, if some hunter is skilled and/or lucky enough to take advantage of the blunder, the aura of invincibility that surrounds such bucks can disappear with the squeeze of a trigger.

Of course, bucks of all ages are especially likely to be caught in a compromising situation during the latter part of the pre-rut on into the breeding period that follows. In most of the Appalachian region, that window of opportunity opens late in October, during bow season. Recently, though, there's been a move afoot to give muzzleloader hunters a crack at deer during the startup of rutting activity as well.

In 1990, Kentucky joined the growing list of states offering a short blackpowder season prior to the regular gun season. The rationale was that such a season—all two days of it—would give hunters more time afield without having a real impact on the deer resource. So now, every year in late October you can find muzzleloader hunters stalking the woods of "Ol' Kaintuck," much as they did in the days of Daniel Boone. Of course, since percussion caps, scopes and stainless-steel barrels have become popular with the blackpowder crowd, primitive-weapons hunting is a lot less "primitive" than it was in Daniel's day.

Delmar Hounshell, born and raised in eastern Kentucky's Breathitt County, is several generations removed from the pioneers who settled this land, but he fully appreciates the difficulties they faced in hunting mountain bucks. The terrain in this area is rugged and the cover thick, so regardless of whether you're toting an old flintlock

Delmar Hounshell's quadruple-beamed trophy, shot in 1990 in the coal-mining country of eastern Kentucky, edged out the Lindemans buck by a fraction of an inch to become the Longhunter's Society record in the non-typical category. Kentucky continues to surprise. Photo by Bill Cooper.

or a modern in-line muzzleloader, the fundamental problems remain largely the same. First, you have to find a buck, which has never been simple in this big country. Secondly, you have to get him to stand still long enough in a reasonably open spot for you to deliver the shot. And finally, because muzzleloaders seldom drop whitetails in their tracks even if you make a lethal hit, you might have a hard time finding your prize in this vast area of unbroken cover.

———————◆———————

Delmar wasn't a trophy hunter. He intended to take a shot at this deer, no matter what his size.

———————◆———————

Delmar began deer hunting in the mountains while still a teenager, and for many seasons, he strictly hunted during the nine-day November rifle season. But when the state's first early muzzleloader season was approved in early 1990, Delmar thought the idea of getting to hunt for two more days with a firearm—*any* firearm—sounded mighty appealing. So, he bought a muzzleloader and began to get acquainted with his new weapon. By the time season rolled around, he was confident in his ability to hit the vitals of a deer within reasonable range, even with the open sights he elected to stick with.

Picking out a good hunting spot is the first challenge when you're hunting an area with a low deer population. Delmar, though, had the great advantage of knowing the country well, for he had been hunting deer there for years. As he pondered his options for the early blackpowder season, he realized his best bet would be to concentrate on feeding areas. That meant he needed to find some old coalmines.

Breathitt County, like much of the rest of eastern Kentucky, is underlain by some of North America's greatest coal deposits, and mining has long been one of the major industries there. Regulations require coal companies to fill in the mines after the coal has been removed and then to replant the surface to minimize erosion. Clovers, alfalfa and grasses are among the favorite plantings, and because this part of the state is somewhat lacking in natural deer foods, reclaimed mining areas are highly attractive to the local whitetail population. In fact, as these plantings have increased, so have deer numbers throughout the region.

Delmar's own house was located on a reclaimed strip-mining site, so the search for potential stand sites began at home. In August, he and a friend began scouting a high hill behind the house and found signs of feeding activity. They erected a couple of permanent tree stands there and waited for opening day of blackpowder season in late October.

When the opener finally arrived, Delmar found himself hunting solo, as his buddy had decided to try his luck elsewhere. Delmar headed out from home before dawn, intending to occupy one of the tree stands until dark if need be. And, he would have, except for one fairly major problem. Between 9 a.m. and 3 p.m., a young guy living in the area walked past the stand no fewer than six times! Though he wasn't intentionally trying to foul up Delmar's hunt, that was the result just the same. Realizing no deer in its right mind was going to wander past that stand with so much human disturbance in the area, Delmar climbed down and walked back home.

There was just enough time remaining in the day for Delmar to drive to a spot on his father's property. Like his own land, this area had been reclaimed recently and had a bench planted in clover and alfalfa that served as a potential deer magnet. The hunter had seen a couple of bucks there in late summer, and now, rubs were sprinkled around the area, especially along a steep, brushy hillside just below the planted bench.

Sure enough, Delmar's late afternoon hunt produced a couple of deer sightings. Unfortunately, by the time the two animals walked into view at the far end of the feeding area, the light was too dim for the hunter to tell if they were bucks or does. He quietly eased out of the area, intent on returning the following morning to give the spot another chance.

Delmar's Sunday morning vigil was fruitless. By 11 a.m., the disappointed hunter had had enough. He elected to head home for a while, planning to return that afternoon to hunt the last few hours of blackpowder season. But first, he needed to use his pocketknife to clear out a couple of limbs that were obscuring his view of the feeding area. Delmar was engrossed in this "landscaping" work when, out of the corner of his eye, he picked up movement down the hill. A buck had burst out of the thicket below the clearing and had run to within 30 yards of the stunned hunter!

Now what? The only weapon Delmar had in hand at the moment was the pocketknife; his rifle

The spectacular "extra main beams" sprouting from near the base of the left antler pushed the Hounshell buck to the No. 1 spot in the muzzleloader records at 232 3/8 non-typical points. The two longest of these abnormal points measure 19 7/8 and 16 6/8 inches! This is a highly unusual antler trait. Photo by Bill Cooper.

was slung over his left shoulder. The buck was still looking around, apparently trying to locate the source of the brush-breaking sounds. Desperately, Delmar tried to figure out what he should do. He knew he would have to move quickly if he was going to touch off a shot. The deer was getting antsy, and within a few seconds, he would surely catch Delmar's scent and bolt away.

The hunter hadn't paid any attention to the rack. All he knew was that a buck was standing before him and that his only chance of the blackpowder season might evaporate at any moment. Delmar wasn't a trophy hunter. He intended to take a shot at this deer, no matter what his size, if he could get one. In a flash, he dropped his pocketknife, grabbed the rifle off his shoulder, cocked the hammer and then drew a bead and fired.

As the echo of the shot rolled through the

mountains, the buck bolted back toward the thick regrowth area from which he had come. Dejected, Delmar figured he had missed his hurried shot. Then, the hunter heard a loud noise from the direction of the deer. Seconds later, when Delmar reached the edge of the steep hillside, he spied the buck lying on the ground 100 yards away. The animal, now dead, had run into a tree with such force that one of his forelegs had broken on impact!

As Delmar approached the deer, he began to appreciate the trophy he had taken. The buck was lying with his head in the leaves and brush, hiding much of the rack. Even so, the hunter could tell he had taken the best whitetail of his career. Finally, Delmar lifted the rack and got a look at all of the deer's headgear—a sight for which he was totally unprepared.

"When I saw all those points sticking every which way, I got so nervous that I had to sit down for a while and catch my breath," the hunter recalled.

No wonder. The rack has 23 scorable points, most of them on the wild-looking left antler that was largely hidden from Delmar's view when he walked up to the deer. We can only imagine this hunter's feelings as he realized he had taken by far the biggest buck in Breathitt County history!

Getting the deer off that hillside proved to be quite a chore. Delmar and his father used a winch-equipped truck to drag the buck up the steep slope, but even that technique proved difficult. Finally, they managed to load the big non-typical into their vehicle and headed for a nearby check station. There, the excitement continued. Everyone who saw the buck was stunned by his size. Apparently, no one had ever seen that deer before Delmar shot him, and it was almost impossible for people to imagine that such a spectacular whitetail had come from this unheralded hunting area.

As Delmar was breaking off a few limbs around his ground blind, a noise turned his attention to the wild-looking buck bounding into a nearby opening as though looking for a fight. Most likely, the giant non-typical believed Delmar was another buck rubbing his antlers in "his" territory. But, he soon learned otherwise! Photo by Bill Cooper.

Getting the rack measured turned out to be easy. John Phillips, head of the deer program for the Kentucky Department of Fish and Wildlife, is an official measurer for both the Boone and Crockett Club and the Longhunter Society's blackpowder record book. In January 1991, he put a tape to the bizarre rack and came up with a net non-typical score of 232 3/8 points. That made the buck not only Kentucky's top whitetail of the season and the state record by muzzleloader, but also the state's all-time No.2 non-typical. And best of all, the huge Hounshell buck was a new *world* record by muzzleloader, edging out the 232-point giant Wayne Lindemans had shot in Wisconsin two years earlier! (See Chapter 25.)

———◆———

It was almost impossible for people to imagine that such a spectacular whitetail had come from this unheralded hunting area.

———◆———

While we can only speculate on what brought the huge Kentucky whitetail out of the brush that October morning, it's likely he simply misinterpreted the sounds Delmar made as he tried to clear a shooting lane. During the pre-rut, bucks spend a lot of time raking trees and brush with their antlers, working off pent-up energy in preparation for breeding. When a dominant buck hears such sounds in his "territory," his instinctive response is to go challenge the intruder. There's a good chance this is exactly what happened when the big non-typical heard Delmar breaking brush near his stand. That would make this deer one of the most noteworthy bucks ever "called in" by a hunter, even though it wasn't done intentionally.

Yes, old mountain bucks are tough to hunt. They live in challenging terrain, and they're usually separated from each other by a lot of real estate. But every so often, one of these deer commits a mistake and an alert hunter makes him pay for it. When that happens, you're talking about a real achievement—world record or not!

DELMAR HOUNSHELL, KENTUCKY, 1990

Measurements	Right	Left	Difference
No. of points	11	12	
Main beam	26 3/8	19 6/8	6 5/8
1st point (G-1)	6 3/8	7 4/8	1 1/8
2nd point (G-2)	9 7/8	8 0/8	1 7/8
3rd point (G-3)	10 2/8	9 1/8	1 1/8
4th point (G-4)	7 3/8	5 3/8	2 0/8
5th point (G-5)	–	–	–
1st circ. (H-1)	4 4/8	6 7/8	2 3/8
2nd circ. (H-2)	4 0/8	3 6/8	2/8
3rd circ. (H-3)	4 1/8	3 1/8	1 0/8
4th circ. (H-4)	3 5/8	2 6/8	7/8
Total	**76 4/8**	**66 2/8**	**17 2/8**
Greatest spread		24 6/8	
Inside spread		23 2/8	
Gross typical score		**166 0/8**	
Assymetry deductions		-17 2/8	
Non-typical additions		+83 5/8	
Net non-typical score		**232 3/8**	

27

FATHER'S DAY IN NOVEMBER

All Jim Smith wanted was his son to send him a legal buck. What he got was a whole lot more.

TITLE: CURRENT BLACKPOWDER
NON-TYPICAL WORLD RECORD
SCORE: 259 7/8
HUNTER: JIM SMITH
LOCATION: WARREN COUNTY,
VIRGINIA
YEAR: 1992

To call Virginia an important place in the whitetail world would be an understatement. After all, the species' scientific name is *Odocoileus virginianus* in honor of the fact that the earliest known whitetail fossil was found here. Perhaps it's ironic, then, that it took nearly 400 years of settlement by white men before a Virginia hunter could lay claim to an official world-record buck.

Just over an hour's drive west of Washington, D.C. lies Shenandoah National Park, one of the largest and most spectacular chunks of public land in the eastern United States. Situated along the spine of the Blue Ridge Mountains, these 196,466 acres—many of them more vertical than horizontal—are home to all sorts of wildlife, including what is literally a sky-high

population of whitetails. It is easy to understand why deer thrive here—the park is an enormous sanctuary with no legal hunting and the surrounding valleys are dotted with farm fields that serve as prime nighttime feeding areas. Several of the East Coast's finest trophies have been shot just outside the park, either on private land or in remote parts of nearby George Washington National Forest.

Jim Smith doesn't need to utilize public hunting land. He owns a tract of private ground near the community of Browntown along Shenandoah's northwest boundary. By day, Jim works at an office in Front Royal, but during deer season, every spare hour finds him in his woods, hunting with a buddy or two and enjoying some of the East's most picturesque surroundings.

That's precisely the plan Jim and his friends, Dana and Chico, had in mind as they prepared to go afield on November 9, opening day of the 1992 blackpowder season. All three had shot deer during the early bow season, and now, they were full of anticipation for the muzzleloader season. A light frost only added to the men's confidence as they headed out in the half-light of dawn.

You might figure that leaving the cabin right at the start of legal shooting time would be a mistake, but it was actually part of the strategy. At night, deer in this area move to the lower elevations to feed and rut then head back into the park around dawn. So, if a hunter moves uphill toward the park boundary in the darkness, he often accomplishes nothing more than to push deer ahead of him into the sanctuary. Waiting for day-

Jim Smith's 259 7/8-point Virginia giant, taken on November 9, 1992, is the highest-scoring whitetail ever taken by muzzleloader and is the overall No.1 buck in Old Dominion. He's just one of several huge deer shot near Shenandoah National Park in the 1990s. Photo by Joe Byers.

light gives a hunter a chance to see what's going on around him and to perhaps catch a buck unaware.

It worked on this particular hunt. Not long after leaving the cabin, Jim spotted a buck and doe off to his left. They were unalarmed and heading into a hollow containing one of Jim's permanent tree stands. Since there was no opportunity to shoot, the hunter decided to ease in that direction as quietly as possible, hoping to cut off the deer. That plan was quickly dashed when, only minutes into the season, the belch of a blackpowder rifle was heard off to the right of Jim's position.

Checking to see what had happened, Jim and Chico separately converged on the hollow where Dana had fired the shot. They found him with a cleanly killed 6-pointer, a good start to the hunt. Dana's friends offered to help him get his buck out of the woods, but the successful hunter insisted they go on to their stands so they wouldn't miss any more of "prime time" than necessary. Leaving Dana to tend to his buck, Jim and Chico decided to walk together up the steep slope, following a logging road through the woods.

Chico eventually peeled off to his stand site, while Jim continued along the logging road. Finally, he came to a switchback that afforded him a good view of the area he wanted to hunt. From his hiding spot beside a downed tree, Jim could see the farms below and the park above. It was an ideal place to catch deer moving up from the fields in the morning or down from the park in the afternoon. The hunter settled in to watch and wait.

Jim had been on-stand for a while when he heard shots fired on a neighboring tract of private land. Soon afterwards, Jim heard men shouting. Then, suddenly, he detected an animal running through the dead leaves. It was a buck coming on the run. Jim quickly rested his rifle on the dead tree, cocked the hammer and tried to draw a bead on the rapidly moving deer. He squeezed the trigger, and a cloud of white smoke burst into the air. But, the shot never found its mark. The buck, which Jim says was a "6 or 8-pointer," went on his way unscathed.

He looked to the sky and said, "Hey, boy, how about running an old buck through here for your old dad?"

At this point, the landowner figured luck just wasn't with him. After all, the season was less than a half-day old and already he had failed on two attempts to down bucks. After issuing a few choice words to himself and reloading his rifle, Jim settled back in for what would prove to be an uneventful remainder of the morning.

Around noon, he headed back down to the cabin for a break. Over lunch, Jim, Dana and Chico talked about the morning's events and plotted out a plan for the afternoon. Based on the amount of sign Jim had observed on the mountain and the fact that he had seen a buck there, he decided to go back to his dead-tree stand for the remainder of the day.

Many thoughts flicker through a hunter's mind during the course of a day afield. You can concentrate all you want on the task at hand—spotting and shooting a deer—but random images have a way of floating through your consciousness. As that opening afternoon dragged on with no more deer either seen or heard, Jim found himself thinking of his family…or, to be more specific, of his late son, David.

Only four years earlier, the boy's life had ended tragically in an automobile accident, leaving Jim to cope with the unbearable void all parents feel in such horrible circumstances. David had been a hunter, and a good one. Now, as Jim reflected on how much he missed his former hunting buddy, he did what he claims he had done many other times in the past four years: He looked to the sky and said, "Hey, boy, how about running an old buck through here for your old dad?"

Undoubtedly, private pleas like this one are whispered countless times every day of deer season from one end of North America to the other. But because what follows is seldom of sweeping significance, we don't hear about them. The difference, in Jim's case, was that something big—very big—was about to happen. For it seems David was listening.

At around 5 p.m., with the mountainside growing steadily darker, Jim noticed movement on one of the many deer trails coursing through the woods. It was a doe, nibbling on the underbrush as she made her way down the ridge toward the fields below. Jim watched her closely, hoping that with the rut in high gear a buck would be bringing up the rear. Then, he saw what he was waiting for—a buck following the same brush-shrouded trail and heading straight for the man who had asked his son to send him one.

By his own admission, Jim didn't realize he was looking at a world-class whitetail. All he could tell for certain was that the deer was "nice," maybe a 10 or even a 12-pointer. Jim had already made the decision to shoot the deer if given a chance, so there was no need to get distracted by counting points. But, getting a shot might not be simple. There was plenty of brush between him and the buck.

Unaware that a hunter was in the vicinity, the giant finally presented Jim with a reasonable shot at 45 yards. Holding his Thompson-Center Renegade as steady as possible on a limb of the dead tree, Jim lined up on the buck's neck, drew a fine bead with the iron sights and squeezed the trigger. *Ker-pow!*

Despite the gray-white shroud of smoke that erupted from the .54-caliber rifle, Jim saw the buck jump straight up and then wheel around to run back up the mountain toward the safety of Shenandoah's unhuntable woods. Seconds later, the hunter heard thrashing in the newly fallen leaves, followed by a silence that could be construed as either very good or very bad. Hoping the buck had fallen dead but not knowing for sure, Jim rapidly reloaded and began to ease up the mountain. The trail was a short one that never reached the boundary of the park. The old buck was nearly dead when

When Jim and friends got the 31-pointer back to the cabin that evening, it was time to celebrate and shoot a few photos. Within hours, folks from all over the area were forming a line at the Smith home to see the biggest buck ever taken by muzzleloader. This buck has it all! Photo courtesy of Jim Smith.

Jim reached him. Another round quickly finished the job. Now, with the deer lying still on the leafy forest floor, Jim could relax and appreciate the moment.

In a clear departure from standard hunter behavior, Jim did not even try to count points at this juncture. Instead, he simply reveled in the sight of the amazing rack before him and wondered why he, instead of someone else, had been honored with such a prize animal. Then, still awestruck and with daylight fading quickly, he rolled the deer onto its back, pulled out his hunting knife and began to field-dress the king of the mountain.

That chore completed, Jim headed down into the hollow below, hoping to recruit Dana to help with the long drag out. Dana had heard the two shots and was eager to find out what had hit the ground. "How big and how many points?" asked the curious voice from down the ridge.

"You know that magazine you were looking at

last night in the cabin?" Jim shouted back. "I got one that looks like those deer, with at least 30 points! This is the biggest deer I have ever seen or shot!"

Naturally, Dana didn't know what to think. But minutes later, when he laid eyes on Jim's gigantic deer, he knew his partner's claims had not been exaggerated. As the two friends huddled around the deer and began counting points, Dana just kept shaking his head, as if his eyes were playing a trick on him. Finally, after picking through the amazing rack, Dana turned to Jim and exclaimed, "Slick, he's got 35 points!" Then, after a pause, he added, "I feel like David had something to do with this."

"That thought crossed my mind, too," Jim replied.

Soon, Chico reached the scene. Like Dana, he needed some time to absorb what had happened. Once his shock had worn off a bit, the trio started the arduous descent to the cabin with one very big-bodied, big-racked piece of cargo in tow. By the time they got there,

Despite the rapid growth in primitive-weapons hunting across North America, Jim's magnificent non-typical remains the only whitetail in the Longhunter Society record book to net over 250 points. It is certainly a worthy No.1. Photo courtesy of Jim Smith.

Chico and Dana had come up with an appropriate name for the deer—the "Browntown Bruiser." Minutes later, Jim phoned his house and asked wife Retha and daughter Shelly to come on out—with a camera and film, naturally.

Later at the check station, Jim's giant would prove to weigh 215 pounds field-dressed, a serious mountain buck with headgear to match. Word began to spread that a "35-pointer" had been shot, causing quite a stir locally. But even after studying the rack and comparing it to some in various magazines, Jim still wasn't prepared for the numbers—259 7/8 net non-typical!—Long-hunter Society measurer Max Carpenter would come up with two months later at the official scoring. The bad news was that Max found "only" 31 points on the massive rack to be measurable; the good news was that the deer was clearly the state-record non-typical—not just for blackpowder, but overall as well!

The Browntown Bruiser certainly is the finest

non-typical whitetail ever from Virginia, but of even more widespread significance is the fact that no other known muzzleloader kill in the world can compare to this one. Jim's 259 7/8-point giant leapfrogged past the 232 3/8-point Delmar Hounsell buck from Kentucky (Chapter 26) to become the standard by which all other muzzleloader trophies are measured. While more and more sportsmen are accepting the blackpowder challenge every year, it will take one serious animal to beat the score of this mountain monster.

———◆———

Word began to spread that a "35-pointer" had been shot, causing quite a stir locally.

———◆———

In 1607 on the Virginia coast, three shiploads of musket-toting colonists founded Jamestown, the first English-speaking settlement in North America. During those uneasy days of colonization, first in struggles with local Indians and later with Britain itself, much of Old Dominion's fascinating history was written with the smell of blackpowder hanging in the air. Perhaps it is only fitting, then, that the most important chapter in Virginia's deer-hunting history was written the same way.

Jim Smith, Virginia, 1992

Measurements	Right	Left	Difference
No. of points	15	16	
Main beam	28 5/8	28 1/8	4/8
1st point (G-1)	7 0/8	6 0/8	1 0/8
2nd point (G-2)	11 2/8	11 0/8	2/8
3rd point (G-3)	12 2/8	10 2/8	2 0/8
4th point (G-4)	8 1/8	7 0/8	1 1/8
5th point (G-5)	–	–	–
1st circ. (H-1)	5 5/8	5 4/8	1/8
2nd circ. (H-2)	5 4/8	5 4/8	–
3rd circ. (H-3)	5 4/8	6 7/8	1 3/8
4th circ. (H-4)	5 2/8	5 2/8	–
Total	89 1/8	85 4/8	6 3/8
Greatest spread		29 3/8	
Inside spread		21 1/8	
Gross typical score		195 6/8	
Assymetry deductions		-6 3/8	
Non-typical additions		+70 4/8	
Net non-typical score		259 7/8	

28

CONTENDERS FOR THE CROWN

With just a little luck, dozens of other great bucks could have been recognized as official world records over the years. Here's a look at some of history's most notable whitetails that for one reason or another never quite reached the throne.

When I set out to write a book about world-record whitetails, my purpose was to assemble all of the information that could be found on these historic deer into an authoritative record that is both accurate and detailed. Hopefully, in the preceding chapters, I have at least come close to achieving that goal.

In the course of investigating these great trophies, I kept discovering other deer that practically begged to be included in this volume. None of these bucks has ever been deemed an official world record and probably never will be. So, why should I consider mentioning them in a book devoted only to No.1 whitetails? Because these trophies might well have been recognized as tops in their categories had fate only been a bit more kind. All were serious contenders for the crown, though none ever wore it. They are nonetheless notable deer in the annals of whitetail history.

Such deer are much more common than you might guess. Indeed, those of us in the whitetail business run into them so often that we've come to call them "what-if" bucks. My good friend and colleague, Dick Idol, coined this term back in the 1980s when he was writing the first-ever features on many of these trophies for the pages of *North American WHITETAIL* magazine. The what-if label is appropriate, for in nearly every case, we can identify a single glitch that kept the deer in question from being officially recognized as a world record. Some examples of what-if shortcomings might include: *What if* the buck had been a clean typical, instead of growing those non-typical points that hurt his net score? *What if* the hunter had had that buck measured right after he got him, instead of waiting 23 years? *What if* he hadn't broken that point? *What if* a record book existed devoted strictly to handgun trophies? And in the case of some of North America's earliest trophy bucks, *what if* the record-keeping groups had been scoring deer back when this one was taken? The problems that can thwart a monster whitetail's bid for immortality are many.

Common sense tells us that king-sized bucks have been harvested by North America's hunters since prehistoric times, and great numbers of whitetail bucks were shot during the first few hundred years of colonization. Unfortunately, precious few racks from distant yesteryear have been preserved for our scrutiny. So, my search for the "complete" history of world-record whitetails could not penetrate the veil of time beyond the early 1800s. Realistically, about the best anyone can do in a search for the record-holders is to check both the record books and private trophy collections across North America. That I have done—not only while conducting specific research for this book, but also as part of my daily duties as editor of *North American WHITETAIL* for well over a decade. In that quest to uncover potential world records, I came upon one fascinating what-if after another and decided to include them in this book. I make no promises that the following list includes every deer that "could have been" a world record in one category or another, though I do believe it to be the most complete such rundown ever compiled.

The most practical way to provide a comprehensive listing of world records (actual or otherwise) is chronologically, sifting down through the years in

Rick Busse shows off the original mount of the 181 1/8-point typical taken by John Bush near Elk River, Minnesota, in 1870. This is the second-oldest typical in B&C. Photo by Gordon Whittington.

search of trophy bucks larger than any documented prior to that time. In the case of potential No.1 bucks for the B&C records, my list includes the overall top-scoring bucks of the time regardless of weapon type or cause of death (hunting versus non-hunting). Potential world records for the P&Y and Longhunter record books obviously have been limited to bucks taken with bow and muzzle-loader, respectively. I've also thrown in a handful of potential miscellaneous "world records," such as handgun and crossbow trophies. As in previous portions of this book, the discussion will focus only on animals that were actually measured by the modern B&C system.

Now, a quick chronological stroll through the years, looking at the what-if bucks that might well have rewritten whitetail history. For a frame of reference, I've also included the official world records described throughout this book in the appropriate years during which they were taken.

1830: In McKean County, Pennsylvania, Arthur Young shot a clean 6x6 that netted 175 4/8 as a B&C typical when scored well over a century later. Arthur's deer is by far the earliest known buck to qualify for the B&C record book, making it in a roundabout way the first world record. The rack is listed in the 3rd edition of B&C's *Records of North*

American Whitetail Deer (1995) as the Keystone State's No.6 typical, even after more than 160 years! Not surprisingly, details of the hunt are lacking, but we can assume the Young buck was taken by muzzleloader since that was the only type of firearm in existence in 1830. So, the deer in effect would have also been the first blackpowder record as well.

This 32-pointer, bagged by Howard Eaton in South Dakota in 1870, was apparently the world's largest known non-typical when killed, but his rack wasn't officially measured until a century had passed. At 250 6/8, it's still huge! Photo courtesy of Jack Brittingham.

1870: For the only time in history, the known upper limits of both typical and non-typical whitetail antlers were redefined in the same year. It happened in bordering states: Minnesota for the typical, South Dakota for the non-typical.

Near Elk River, Minnesota, self-described "gold

hunter" John Bush downed a typical that many years later would be scored at 181 1/8 net points. John shot the buck with an 1849 Plainsman rifle, in effect making him not only the B&C world-record typical but the record by muzzleloader as well.

Meanwhile, to the west in South Dakota, Howard Eaton was setting a lofty standard for non-typicals, shooting a 250 6/8-point giant. Little is known of the hunt that produced this brute, but B&C has accepted the hunter's name, year of kill and score for its record book.

Circa 1892: Jeff Benson reportedly either shot or found dead the so-called "Brady" buck in McCulloch County, Texas. The 49-point monster non-typical netted 284 3/8 (Chapter 9), easily setting a new upper limit for antler score in whitetails. For almost a century, no known buck would exceed that mark.

1903: In Frio County, Texas, hunter Basil Dailey was sitting near a pond on a large ranch when an incredible buck suddenly ran out of the brush and into the pond, splashing water everywhere! The startled hunter drew a bead on the beast and fired. The deer wheeled to run, then dropped. Many years later, the rack was measured at 193 2/8 net points, making him the highest-scoring known typical in the world at the time he was killed.

That same year in New Brunswick, hunter George Lake shot a 203 6/8-point non-typical. According to information turned up by New Brunswick whitetail enthusiast George Chase, this Canadian brute was taken with a muzzleloading shotgun. Would that have made him the first known muzzleloader non-typical record? Perhaps, but perhaps not. We don't know whether the aforementioned 1870 monster from South Dakota taken by Howard Eaton was shot with a muzzleloader or one of the "newfangled" blackpowder cartridges just coming into widespread use. No attempt has been made to have any of these early deer entered into the Longhunter records.

1905: Near Elk River, British Columbia, Jim

Basil Dailey downed this magnificent 15-pointer in Frio County, Texas, in 1903. A 22 6/8-inch inside spread helps propel the deer to 192 net typical points, the highest verifiable typical score as of that time…and still one of the all-time greats! Photo by John Stein.

Brewster shot his 245 7/8-point non-typical, which would be recognized as B&C's No.1 non-typical when the first modern record book came out in 1952 (Chapter 8).

1906: On December 20, Milton George went looking for meat on his ranch in McMullen County, Texas, and came back with a 196 1/8-point typical that was at the time not only the biggest in Texas but also in the rest of North America as well. Some 82 years would pass before the huge 6x7 was officially scored. By that time, he had slipped far down the list of top B&C typicals. The world was lucky to have ever heard about this head, for during the 1960s, the George family's ranch house burned to the ground. Fortunately, the rack had been moved to a more secure place in San Antonio.

1914: Wisconsin's Jim Jordan shot his 206 1/8-point typical in Burnett County (Chapter 6), raising the bar to a point no typical whitetail would be able to clear for almost 80 years. But, the Jordan buck wouldn't be accepted as the world record until 1966, by which time three other bucks had taken their turns atop the B&C rankings.

1914-1918: Sometime during this period, Lewis Bissell of Madeline Island, Wisconsin, reportedly arrowed a 239 7/8-point buck while hunting near Green Bay. If it could be proved that the deer was taken by bow, he would be the earliest known buck big enough to qualify for listing in P&Y and, indeed, the easy "world record" by bow for nearly 50 years! In the 1980s, both P&Y and the Wisconsin Buck & Bear Club opened an investigation in hopes of finding photos or eyewitnesses to prove a bowkill. The late hunter's niece, a Mrs. Anderson,

With a gross typical score of 210 2/8 points, the Milton George buck from McMullen County, Texas, has more inches of typical antler on his head than any other buck from the Lone Star State. The wide, heavy 6x7 rack was the world's biggest when the deer was shot in 1906 and still ranks as the No.2 typical in Texas with a whopping net score of 196 1/8. Photo by John Stein.

At 328 2/8 net non-typical points, the famous "Hole-in-the-Horn" buck was the world's highest-scoring whitetail when found dead around 1940 in Portage County, Ohio. Unfortunately, he hung unnoticed until 1983, when Dick Idol discovered him, and by the time the rack finally was submitted for panel-measuring in 1986, the 333 7/8-point Missouri Monarch had been certified as B&C's world record. Here, original taxidermist Al Morgan puts finishing touches on the mount. Photo courtesy of Dean Ziegler, Ohio Hall of Fame Whitetail Museum.

had suggested that the deer was an archery kill because Lewis hunted with a bow and arrow "all the time." Naomi Torey, then P&Y secretary, actually went to California to visit with Mrs. Anderson in hopes of substantiating her claims, but the woman was well up in age and had difficulty recollecting details of the events. Citing a lack of evidence, P&Y officials refused to accept the Bissell buck.

Even if there had been proof that Lewis took the buck with archery equipment, a second question might have been enough to bar him from P&Y acceptance anyway. Was it legal to hunt with a bow in Wisconsin at the time the deer was shot? The answer depends on exactly when the buck was taken. According to the Wisconsin Department of

Natural Resources, bowhunting was allowed through the 1916 season but then was banned from 1917 through 1930. All Mrs. Anderson said she could remember was that the deer was shot "between 1914 and 1918." So, doubts linger about the weapon used and whether or not the deer was legally harvested. What no one doubts, however, is that the Bissell buck remains a world-class whitetail.

1918: John Breen's 202-point typical was taken by gun in Minnesota and would go on to be ranked No.1 in B&C nearly 40 years later (Chapter 5).

1923: In Bucks County, Pennsylvania, Robert Weaver arrowed a 144 2/8-point buck that would have been the world-record typical by bow had there been a bowhunting organization around to recognize it as such. Robert's 4x4 remains the earliest whitetail kill in the P&Y listings.

Circa 1940: Near a railroad track just outside Ravenna Arsenal in Ohio's Portage County, workers came across the bloated carcass of a huge animal lying next to the arsenal's chain-link security fence. The workers weren't even sure what the beast was—one claimed it was an elk, another a moose. Meanwhile, standing inside the fence was a young laborer named George Winters, who announced that the animal was a whitetail—a gigantic whitetail!

The process of recovering the dead buck's antlers and cape wasn't easy. The deer, apparently killed by a passing train, had died with his right antler wedged beneath the fence. As the railroad workers tried to pull the buck away from the barrier, George noticed that a piece of fence wire had been forced through one of the deer's flattened drop tines, apparently during the animal's death struggle. George helped dig that right antler out of the frozen ground, and the chief of the railroad crew, Charlie Flowers, claimed the head as his own.

Later, the distinctive rack was shoulder-mounted by Akron taxidermist Al Morgan and became a fixture at the nearby Kent Canadian Club, whose members were a group of local outdoorsmen. In 1983, Dick Idol visited the club, recognized the rack as that of a potential world-record non-typical and purchased the mount. Veteran B&C measurer Phil Wright gave the deer, now known as the "Hole-in-the-Horn" buck, a net entry score of 342 3/8 points, substantially higher than the official 333 7/8-point score of the then-No.1 buck from Missouri (Chapter 10).

But, the Ohio deer never became the world record. At the next panel-measuring session in Albuquerque in 1986, Boone & Crockett officials granted the deer a final score of 328 2/8 points, making him No.2 on the list. Although many antler enthusiasts still believe this deer has more antler than any other whitetail in history—including

Missouri's world record—the panel's judgment was final.

1947: The earliest known P&Y non-typical was taken by Elwood Snell in Michigan's Allegan State Forest. The 8x5 scored 152 3/8 and was in effect the first No.1 bow non-typical, though never proclaimed as such. Because the minimum net score for non-typicals has since been raised to 155 points, this trophy no longer even appears in the all-time P&Y record book.

1953: Gilbert Guttormson arrowed the highest-scoring typical taken by a modern archer to that point, a 164 3/8-point 7x7 in Norman County, Minnesota (Chapter 13).

1954: In Bayfield County, Wisconsin, Claude Butler took an 8x12 that netted 153 7/8 points. It was then the largest verifiable non-typical bagged by bow, but by the time he was officially measured some years later, higher-scoring P&Y bucks had been registered. This deer no longer appears in the all-time record book.

1955: On the last afternoon of Minnesota's month-long season, Lawrence Sowieja needed a miracle if he was to arrow the first deer of his three-year bowhunting career. And, a miracle he got. As several friends conducted a drive through a small woodlot in Dodge County, Minnesota, Lawrence hid in the brush and waited. Suddenly, he spotted a big buck running his way. As the deer flashed through an opening in a deadfall, Lawrence instinctively released his arrow. Despite the buck's speed and the distance of 25 yards, the broadhead caught the brute right in the vitals.

The trophy whitetail lying at the end of that short blood trail had 7 points on one antler and 13 on the other, a miracle indeed. In fact, at 203 4/8 net P&Y points, he was easily the top non-typical yet taken by bow! Sadly, family medical problems shortly after the hunt rearranged Lawrence's priorities, and until the 1970s, he made no attempt to get the buck officially measured. By the time that finally happened, much bigger non-typicals had been cer-

Had Lawrence Sowieja not waited so long to have his 1955 non-typical from Dodge County, Minnesota, officially measured, he would have become the first-ever record-holder in P&Y's non-typical category at 203 4/8 points. Photo courtesy of Lawrence Sowieja.

tified. As a result, neither the hunter nor his fine buck ever got the recognition they otherwise would have received.

1957: George Ferber arrowed a 149 3/8-point typical in New York (Chapter 11). In effect, this deer became the archery world-record typical since he won the first-ever National Field Archery Association (NFAA) big-game competition in which the B&C scoring system was used.

1958: In North Dakota, bowhunter Bobby Triplett shot a 163 4/8-point typical whitetail to take over the top spot by bow in the NFAA's record listings (Chapter 12).

Even though never a record of any sort, a buck taken in 1958 in a Louisiana swamp was so memorable that he deserves mention. On January 2, Sammy "Peanut" Walker and friends were dog-hunting for deer in Gross Tete Parish near a backwater called Bayou Blue. Conditions were bitter as the area was in the grip of a freak ice storm. After the dogs were turned loose and the other hunters in the group dropped off at their stand sites, Peanut set up along a narrow logging road and waited. Soon, he heard the dogs turning his way. Minutes later, a

The author displays Sammy Walker's amazing 1958 buck from Louisiana. Although an official measurer came up with a score of more than 290 non-typical points – higher than any other known whitetail at the time of the kill – B&C ultimately ruled the rack unscorable. Photo by Tom Evans.

buck came bouncing through the brush. The deer's rack was covered with vines and branches, but that didn't stop the hunter from shooting. The 12-gauge shotgun's blast put the buck down on the spot. When Peanut unwrapped his "present" moments later, he discovered one of the oddest racks in whitetail history. Instead of the usual main beams with points sprouting up from them, this buck had two huge clumps of velvet-covered bone adorning the top of his head, resembling the snake-covered head of Medusa, the figure from Greek mythology!

Many years later, veteran B&C measurer Dave Boland was asked to come up with a score for this strange rack. Despite great difficulty in distinguishing main beams, typical tines and, thus, places at which to measure circumferences, Dave got a net non-typical score of 291 3/8 points. If accepted, that score would make the Louisiana buck bigger than the 284 3/8-point "Brady" buck from Texas, the official world record at the time Peanut shot his deer.

Ah, but wait. B&C reserves the right to deem any trophy "unscorable," and that was the decision on this one. (It has happened with other bucks, too. See Chapter 29.) Thus, Peanut's bizarre buck currently appears in no record book, not even in Louisiana's list of top trophies. Perhaps all of this

makes the strange creature from down on the bayou a "pretender" rather than a "contender." But, that label seems a bit harsh for any rack that weighs more than 10 pounds and has been taped at 291 3/8 points by an experienced official measurer, whether the score was accepted or not.

1959: Two bucks that would go on to become official P&Y world records were shot this year: Jerry Polesky's 164 3/8-point typical in Montana (Chapter 14) and Don Vraspir's 186 2/8-point non-typical in Minnesota (Chapter 18).

1961: Can you imagine what would it be like to shoot a world-record whitetail and never get credit for it even though you followed the entry procedures to the letter? Well, that's just what happened to a couple of bowhunters in the fall of 1961.

When William Cruff arrowed a 188 1/8-point North Dakota buck, he had every reason to think he had shot the new No.1 P&Y non-typical. At 188 1/8 net points, the buck was 1 7/8 inches bigger than the record whitetail Don Vraspir had taken in Minnesota two years earlier. Unfortunately for William, there was too much time left in that three-year P&Y competition period before his buck could be declared No.1.

As it turned out, his "record" didn't even last

When Ivan Mascher arrowed his 198 5/8-point non-typical during the 1961 season, it became the highest-scoring P&Y non-typical on record. Unfortunately for Ivan, by the time that recording period had ended, another Nebraska trophy – Del Austin's 279 7/8-point giant – had also been entered. Thus, the Mascher buck beat the world record but never became one! This great rack now hangs in Cabela's archery department in Sydney, Nebraska. Photo courtesy of Ivan Mascher.

Had the right G-2 tine on Larry Gibson's huge 6x6 typical not been injured in velvet, the deer almost certainly would have become the B&C world record. As is, this 1971 Missouri trophy ended up at 205 net, a mere 1 1/8 inches below Jim Jordan's No.1 mark. Photo by Jim Rathert, Missouri Department of Conservation.

through the 1961 season. On the afternoon of November 27 while standing on a sparsely covered sidehill in Douglas County, Nebraska, Ivan Mascher watched in disbelief as a rutting buck nonchalantly walked straight toward him. At first, the bowhunter wasn't sure what to do. Then, the massive deer began to angle off to Ivan's left, offering a nearly broadside shot at close range. Ivan drove a broadhead through both lungs of the 19-point monster, which traveled only 50 yards before dropping. "It was about the shortest hunt there ever was," Ivan later recalled.

That whitetail would be entered at 198 5/8 non-typical points, making him the frontrunner for the next world record. However, by the time the competition period ended in 1963, he too had been bumped out of contention for the No.1 spot, sur-

passed by a Nebraska trophy from the 1962 season.

1962: Once again, both bowhunting records fell to bucks taken in a single season. In fact, *three* whitetails shot this year would go on to be recognized as official world records by P&Y. On the typical side, Kent Price's 165 4/8-pointer in Maryland (Chapter 15) and Lloyd Goad's 197 6/8-pointer in Iowa (Chapter 16) both broke to top mark. As for the non-typical side, Del Austin arrowed his incredible 279 7/8-pointer in Nebraska (Chapter 19), blowing away Ivan Mascher's 1961 Nebraska trophy and every other bow-killed whitetail as well. The Austin buck remains No.1 as of this writing.

1965: Illinois bowhunter Mel Johnson bagged his 204 4/8-point typical (Chapter 17), breaking the Goad buck's P&Y record. Mel's giant has held top ranking ever since.

1967: A buck from Beaverdam Creek, Alberta, seriously challenged the B&C typical world record.

Larry Raveling's "Raghorn" buck from Iowa, displayed here by the author, scores 282 non-typical and probably would have set the B&C record at around 290 if not for at least one broken drop tine. Photo by Tom Evans.

Stephen Jansen's massive 17-pointer had a typical frame that netted 211 1/8, easily enough to beat the Jordan buck's 206 1/8 for No.1 in B&C. But, the Alberta trophy also had 6 7/8 inches of abnormal points, which had to be subtracted to get the final score of 204 2/8 typical.

1971: The next serious threat to Jim Jordan's typical B&C emerged this year, and it came from Randolph County, Missouri. Larry Gibson's wide, high-racked 6x6 netted 205 points, only 1 1/8 below the Jordan buck. It might have been No.1 except for one of those dreaded *ifs*. *If* his right brow tine were as long as his left, he would have picked up enough score to push him over the top. Even more intriguing is the Missouri buck's deformed right G-2 tine. Near its tip is a pronounced "knot," almost certainly caused by an injury during velvet. *If* this injury hadn't occurred, that tine well could have been another inch or more in length. Because the injured G-2 tine is noticeably shorter than its mate on the left antler, even an increase of 5/8 inch in the deformed tine would have resulted in a net scoring gain of 1 2/8 inches, enough to make the Gibson buck the world record. But, that didn't happen and the Missouri deer settled in as the all-time No.2 typical in B&C records.

1973: In Clay County, Iowa, Larry Raveling got his first whitetail and what a deer it was! With 29 scorable points, Larry's buck would likely have been a new world-record non-typical—*if* he hadn't snapped a drop tine off his right antler. The deer still netted 282 points, just behind the Brady buck from Texas. Had that broken tine been intact, there's every reason to believe the Iowa buck would have been No.1. But as it is, the world will never know.

1974: During the Iowa shotgun season, Wayne Bills shot the state-record typical and a near-world-record. The tall-tined Hamilton County 5x5 burst out of cover on a drive, and Wayne, who had never even shot a deer, dropped him on the run. The antlers floated around in various collections for 17

A chipped brow tine and years of shrinkage before being measured might well have kept Wayne Bills' 1974 Iowa buck from edging out the Jordan buck as the B&C typical world record. The giant 10-pointer nets a phenomenal 201 4/8. Photo by Gordon Whittington.

years before being officially scored by B&C measurer Dave Boland at 201 4/8 net points. A year later, a B&C panel confirmed that score, making the Bills buck No.6 all time. But *if* several inches of the deer's left brow tine hadn't been snapped off and *if* the rack didn't have 3 2/8 inches in abnormal points, he certainly would have beaten Jordan's 206 1/8-point record. The gross typical score of the Bills buck is 212 7/8, stunning indeed for a basic 10-pointer.

1979: In Pennsylvania, muzzleloader hunter Frank Moldovan's "old faithful" stand in a cherry tree paid off in spades on the morning of December 4. Frank was keeping an eye on an adjacent apple orchard when he spotted a big buck following a couple of does. The rifle's payload caught the buck right behind the shoulder, and he went straight down. At 142 1/8 net typical points, Frank's Somerset County 4x4 remains the earliest known qualifier for the Longhunter Society records. As such, it might be argued that this deer was the world record by muzzleloader at the time he was bagged. However, the trophy wasn't entered until 1992, by which time a number of larger typicals had been entered.

Frank Moldovan used his muzzleloader to down this 142 1/8-point Pennsylvania buck in 1979. By the time Frank had the 4x4 scored for the Longhunter Society listings in 1992, much larger typicals already had been entered. Photo courtesy of Frank Moldovan.

1981: During the November gun season on the outskirts of St. Louis, Missouri, the highest-scoring buck of all time was found dead (Chapter 10). When panel-measured by B&C two years later, The Missouri Monarch received a final score of 333 7/8,

a mark that remains unmatched by any other whitetail.

Meanwhile, in Lincoln County, Montana, black-powder hunter Huston Hanson shot a 153 2/8-point typical, officially the largest taken by muzzleloader to that point. But as with the Moldovan buck that had been taken two years earlier, the timing of this kill was a bit unlucky. The hunter never received recognition as an official Longhunter record-holder, though his deer was plenty big enough.

1983: In Tennessee, Terry Burns claimed the earliest non-typical ever to make the Longhunter Society listings, a 185 3/8-point trophy that in effect became the world record by muzzleloader (Chapter 23).

1984: Kansas blackpowder hunter Tom Mosher shot his 184 4/8-point typical, the earliest Longhunter record in that category (Chapter 20).

1985: Bob Bromm's grueling quest for an Indiana trophy buck ended during the muzzleloader season. Bob's magnificent buck netted 226 3/8 non-typical points, easily taking over as the Longhunter Society's new No.1 whitetail (Chapter 24).

Meanwhile, in Wapello County, Iowa, shotgun hunter Robert Harding downed a buck with enough antler to become No.1 in the B&C typical records—*if* it weren't for his abnormal points. Without them, the brute would have netted 208 2/8 typical, sufficient to break Jordan's 206 1/8-point record. But with 21 1/8 inches of non-typical points, the final typical score would have been lowered to a disappointing 187 1/8 net. So, Robert decided to list the deer as a non-typical at 229 3/8 net. (Few other non-typicals in any record book have achieved such a high score with so few inches of abnormal antler growth.)

1986: Two giants killed that fall were legitimate contenders for world-record status. One came in a bit short of the P&Y typical mark because of scoring deductions, and the other was the biggest non-typical whitetail ever taken by crossbow.

Bowhunter Bill Kontras tagged this magnificent 201 1/8-point Ohio typical in 1986. The buck grosses 215 5/8 points as a basic 6x6, but heavy deductions kept him from challenging Mel Johnson's 204 4/8-point P&Y world record. Photo courtesy of Bill Kontras.

Although on the mend from a bout with cancer, Ohio bowhunter Bill Kontras still managed to get into the woods of Clark County and bag a sensational buck, one that easily had enough antler to beat Mel Johnson's P&Y typical record of 204 4/8. Bill's trophy grosses 215 5/8 as a basic 6x6, but asymmetry and three short abnormal points reduced his net score to 201 1/8 typical. (Without the abnormals, he would have tied for the P&Y world record at 204 4/8.) As is, the deer well could have become the official No.2 P&Y typical; however, for personal reasons, Bill ultimately decided not to enter the rack into the record book.

Meanwhile, in Cross County, Arkansas, Randal Harris took what remains the world's top non-typical by crossbow, a monster scoring 223 1/8 points. (Arkansas has a liberal policy regarding the use of crossbows during its archery season.) Randal had found one of the buck's hefty shed antlers in the spring of 1986 and had seen him several times early in the bow season. After spending "40-something" straight mornings in pursuit of the buck, he finally connected in mid-November. Unfortunately, despite Randal's tireless efforts to recover him, it took 35 days to do so. By then, of course, the meat and cape were unsalvageable but the antlers remained as stunning as ever. Few basic 4x4s have ever even grossed 193 4/8 points, but that's what this one *netted!* He did so largely on the strength of 29 2/8-inch and 30 4/8-inch main beams and an inside spread of 28 4/8! It seems reasonable to consider

If a separate listing for crossbow-taken deer existed, Randal Harris's stunning non-typical from Arkansas would rule it. The 16-pointer scores 223 1/8, thanks largely to 89 2/8 inches' worth of main beams and inside spread. What a buck! Photo by Kenn Young.

this deer the "world record" for crossbows, though the title is unofficial.

1988: Two noteworthy whitetails were taken this year. One was a true world record; the other a what-if buck.

In Wisconsin, Wayne Lindemans used a muzzle-loader during the regular gun season and killed what would become the new No.1 non-typical in the Longhunter Society record book at 232 net points (Chapter 25).

To the south in Macoupin County, Illinois, shot-gun hunter Kevin Naugle took his first whitetail. The massive, long-tined giant had a 6x6 typical frame big enough to net 210 B&C points…*if* it weren't for his forked brow tines. Unfortunately, those forks combined for a 12 7/8-inch deduction, more than enough to prevent this great typical from shattering Jordan's record. As it was, the Naugle buck netted 197 1/8.

Only a pair of forked brow tines kept Kevin Naugle's massive 1988 Illinois typical – the first deer he had ever shot!—from shattering the Jordan buck's B&C typical world record. Photo by Gordon Whittington.

1990: Delmar Hounshell downed a 232 3/8-point non-typical during muzzleloader season in Kentucky, taking over the top spot in the Longhunter record book (Chapter 26).

Just three weeks later in neighboring Indiana, Bedford resident Larry Deaton dropped the biggest whitetail ever taken by handgun. Larry was hunting for *another* big non-typical he had seen earlier in the year, but when this one stepped into a weed field in late afternoon, he didn't hesitate to shoot. A 180-grain bullet from the hunter's .35 Rem. did the job. The huge buck officially scored 229 7/8 B&C points and is in effect the handgun world record.

1991: The whitetail world was hit with jolt of electricity coming from the vicinity of Red Deer, Alberta. Local hunter Ed Koberstein reportedly had shot a typical big enough to dethrone the Jordan buck once and for all. At the end of the 60-day drying period, official B&C measurer Randy Bean gave the rack a net entry score of 207 2/8 typical points and a gross typical score of 235 6/8! This scoring was based on his opinion that the rack could be called a rare 9x8 typical with three short abnormal points.

In the end, whether or not this deer was indeed a potential world record hinged on two key questions. First, should a "fused" common-base tine on the rear edge of a typical tine on the right antler be considered typical or non-typical? Second, were a matched pair of upright points (called G-6 tines on the score sheet) really part of the typical frame or merely symmetrical abnormals? They were slightly out of line with the other typical points, but the debate was essentially, how far is *too* far out of line? When the rack went to panel in 1995, measurers there decided to call the G-6 points abnormal, making them deductions from the typical score rather than additions. Thus measured, the Koberstein buck's net typical score plummeted to 188 3/8, still high but nowhere near what the deer would have scored with a different ruling. Though the buck's non-typical score is 224 5/8, which is proportion-

Should Ed Koberstein's massive 1991 Alberta buck have become a world-record typical? An entry score of 207 2/8 net points raised the question, but a 1995 B&C panel said otherwise. Photo by Gordon Whittington.

ately higher than his typical score, Ed exercised his prerogative to list the trophy in the typical category anyway.

1992: It again was time for Canadian bucks to be in the spotlight. First, as profiled in Chapter 22, Dave Wilson shot his 193 2/8-point blackpowder typical in Saskatchewan, setting the Longhunter Society record in the process.

Near Saint Paul, Alberta, Larry Youngman bagged a whitetail with an even more impressive typical frame—a basic 5x5 grossing 220 7/8 points! Indeed, Larry's buck would have netted a shocking 211 6/8 typical...*if* he hadn't had 14 3/8 inches of abnormal points knocking his final score down to 197 3/8. Once again, a deer had grown more than enough antler to beat the Jordan buck but hadn't put it together in just the right way to satisfy the scoring system.

1993: The seemingly interminable wait for a new world-record typical finally ended when Saskatch-

ewan's Milo Hanson downed his 213 5/8-point giant (Chapter 7) to break the Jordan buck's long-standing mark of 206 1/8. Clearly, this was the biggest news in whitetail hunting in many years. However, it wasn't the *only* noteworthy event of 1993. In the 17 days preceding Milo's fateful hunt, two other phenomenal typicals also were taken.

The first was Daniel McDonnell's buck shot near Spiritwood, Saskatchewan, on November 6. Daniel rattled in the buck and caught a glimpse of a world-class right antler. Unfortunately, the hunter discovered after the shot that approximately half of the left beam had been snapped off. Amazingly, though, Daniel located the buck's left-side shed from the previous year (in a friend's shed pile!) and had taxidermist Brian Stein splice the front half of the shed onto the broken left beam of the actual rack. When that tricky task was completed, Daniel was amazed

Only the presence of six abnormal points prevented Larry Youngman's 1992 Alberta trophy from knocking off the Jordan buck and becoming B&C's top-ranked typical. Photo courtesy of Larry Youngman.

We'll never know if Daniel McDonnell's 1993 Saskatchewan buck could have kept Milo Hanson's 213 5/8-point buck from becoming the current No.1 B&C typical. But as repaired, Daniel's 7x7 rack nets 214 4/8 typical! Photo courtesy of Daniel McDonnell.

to learn that the 7x7 "rack" would net 214 4/8 typical, even higher than Milo's new record! Because altered racks can't be entered, the McDonnell buck won't ever show up in the official B&C listings. To his credit, Daniel never claimed his deer had once been a world record "on the hoof"—only that he *might* have been.

A few weeks later, Illinois shotgun hunter Brian Damery made a stalk on an outrageously big typical that had been courting a doe in a cut soybean field. The Macon County buck finally passed within slug range, and Brian nailed him. Within hours, word started spreading that the Damery buck possessed ample antler for becoming a world record. He had sweeping main beams of 32 and 32 4/8 inches, and the inside spread of his 6x6 typical frame was 28 3/8 inches. The 92 3/8 net inches comprised by those

three measurements is the highest such figure in whitetail history, as is his official gross typical score of 231 1/8. Had the rack carried no abnormal points, it would have netted an incredible 222 7/8! But, it did have abnormals, five of them totaling 22 5/8 inches. Once they were figured into the score, the net typical total dropped to 200 2/8, just enough to squeak the deer into B&C's all-time Top 10. Despite the reduced net score, Brian's Illinois giant is widely recognized as one of the all-time greats. You can't grow that much typical antler and not be!

No other whitetail in history can match the Damery buck's gross typical score of 231 1/8. With fewer deductions for abnormal points, this 1993 monster from Illinois would have beaten the Hanson buck out of B&C's top spot. As is, the basic 12-pointer nets 200 2/8. Photo by Tom Evans.

1995: January isn't normally a month in which big whitetail news is made, but it occasionally happens in those parts of the South with a late rut and lengthy gun seasons. During the first week of 1995, Mississippi hunter Tony Fulton shocked the world with a potentially record-breaking deer. On January 5, the Winston County resident decided to spend the last hour or so of the day watching a nearby

Tony Fulton's massive Mississippi 45-pointer from 1995 made a run at the top non-typical spot but fell short at 295 6/8 net non-typical points. The 13 pound-rack now ranks No.3 all time. Photo by Ron Boucher.

field of wheat and oats. Just before dark, a huge buck ran out into the field. Tony's rifle barked, and minutes later, the hunter walked up to his trophy.

When first scored, the complex rack, which weighed an unprecedented 13 pounds, received an official B&C entry score of 255 5/8 points, blowing away the Mississippi record of 225. But a year later, another measurer, Ron Boucher, was asked to take a second look at the rack and came up with a very different score—329 6/8 net and 342 3/8 gross! Those are world-record-class dimensions! Because the buck had already been entered in B&C, this second scoring was done unofficially. Even so, there was compelling reason to call the Fulton buck in for verification of final score when B&C's next panel convened in the spring of 1998.

Just as this book was going into production, I received word that the panel's final tally, reached after hours of painstaking scoring, came in at a net 295 6/8 non-typical points! This makes the 45-point Fulton buck the third largest non-typical on record! And while it falls short of the official world record, that incredible score does allow it to lay undisputed claim to being the largest whitetail ever killed by a

known hunter, eclipsing the 282-point Raveling buck from Iowa that formerly held that title! This Southern buck shows that not all giants come from the Midwest and Canada.

In November 1995 in Columbia County, Ohio, crossbow hunter Rick Williams bagged a massive typical officially measured at 193 2/8 B&C points. The deer, now part of Dean Ziegler's Ohio Hall of Fame Whitetail Museum collection, has never been entered into the B&C record book but apparently would be the largest crossbow typical on record if he were.

Ricky Williams shows off dad Rick's stunning 1995 Ohio buck that is likely the highest-scoring typical downed with a crossbow in modern times, but the rack hasn't been entered into any record book, though officially scored at 193 2/8. Photo courtesy of Rick Williams.

1996: The first week of January produced another surprise contender, just as it had in 1995—only this one came from much farther north. On January 4, the opening day of Ohio's muzzleloader season, Doug Rhodus decided to hunt in a lightly timbered part of Preble County. While waiting near a small tree in a grassy area, he spotted a huge buck 75 yards away. The deer was looking behind him, as if concerned about an approaching hunter or predator. With the buck thus preoccupied, Doug raised his open-sighted .45-caliber smokepole and squeezed off a shot. The whitetail dropped instantly.

When Doug walked up to his trophy, he was in awe of the wide, massive rack. Then, a minute later, another hunter walked up to see what was going on. Doug learned a deer drive was underway, and soon, all of the hunters came over to see what sort of deer they had pushed out. After everyone had taken turns gawking at the trophy, Doug decided it was time to start dragging him out. To the hunter's horror, as soon as they started pulling on the big-bodied animal, one antler popped free—then, the other! Against all odds, Doug had managed to shoot the buck just as he was about to shed his rack!

Incredibly, right after Doug Rhodus shot his great Ohio buck in January 1996, one antler popped off…and then the other! That rendered the deer unscorable, though he would have been the No.1 Longhunter typical "on the hoof" with a net score of over 200 points. Talk about bad luck! Photo by Rick Busse.

An undeniable irony of the scoring system is that sometimes, growing more antler can make a buck smaller!

Because shed antlers can't be measured officially for the Longhunter record book no matter what the circumstances, Doug's deer wasn't eligible for entry into the B&C listings and wasn't recognized as a new blackpowder world record, which he clearly had the size to become! Giving him a 22-inch inside spread, which appeared to be appropriate, his typical frame would have netted 211 4/8 and grossed 225 6/8. Even subtracting his 9 1/8 inches of abnormal points still would have left a stunning final score of 202 3/8 typical, far bigger than Dave Wilson's 193 2/8-point world record from Saskatchewan! In fact, that net score would have

placed the deer well up in B&C's Top 10.

Very few known typicals ever have grossed more than 100 inches on each antler; in fact, none of the official world records in this book do so. However, Doug's Ohio giant did, tallying 101 2/8 on the right side and 102 4/8 on the left! Without a doubt, he was plenty big enough to become the world record by muzzleloader. Had Doug shot him even a day or two earlier, the rack would not have fallen off and the Rhodus buck would be the Longhunter Society's top entry of all time.

In the fall of 1996, bowhunter Sam Collora shot the year's other legitimate contender for world-record status. But in the end, he too ran into some bad luck. Sam and wife Judi own and operate Mrs. Doe Pee deer lures in Mt. Pleasant, Iowa. Naturally, as part of Sam's "field research," he spends a lot of time each season "testing" these urine-based lures on trophy bucks. (It's a dirty job, but…well, you know the rest.)

On the afternoon of October 11, Sam looked downwind of his tree stand and spotted a huge buck following the estrous scent trail the hunter had made minutes earlier. When a shot was presented, Sam's arrow flew true. He soon found himself putting his tag onto one of the world's greatest bucks. A P&Y panel eventually gave the massive 8x6 a net score of 193 3/8 typical, good enough to be No.10 on the all-time list.

Sam Collora's massive 1996 Iowa buck fell short in his run at the P&Y typical record only because two typical-looking points on the right beam were judged to be non-typical, resulting in a net score of 193 3/8. Photo courtesy of Sam & Judi Collora, Mrs. Doe Pee's Buck Lures.

As high as that score would seem to be, anyone who has seen this rack will tell you the deer would have been an easy world record by bow—*if* he had not grown as much antler as he did! The panel ruled that the two extra points on the right antler were "non-symmetry" points. That means that, though the points appear to be typical, they are counted as non-typicals because they don't have matches on the other antler. This decision resulted in a whopping deduction of 12 5/8 inches. The bottom line is that had the Collora buck never grown those unmatched points at all—or broken them off before Sam shot him—he would have netted 206 typical! That would have made the Iowa monster the P&Y world record by 1 4/8 inches, and he would have become the No.3 B&C typical in the world, behind only the Hanson and Jordan bucks. But, it didn't happen that way. In the end, trophy enthusiasts were left to ponder an undeniable irony of the scoring system: Sometimes, growing more antler can make a buck *smaller!*

By now, it should be clear that a host of problems can prevent a potential world-record buck from actually becoming one. Judgment calls in scoring have kept some deer from reaching the pinnacle, while injured tines or even loose antlers have eliminated others from contention. Some bucks weren't entered soon enough, forever missing their chance to lay claim, even if only temporarily, to world-record status. Maybe what all this boils down to, as much as anything else, is simply bad luck. But then again, luck is a relative term. When you look at the incredible bucks we've just profiled, calling any of these hunters *un*lucky seems out of the question!

29

FACT
OR
FICTION,
RUMOR
OR
REALITY?

If you have ever wondered what it's like to be on the front lines in the search for the next world-record buck, now is your chance to find out. But, be forewarned—things aren't always as they seem!

There once was a boy who cried, "Wolf!" —not because he had actually *seen* one, of course, but because he loved the attention the resulting hysteria brought him. Did you ever wonder what became of that kid? Well, the older I get the more certain I am that he grew up to be a whitetail hunter!

For as long as record books have been around to honor trophy bucks, there have been wild claims about deer rumored to be even bigger. Many such "lies" start out innocently enough, perhaps nothing more than erroneous information dispensed by someone who doesn't know better. Others are outright fabrications meant to delude or even defraud. But regardless of the intent, the immediate result is much the same— plenty of frenzied scurrying as writers, record-book

measurers and antler collectors all seek to uncover the truth, if any, behind the rumor.

I decided to include a chapter on such tales because they play an annoyingly big role in the search for information about world-record deer. Rumors of this sort are rampant, and unfortunately, they can't very well be ignored. After all, every *true* story of a new No.1 buck essentially starts out unproved, so who is to say the next one won't be true? As a result, those of us in the whitetail media spend a fair amount of our time chasing down every lead we get, hoping the next rumor of a great deer will turn out to be legitimate—even if the last 50 haven't.

It takes a person with the right instincts, experience and contacts to excel at this search for the truth. Still, even accomplished antler-chasers get caught responding to far more false alarms than they would care to admit. All the following stories got the whitetail community buzzing at one time or another, though none concerned a legitimate world-record buck.

While this chronological review by no means includes every juicy world-record rumor, these tales should give you a good idea of the frustrations involved in searching for the next *real* record deer. Enjoy them all, if only for their entertainment value, and be glad you weren't the one left red-faced at the end!

This novel postcard, distributed around northern Wisconsin years ago, clearly claims the buck Mr. and Mrs. Homer Pearson shot in 1937 was a "world record." Someone mistakenly counted 103 points on the rack, leading to the inaccurate conclusion that the deer had to be the biggest ever. The buck ended up scoring 233 7/8 non-typical points. Postcard courtesy of John Pritzl.

FRIENDLY BUCKHORN," a bar in the town of Rice Lake, and proclaimed the animal as a "WORLD RECORD DEER."

The rack wasn't officially measured until years after the kill, and at no time was it given a potential No.1 score. What apparently led to the assertion that this buck was a "world record" was the unfounded claim that his rack had 103 points. That figure first popped up in a newspaper article shortly after the kill, and for some reason, it persisted. Officially, though, the rack has 31 points an inch or more in length—plenty, to be sure, but 72 fewer than claimed.

Wild exaggerations of the number of points on a whitetail's rack definitely can elicit rumors about world records. Fortunately, as the hunting public has become better versed in the nuances of the measuring system, such problems have diminished. Now, talk of a deer with a lot of points seldom goes far before someone rightly asks, "What does he actually *score?*"

72 POINTS TOO MANY

It would not be fair to classify Homer and Bea Pearson's 1937 non-typical from Polk County, Wisconsin, as any sort of a "hoax." He's very much a real buck, and a great one at that, netting an impressive 233 7/8 points. Even so, he belongs in this chapter because he was perhaps the first whitetail ever falsely touted as a "world record." Proving that such a claim was made is simple. Old postcards still exist that show the Pearsons and their rifles posed in front of the full-body-mounted buck. The postcard says the mount is "on display at the

POINT-SHAVING SCANDAL

In 1956, Minnesota produced one of the greatest typical whitetails the world has ever seen. Sal Ahrens, then a 29-year-old farmer, shot the buck on family property near Sauk Centre, but the huge typical wouldn't be measured for another 27 years. When that finally happened, the tape showed a net typical score of 212, enough to blow away Jim Jordan's B&C record of 206 1/8 (Chapter 6).

This naturally caused a major stir in the whitetail community. However, before the deer could be certified as a world record, taxidermist Alex Martin surprised everyone when he produced an old photo showing the same rack with *additional* short abnormals on the G-2 tines and the end of the left beam. Had those additional points been present when the rack was measured, it would have probably netted above 200 points but below the world-record mark. Someone, sometime, somewhere had altered the rack in an attempt to improve its net score.

Once that secret was out of the bag, the notion of the Ahrens buck ever becoming a world record quickly died because B&C has strict rules against accepting altered racks. Thus, one of the greatest bucks that ever walked was relegated to being a historical footnote rather than the star he really deserved to be. In case you're wondering, nobody ever quite figured out who removed those unwanted

Sal Ahrens' huge 1956 Minnesota typical looks like a world-record contender, but since several short abnormal points had been removed in an attempt to increase the rack's net typical score, the great buck was tragically disqualified from record consideration. As is, the buck nets around 212, easily enough to top the Jordan buck's then-B&C mark of 206 1/8. Photo courtesy of Tom Brown and John Morgan.

inches of antler. Truly, it was a point-shaving scandal of the first order!

BUSTED *PIÑATA?*

My own initial experience with world-record rumors came in 1983 when I was a freelance outdoor writer living in the Hill Country of Texas. I heard the rumor from an old hunting buddy, Pete Gipson, who had grown up on a ranch just down the road from my family's place. Through his contacts at work, Pete had heard that a guy from the South Texas town of Devine had a potential No.1 typical mounted in his garage, a buck he had supposedly shot the previous season in northeastern Mexico. The rack was gigantic by all accounts, supposedly netting in the ballpark of 245 B&C typical points. Now, that would be an incomprehensibly huge "ballpark" even today, but it was even more astounding back then since the Jordan buck had seldom even been seriously challenged as the world record. Then, as now, no known whitetail had ever even *grossed* 245 typical points, and here was a buck that supposedly would *net* that much! I had to learn more.

When I heard this rumor, I immediately phoned the offices of *North American WHITETAIL* magazine in Marietta, Georgia, and asked then-executive editor David Morris if he wanted me to do some digging. That's when I found out how quickly deer rumors spread. "We're working on it already," David informed me.

Here was a buck supposedly only a couple of hours from my home, and somebody halfway across the nation already knew more about it than I did! I could only sit back and wait to hear the news, which came in short order. The "antlers" turned out to have been more like a Mexican *piñata* than a real rack , for you see, they were made of *papier-mache!* The whole story was an outright hoax.

No known whitetail had ever even grossed 245 typical points, and here was a buck that supposedly would net that much!

Based on the outcome of this rumor, you might think the entire incident was a waste of time. Yet, from that single episode, I learned a lot about the pattern that world-record rumors often follow. Let's look specifically at three main points:

There was indeed a huge set of "antlers" to serve as a catalyst for the story. Once a credible person actually saw the "trophy," it was immediately recognized as a fake. In the meantime, just the rumor that somebody had seen a huge, mysterious deer head hanging in a hunter's garage fueled hopes that it was indeed real. Remember, this was less than two years after the shocking revelation that a new No.1 nontypical scoring 333 7/8 points really had been found dead in St. Louis County, Missouri, beating the old world record from Texas by nearly 50 inches. As a result, many whitetail fanatics woke up every morning half-expecting to hear that the Jordan buck had

been bumped off the top of the typical category. In such an atmosphere, it was only natural to mobilize the troops in a hurry whenever a rumor surfaced.

The deer reportedly had been killed in a region known for producing trophy bucks. It wouldn't do much good to spread a lie about a world record from an area where huge-racked deer were extremely rare or even non-existent. But in this case, the location—the Rio Grande region of Mexico—made it plausible. While that part of the world had no track record of producing 200-inch typicals, the fact that it contained so many vast, relatively unexplored ranches led many observers to believe it capable of such a stunner. Even if the buck didn't net 245, he might still be bigger than 206 1/8. After all, Mexico had produced some real bruisers over the years.

The hunter at first insisted that the story was true but then backed off as serious investigators pressed for details. The "rack" had apparently been something of a practical joke to start with, but then, the situation escalated out of the guy's control. He could have doused the fire early on by being honest about his little gag, but he apparently thought it was fun to string everyone along. Once he realized the callers were persistent and more knowledgeable about antlers than he was, he at least had the good sense to 'fess up. Of course, by then the damage to his reputation had been done.

For me, this episode proved to be not only fascinating but also educational. I had always known there were individuals who wouldn't hesitate to poach a trophy buck, but now, I realized some folks were just as willing to *build* one. As we'll see, it wouldn't be the last time, either.

WHITETAIL, MULIE OR BOTH ?

Most serious deer hunters would claim that, even at a glance, it's easy to tell big whitetail antlers from those of mule deer. And in the majority of cases, they would be right. The G-2 tines of mature mulies usually are noticeably longer than those of whitetails and are often forked. Plus, the main beams and brow tines commonly are shorter than those of mature whitetails. And, some fairly obvious differences in the patterns of beading around the bases and brow tines are often indicators of species. When several of the mulie-like traits are present in a rack from the Great Plains or Rocky Mountains regions, the logical assumption is that you're looking at mulie antlers. Throw in a wide spread, and the chances are even better that the rack didn't come from a whitetail.

But oh, those exceptions to the rule will get you. Mulies sometimes have G-2s of moderate length, and they aren't always forked. Mulies don't always have wide racks, either, or short brow tines or short main beams or distinctive beading, for that matter. As a result, when several "whitetail" features are seen on a mulie rack, confusion quickly arises. What makes this relevant to our discussion is that every so often a huge rack turns up with no photos or other proof of which type of deer it adorned. In such instances, proper identification of species is especially critical to keep a rack from going into the wrong category, perhaps even as a bogus "world record."

A set of antlers evoking considerable confusion as to what species it belonged turned up after the 1986 Saskatchewan deer season. The hunter in question, young Rick Peters, was at the time a novice, so when he described the deer carrying this huge rack as a "whitetail," there was some skepticism. However, no such dispersions were cast upon the quality of the rack, for it clearly was that of a gigantic deer. The basic 5x5 was scored by a measurer for the provincial record book at 202 1/8 net points, which would have made it the second-best 10-pointer in the world behind only the Jordan buck. And if an 8 6/8-inch abnormal point off the right G-3 tine weren't absent, the net score would have been over 210, easily enough to make Rick's trophy a world record!

What is it? A contender for the B&C crown as the world's biggest typical whitetail? Maybe – but probably not. While young Rick Peters believed his 1986 Saskatchewan giant is a whitetail, he couldn't provide any real evidence to back up the claim. Most experts believe the rack is from a mule deer or perhaps a mulie-whitetail cross, rather than a pure whitetail. Whatever the rack is from, it's tremendous! Photo by Don Schwab.

Was the Saskatchewan deer indeed a whitetail? Good question. Rick claimed it was but didn't take a single field photo to provide proof. Nor did he save the cape since he merely whacked off the skull plate and had the rack mounted on a plaque. By the time Rick started showing off the antlers that winter, there was little tangible evidence to support his claim that he had taken one of the world's biggest whitetails.

In 1998, I carried the accompanying photo to an annual meeting of some of the brightest minds in the field of whitetail management and research. When I showed the photo around, each person was stunned by the rack's size but serious questions were raised about whether the rack had been grown by a whitetail or a mulie. Several researchers, in fact, noted that it had some trademark features of each, suggesting that perhaps the buck was a hybrid. When I then noted that the deer had come from an area containing both species, several of the experts had even greater doubts about the animal having been a pure whitetail.

Don Schwab of Saskatoon, Saskatchewan, who sent me the photo of the rack, has changed his own mind about the deer's bloodlines over the years. "Originally, I thought it was a whitetail," he told me. "But the more I looked at it, the more I decided it wasn't. Virtually everywhere you find whitetails in Saskatchewan, you'll find some mulies as well. In my 30 years of hunting in the province, I've seen at least three deer I fully believe were hybrids. Maybe Rick's deer was one, too."

The buck never was entered into the B&C whitetail records, so perhaps the question is moot. To Rick's credit, I really doubt the young hunter was trying to fool anyone. It just seems more likely that he shot either a hybrid or a very whitetail-looking mulie. In case you're wondering, a hybrid *can* be entered into the B&C, P&Y or Longhunter records, but only in the species listing with the higher minimum entry requirement, meaning it must be entered as a mulie.

BIG AS A "MOOSE"

As noted, a world-record rumor that originates in a well-known trophy area is much more likely to be taken seriously than one that isn't. Add in a backwoods hunter with no apparent reason to draw attention to himself, and the rumor sounds even better. The combination of these elements is why a story coming out of eastern Canada in the late 1980s got so many folks buzzing. A guy reportedly had shot a new No. 1 typical in New Brunswick, which in 1937 had produced a world record and is still considered to be a "sleeper" area for trophy whitetails. By all accounts, the hunter who had taken this new buck was low key and generally uninterested in all the commotion surrounding his deer.

The most suspicious part of the equation was the dimensions of the buck in question. Rumor had it that the rack had an inside spread in excess of 30 inches and main beams somewhere in the neighborhood of 40 inches apiece! (Thirty-inch inside spreads are extremely rare, and only a handful of known bucks have had even one beam of over 31 inches, with none in any record book as long as 34.) I was told that the gross typical score was in the 240 range and that the basic 7x7 would net well in excess of 220!

I pondered whether or not to pack my bags and head for the airport to see this marvel of nature but elected to stay put. The deer simply sounded too big to be real, and there was no guarantee I would be allowed to see it even if I traveled to the hunter's rural home. I decided to wait for more "facts" to surface. Fortunately, that didn't take long.

◆

I was told that the gross typical score was in the 240 range and that the basic 7x7 would net well in excess of 220!

◆

It was a rack, all right—a *moose* rack! Your first reaction is that nobody smarter than a turnip could confuse the rack of a Canadian moose with that of a whitetail. However, in this case, the antlers had been altered considerably, with the clear intention of passing off the rack as something it wasn't. The guy had done it by sawing away large areas of the "palms" of the moose rack and rounding off the edges so that what was left simulated a huge-framed whitetail rack. I was glad I hadn't made the trip, though it might have been intriguing to see the concoction firsthand.

Shortly after the New Brunswick hoax was defused, I decided to try making my own "whitetail" rack from moose antlers just to see if it could be done convincingly. Rather than break out a saw, though, I went looking for a moose rack that already resembled the headgear of a big buck. I found it in the taxidermy shop of a friend. One of his clients had shot a moose in Siberia sorely lacking in palmation. To set up the accompanying photos, I laid a whitetail cape in the snow and then positioned the moose rack *backwards* on it. With the "beams" pointing at the viewer and a little strategically placed snow to reduce the amount of palmation visible, the rack bore a remarkable resemblance to a big-framed whitetail rack. By the way, scored as a whitetail rack, this smallish moose would have grossed just over 210 B&C points, making it the highest scoring basic 4x4 "whitetail" of all time!

While I never actually saw photos of the New Brunswick fake, my impression is that it didn't look as much like a whitetail rack as did the moose rack I turned into a set of whitetail antlers. So, how did that wild rumor ever find its way out of Canada?

Good friend George Chase, an avid New

Brunswick hunter, outfitter and record-book organizer, told me he believed the rack's owner had taken the fake, presented as the antlers of a whitetail, to his taxidermist to have it put on a plaque. The taxidermist apparently then spilled the beans to a measurer for the provincial record book, who in turn went to the home of the rack's owner and asked to see it himself. He was met with a rather icy reception, though he previously had scored one of this fellow's legitimate deer racks. Finally, after rattling off an imaginative tale about having found the antlers in a frozen pond (or was it on a remote snowmobile trail?), the owner reluctantly consented to give his visitor a peek at the mounted rack. It was being kept in a wood-shed just dark enough to make the measurer think what he was seeing and measuring was real.

Only after George finally got his hands on the measurer's photos of the rack, saw how weird the antlers looked and started asking hard questions did the truth about the hoax finally come out.

Just an interesting side note. While reviewing my documents regarding the moose-rack events in preparation to write this chapter, I came across a note I had received from someone with information to share about the "whitetail." From his assertions,

With a bit of effort and imagination, a moose rack can be made to resemble a gigantic whitetail rack. The author combined this small rack of a Siberian moose with the cape of an Ohio deer to show how it might be possible to pass off the "trophy" as a world-record whitetail. Photo by Tom Evans.

all admittedly from secondhand sources, you can see how even total fabrications can be made to sound authentic. This is the gist of what his note claimed: (1) the rack was real; (2) the owner had turned down $10,000 for the rack from two potential buyers in the U.S.; and (3) the owner had the idea that if he talked much about this "deer," his hunting area would be flooded with "every hunter in North America." Sounds authentic, doesn't it?

THE "BARNACLE" BUCK

A rack's frame need not be shockingly big to send a jolt through the whitetail community. Proof of that came from Mahoning County, Ohio, in 1989, when Lionel Crissman came forth with an amazing buck skull that one of his friends had found in a local swamp.

I met Lionel at the Deer Hunters' Rendezvous at Pine Lake that December and saw the strange rack firsthand. It was clearly from what is known as a "cactus" buck, i.e., a sterile buck lacking the hormonal triggers necessary to regulate antler growth. Unlike Sammy Walker's Louisiana freak from 1958 (Chapter 28), this deer had an easily distinguishable typical frame and all the abnormal points sprouted from the main beams or typical points, giving the

Ohio's bizarre "Barnacle" buck raised new questions about scoring non-typical whitetails. The animal that grew this strange rack apparently had hormonal problems, causing his antler growth to continue long after it should have ended. Official measurer Bill Cooper counted 72 legal points on the rack, but in the end, B&C decided to reject all entries of such "cactus" racks. Photo by Gordon Whittington.

appearance of a normal set of antlers encrusted with barnacles. This unique look gave rise to the deer's nickname, the "Barnacle" buck.

Though the antlers were most interesting, I gave little thought to their score since literally hundreds of the "points" obviously were less than an inch in length. Then, several months later, I got a call from friend Paul Thomas, a taxidermist in North Lima. According to Paul, he and another deer enthusiast had unofficially measured the highly unusual rack. It took them hours to do so because many of the points were in the form of exaggerated beading and were wedged tightly together. The only way to measure them was by inserting a flexible wire down through the "crevices," marking the length of each point and then laying the wire against a steel tape to get the measurement. When this was done, the men were stunned to learn that they had come up with *134 measurable points*—50 on the right antler, 84 on the left—and a net non-typical score of 343 1/8!

Would this strange deer really outscore Missouri's 333 7/8-point world record? It seemed incomprehensible, and Paul certainly wasn't making any promises. Still, the deer obviously had to be checked out by an expert, so when the rack was at the offices of *North American WHITETAIL* a few weeks later, I asked official B&C measurer Bill Cooper to give me his opinion. Bill studied the rack for a long time and then began to make his first exploratory measurements. When he finished the laborious measuring process several hours later, his numbers showed "only" 72 scorable points and a net non-typical score of "only" 257 7/8. Bill disallowed 62 of the projections that earlier had been ruled to be a full inch in length.

Even at this drastically reduced score, the Barnacle buck would have the distinction of possessing far more scorable points than any other deer in the record book. (At this writing, the 50-mark has never been broken.) However, that honor failed to materialize. A few months after Bill measured the rack, B&C's Records Committee announced that any "cactus" buck was ineligible for entry, even if the rack in question had a recognizable typical frame. So, the buck never made it into the record book at *any* score. Still, he remains one of history's special deer.

A LOT OF BUCK …OR ALL BULL?

Rumors spread quickly enough by word of mouth, but if you really want something to travel at warp speed, get it onto one of the wire services that newspapers and broadcasting companies use to stay informed of breaking events. By utilizing such technology, a lie can be spread all over North America in less time than it takes you to read this paragraph.

Sadly, that's just what happened in the fall of 1988 when a strange deer-hunting story hit the wire. It originated in the eastern Kentucky town of Harlan but quickly found its way into the far corners of the continent. And, it apparently ended up costing at least one newspaper reporter his job. Here's how the story appeared on the wire, except that I've substituted fictitious names for those of the jokers involved:

Harlan, Ky.—Every sportsman dreams of bagging a trophy size deer when he takes to the woods.

Every hunter hopes that his trophy will be of sufficient size to make an attractive addition to the den wall.

Fred Smith is no exception. Only the latest addition to be added to the Jones trophy wall is not just trophy size and is not just large enough to make an attractive display—it is world record size.

Smith's latest deer has been certified as the Boone & Crockett world-record-holder typical buck, based on antler size, spread and configuration.

Smith bagged the record-breaking whitetail deer Dec. 10, his first day of a hunting trip in Barnhart, Mo., a rural community in the southeastern part of the state along the Mississippi River.

He was accompanied on the trip by hunting companions Bob Bullet and Sam Slug.

"We went to Missouri to hunt after we got our limit of six deer, one each with bows and one each with guns," Smith said.

The deer Smith bagged broke the world record of 234 points that had stood for more than 12 years, and he broke it by more than 60 points.

The trophy buck was taken on land owned by a power company in Missouri that gave the three men permission to hunt there.

"We got to Barnhart early in the morning on Dec. 10. We got our licenses and tags and got to the field about nine in the morning. We drove across this field of grass to the edge of the woods and left our vehicles there and split up to hunt," Smith recalled.

He told of taking a portable tree stand, a device that locks around a tree and provides the hunter with an elevated seat from which to watch for his quarry, into the woods to begin looking for "deer signs," some rubs and scrapes (signs male deer leave to mark their territory). "I figured that would be a good place to set up," he said.

"About an hour passed and I glanced over my left shoulder and saw this big buck grazing his way across the same field we had crossed. The wind was blowing

away from me and toward him, and he would lift his head and wind the air, sniffing the deer lure I was using," he said.

He said the lure was a combination of commercial deer attractor mixed with a homemade formula he and his hunting companions have been having pretty good luck with over the past four years.

"I just turned around and, using a limb for a rest, I just waited for him. All I could see through the scope was this massive set of antlers. I let him get to within about 150 yards and then shot him broadside. He ran for about 100 feet and took a nosedive into the dirt."

------◆------

Don't rely too heavily on big-city wire services for the straight story on world-record whitetails.

------◆------

"I went over and field dressed him, knowing I had a big deer, but never guessing just how big. I sat down on him and waited for my buddies to come in. I sat on the deer because I have had five big bucks I have killed stolen, including one this year. I wasn't about to take a chance on letting somebody get away with this one."

The animal was taken to a deer check station, and it was only then Smith began to get the feeling it was something special.

"They seemed to get kind of excited about it. We took a yardstick and could move it back and forth between the widest part of the antlers. They called a game warden, and he came over and told me I likely had a Missouri state record buck and if it proved to be one, they would mount it free of charge."

The deer was skinned and the head, cape and antlers were left in Missouri. Since then, Joey Lucas, commissioner of the Missouri Department of Conservation, has since called him with details of the record and how the determination was made that the buck was in fact sporting the largest rack of antlers of

any whitetail deer ever taken, anywhere in the world.

According to Lucas, Smith's record was calculated by three Boone & Crockett officials to be 298 and four-eighths typical points on the B&C scale.

"This means quite a bit of money for John Smith," Lucas said, indicating Smith will be receiving requests for endorsements and promotions of hunting products and purchases of his story from hunting magazines and enthusiasts.

"I've killed a whole lot of deer and some pretty big ones, but never anything this big," Smith said.

Smith, a coal miner for 14 years and former coal mine operator, has been told there is a lot of notoriety that accompanies taking a world record deer and he looks on the possibility with a certain degree of skepticism.

"It would be nice, though, to be able to make a little money off of something you love to do as much as I love to hunt," he said.

The trophy is now in the hands of the Missouri taxidermist, and it may be as much as three months before the job is completed and Smith gets his prize here.

"But, it'll be worth waiting for," he said.

Following this text was a more specific description of the rack:

Smith's deer measured 10 inches in circumference at the base of the main antler beams, 39 inches in length for each beam, 32 inches in the spread of the beams from tip to tip, 41 inches of outside spread at its widest point, and the buck weighed 278 pounds field dressed. The animal was approximately six years old.

Well, I guess if you're going to tell a bald-faced lie, you might as well make it a good one—and whoever originated this story did exactly that. Of course, to anyone even halfway familiar with the B&C scoring system and/or Missouri deer hunting, this was obviously a hoax from the first moment. But, it still managed to get onto nothing less than the New York Times Wire Service, just because a bunch of non-hunters blindly assumed every bit of it was the gospel truth. In retrospect, *nothing* about it was.

The "hunters" in question couldn't be located. Missouri's gun season wasn't even open on December 10. The typical B&C record was 206 1/8 points, not the 234 points mentioned. No Joey Lucas was serving as commissioner of the Missouri wildlife department. We could go on but you get the idea.

How this mess ever reached print remains one of the more vexing mysteries of modern journalism. There was a byline on the article, but when I contacted the *Harlan Daily Enterprise* to speak with that writer, I was told he was "no longer employed" there. The general impression I got was that everyone in the newspaper office wished the entire episode had just been a bad dream, but that wasn't the case.

The moral of this bizarre story? Just as you probably shouldn't count on outdoor writers to explain the inner workings of Congress, don't rely too heavily on big-city wire services for the straight story on world-record whitetails!

It's not a crime to use a wide-angle lens to make a buck look bigger, but it can be if the resulting photos are used to defraud someone. Here, Barry Leach recreates how an unscrupulous outfitter used a wide-angle shot of Barry's big Nebraska typical, which actually scored 173 6/8, to make the deer look like a potential world-record specimen. The outfitter's photo of the unmounted rack was even more exaggerated than this. Photo courtesy of Barry Leach.

ANYTHING FOR A BUCK?

I suppose we'll never know if the motivation for spreading that rumor of a 298 4/8-point Missouri buck was pure greed, but a 1994 scam involving a Michigan outfitter clearly was. The guy wanted to drum up some attention for his Nebraska whitetail hunts, and he knew exactly how to do it—by suggesting that a potential world-record typical had been taken on land he and his partner had leased for hunting.

Barry Leach, a resident of Hyannis, Nebraska, had legally shot a gorgeous 173 6/8-point B&C typical in Grant County in the fall of 1991. But before anyone outside the small town even knew the deer was dead, the outfitter in question tracked the deer to a local taxidermy shop and had his partner shoot some photos of him holding the rack. The photos were taken with a wide-angle lens that so grossly exaggerated the wide, heavy rack that it really did have the look of a world-record contender.

Within two months, the outfitter was flashing these photos at major hunting shows. At one, he cornered a writer and assured him that the rack was as big as it looked, with a gross typical score around

230 and a net in the range of 220. The guy repeatedly told everyone that his partner had shot the deer the previous season on the ranch they had leased, and—in case any potential clients might be wondering—this wasn't the only monster on the place. (Surprise, surprise.)

What brought the deer into public view was a magazine article in the spring of 1994, in which the alleged "new potential world-record typical" was shown and discussed in print for the first time. Not coincidentally in my opinion, this article came out shortly after the magazine publishing the story had been scooped on the breaking story of Milo Hanson's *real* world-record typical from Saskatchewan. That prompted many whitetail insiders to figure the story was as much a marketing ploy by the publication as a serious "news" report. The photos of the Nebraska buck had been circulating for three years at that point, but no one else had chosen to publish them. There were simply too many hints that something about that deer story wasn't quite right.

The writer who had authored that magazine article eventually told investigators for the Nebraska Game and Parks Commission that he suspected something about the outfitter's story was amiss. The

A simple clerical error caused Iowa shotgun hunter Don Boucher's huge 245 3/8-point buck to be incorrectly listed as a typical rather than a non-typical in the Iowa Department of Natural Resources' all-time whitetail rankings. Because no photo of the buck accompanied that printed list, many assumed the deer was a new world-record typical, kicking the rumor mill into overdrive. This photo should help end any remaining speculation that the rack is typical. Photo courtesy of Don Boucher.

investigator began to check into the situation, and in no time at all, the outfitter's story unraveled because he had overlooked one critical detail—a metal tag on the rack.

That tag, quite visible in the magazine photo, proved the deer in question had been checked in at a Commission check station. But, a review of state records showed that the outfitter's partner, who had reportedly shot the buck in 1991, had not even received a Nebraska firearm permit for that area that year. The state investigator told U.S. Fish and Wildlife Service agents that he had reason to think the rack had been illegally tagged, leading federal agents to pay the outfitter a visit at his home in Michigan. Upon being confronted with the possibility of heavy-duty charges regarding interstate transport of illegal wildlife, he immediately confessed his elaborate scheme.

In the end, no state or federal charges ever were brought against the outfitter. Technically, he hadn't done anything worse than lying. Had a client booked a hunt with him strictly on the basis of this photo, however, that well could have constituted fraud. But, apparently no such case ever was made and the scheme went unpunished.

The real shame in this story is that Barry Leach and his beautiful buck were indirectly involved in this whole ugly scene. Both deserved better!

ONE BIG CLERICAL ERROR

As we've seen, a very real trophy buck can become a world-record "pretender" in quite innocent fashion. If you need still more proof, ask Iowa's Don Boucher.

In 1996, the Albion resident was participating in a Marshall County deer drive when a tremendous non-typical buck appeared. Don's aim was true, and seconds later, he had the buck of his dreams on the ground. In short order, Iowa's biggest whitetail of the season was officially measured and entered into the state record book maintained by the Department of Natural Resources (IDNR).

Everything was going perfectly to this point. Then, while preparing the list of Iowa's all-time top whitetails for inclusion in the September-October 1997 issue of *Iowa Conservationist* magazine, someone made an unfortunate mistake. Don's great non-typical—all 245 3/8 points' worth of him—accidentally got placed onto the *typical* list instead. You can

Several copies of this fake "world-record typical" are floating around North America at present. The anonymous joker who submitted this photo to North American WHITETAIL *in 1997 claimed the "buck" had been shot in Iowa by his/her cousin and would net over 229 typical points. Not surprisingly, no further information was provided.*

probably imagine what followed.

Even though the listings were printed in very small type, as soon as that magazine reached readers, calls started pouring into IDNR. Hunters all over the state wanted to know about this Iowa deer that was going to blow away Milo Hanson's 213 5/8-point Saskatchewan buck (Chapter 7) as the world-record typical! Compounding the problem was the fact that the year of kill for Don's deer erroneously was shown as 1961, suggesting that someone had dragged an old, moth-eaten mount out of a closet and had it measured for the first time. Before long, folks from all over were calling me and asking about this new "mystery" buck.

Today, the only "mystery" was how such an error could be made. Of course, being in the magazine business myself, I would be the last to throw stones. Such a glitch certainly could happen to anyone. And hey, look at the bright side: It did prove that people actually read the fine print!

FIBERGLASS FINAGLINGS

When industry began to develop synthetic materials for a variety of uses, it was only "natural" that these began to find their way into the taxidermy business. Various wood putties and assorted polymers, including fiberglass, have given the modern taxidermist more ability than ever to repair broken antlers, chipped bear teeth, etc. Unfortunately, in the hands of the wrong person, such materials also are tailor-made for manufacturing big racks.

Although altered and even completely synthetic whitetail antlers have been around for some time, until fairly recently they had spawned few good world-record rumors. As recently as 1980, taxidermy materials and techniques were still relatively crude, antler collectors were few and far between and there was no network of specialized media clamoring to publicize every new No.1 deer. All of those factors reduced the probability of high-quality fakes showing up. After all, fabricating racks was difficult and there simply wasn't much incentive to try to fool anybody with one. Sure, guys occasionally would come up with the idea of attaching more points to an old rack lying in the rafters, but it was usually just to play a joke on a hunting buddy.

While it is difficult to pass off as the real McCoy a fiberglass replica to a seasoned collector or measurer, some unscrupulous types are becoming ever-

Several years ago, this "rack" showed up in Arkansas and caused quite a stir among those who wondered if it was a real world-record typical. The person who owned it claimed to have received it in trade for a mule deer while hunting in the Colorado mountains the previous fall. Ultimately, this 240-class "rack" was traced to an antler fabricator from the Southwest. Photo courtesy of Kenneth Mullins.

more skillful at "improving" real antlers. One of the more common ways is by adding or lengthening points to achieve the desired net score. If there's reason to doubt the authenticity of antlers, X-raying them will answer many such questions in a hurry. But, not many of us keep X-ray equipment around so this technique requires time, trouble and expense. And on a typical rack, even a high-tech approach can't prove broken abnormal points weren't intentionally snapped off or otherwise shortened to achieve a higher net score.

At any rate, there have been many attempts to fool the whitetail world with manufactured or altered antlers of outlandish size. The accompanying photos show a few of the more notable world-record fakes (some, of course, more realistic than others) that have been "discovered" in the past few years.

NO END IN SIGHT?

One day, perhaps, the jokers out there will grow tired of such games. But, I believe it's wishful thinking to believe the rumor mill ever will stop turning. To prove it, I kept track of the rumors of "new world records" I heard during and following the

1997 hunting season, which was pretty average in terms of stories spun.

Leading off was a rumor coming out of the mountains of northern Virginia. The tale had it that a guy named Roy Hilliard had shot what might well turn out to be a new No.1 typical by muzzleloader. The person who called our office at *North American WHITETAIL* to tell us about the buck didn't insist he would outscore Dave Wilson's 193 2/8-pointer from Saskatchewan, but he felt the buck had a good shot at that title. I spoke with Roy shortly thereafter and learned that the buck had a gross score in the high 180s. This 27-inch-wide 5x5 ended up netting just under 180 and was a new state record by blackpowder, but far from No.1 in the world.

By early December, another intriguing tale was floating on the wind. This one involved a new No.1 B&C typical that reportedly had been shot in western Saskatchewan. The deer was rumored to score in excess of 215 net typical points and was said to have come from the town of Macland, roughly an hour west of where the 213 5/8-point Hanson buck had been shot in 1993. Despite considerable effort, I never could find anyone who had actually seen the Macland buck. Finally, the truth surfaced.

Apparently, a 215-point-class buck had been shot in those parts…a 215-point non-typical! Big but no world record.

A week or so later came word of a southern Kansas typical that would net "around 220 points," again several inches bigger than the Hanson buck. Nothing more ever came of that story.

Next was talk about a non-typical taken in the Rio Grande Valley of South Texas that somebody claimed was a "new world record." According to the story, the buck bore 41 scorable points and was bigger than the 333 7/8-point Missouri Monarch. In truth, the buck turned out to have 29 scorable points and a net non-typical score of just under 200 points. It was a monster, to be sure, but far from the world's biggest. Indeed, at least two other Texas bucks from that same season outscored him by a wide margin.

Then, it was Ohio's turn. A friend called me in January to report that he had heard a 5x5 netting in the neighborhood of 230 typical points had been confiscated from a poacher in the southern part of the state. As the story went, the deer had been shot at night, and on top of that, the deed had been done with a high-powered rifle, both serious no-no's. Given all of this, I suppose it is fortunate that the

Fortunately, not everyone who owns a fake or altered "world record" tries to pass it off as real. The antler enthusiast who had this one crafted makes no claim that it's real but simply gets satisfaction from looking at the mount and showing it to fellow hunters. The owner won't even tell anyone what the "rack" would score if it were real, but the tally likely would approach 230 net typical points.

poached deer ended up scoring "only" 183 typical, far less than rumored.

Finally, another phone call turned up word of a new world-record non-typical from central Ohio. The rumor sounded good, and because it was coming from a state with a history of gigantic non-typicals, I knew it had to be pursued. Several phone calls later, I found myself talking to one of the proprietors of a taxidermy shop north of Columbus, a woman who quickly dispelled any notions about world records. "I'm afraid," she said, "that somebody's been pulling your leg." Well, it obviously wasn't the first time, and unfortunately, it won't be the last. That comes with the territory, I suppose.

As long as folks are interested in world-record whitetails, some of us will be out there looking and listening for any sign of that next historic buck. With each new rumor, we feel that surge of adrenaline because we can't help but wonder if this is the one that will pan out. What keeps us waiting and wondering is the fact that every so often a buck does come along big enough to dethrone every buck that has ever preceded him.

Nowadays, with the great bucks that already sit atop their respective heaps, that makes for a very BIG story indeed!

Usually, a person who goes to the trouble of fabricating a rack makes it outlandishly big for greater shock value. Sometimes, copies of the artificial rack are made. This was the case with this fake whitetail "rack" adorning the wall of a Wyoming restaurant. Another one identical to it (except for darker coloring) hangs in a South Dakota establishment, and there might be even more copies out there. Photo courtesy of Tim Condict.

PULLING IT ALL TOGETHER

"No matter how well conceived such a strategy might be, it almost certainly is destined to failure when a world record is the target because of extraordinarily long odds. But even if I came up empty, I don't know that we should call it failure."

I just might know as much about world-record whitetails as anyone ever has. This certainly shouldn't be construed as bragging, but rather as a simple acknowledgment of the unique path my career has taken. You can't serve as editor of *North American WHITETAIL* for 14 years without coming to know history's biggest bucks and the hunters who took them almost as family. And, you certainly can't write a 100,000-word book on these amazing trophies without discovering whatever common ground exists among them. This ground is well worth exploring, for within its borders must lie the "secret," if there is one, to bagging a record-breaking buck.

Because history so often has a way of repeating itself, it would seem logical for the hunter who wants to shoot a No.1 whitetail to study how it has happened in the past. If that's the case, what can we learn from a century's worth of these trophies that might improve your chances of bagging a top-ranked trophy? When we objectively analyze the facts behind the great deer presented here, some interesting patterns do emerge. Among them are several I believe are worth noting:

1. Most world records and world-record contenders have come from north of the 37th Parallel.

This east-west line intersects North America in southern Virginia and extends westward to just south of San Francisco, California, separating Oklahoma from Kansas en route. In a rough sense, it also separates the historic ranges of several of the bigger-bodied whitetail subspecies, such as *Odocoileus virginianus borealis* and *O. v. dakotensis*, from those of some smaller ones, such as *O. v. texanus* and *O. v. mcilhennyi*.

A biological axiom known as Bergman's Rule essentially states that as you move closer to the earth's poles, animal populations tend to be made up of progressively more robust (larger) specimens, a necessary adaptation for retaining body heat. If you care to look at it another way, you could say that animal populations living closer to the equator tend to be made up of less robust (smaller) specimens so as to better shed excess body heat. No matter how you choose to express the principle, what it means is that if you're looking for bigger deer head to colder climes.

———◆———

When we objectively analyze the facts behind the great deer presented here, some interesting patterns do emerge.

———◆———

What does body size have to do with antler size? Plenty. On average, the larger a buck's body, the less genetically exceptional he must be in order to produce world-class antlers. Interestingly, the very largest-bodied *individual* bucks seldom seem to have the highest-scoring racks, but there is clearly a relationship between a *subspecies'* average body size and average antler mass. As the top whitetail scores continue to inch upwards, the advantage of Northern deer over Southern deer likely will become even greater –particularly in the non-typical category, in which the next world-record rack is likely to weigh at least 13 pounds!

2. Most world records and world-record contenders have come from areas with restricted hunting pressure on bucks.

While a single gigantic whitetail could turn up virtually anywhere, the odds of taking a world-record specimen are best in areas where mature bucks make up a fair percentage of the overall deer population. Many years ago this was fairly common, but in more recent times, heavy hunting pressure has greatly reduced the average age of bucks in most herds.

Good buck:doe ratios and a balanced age structure can be achieved through various means, such as setting a short firearms season; not allowing firearms hunting during the rut; limiting the number of hunters; restricting the type of weapon; lowering bag limits; and/or restricting the buck harvest to older animals via some type of size limit. Today, as a rule, the best trophy hunting is in areas where one or more such restrictions are in place or in the remote fringe regions of the whitetail's range.

3. Most world records and world-record contenders have had access to agricultural plantings.

North America's whitetail range is dotted with literally millions of fertile fields, many of them planted with crops that are both attractive and beneficial to deer. It is no coincidence that the record books are dominated by bucks from agricultural regions. The Midwest and central Canada in particular have big edges in this regard. Large areas of the fertile prairies are intensively farmed and provide deer with an ideal blend of warm-season protein (soybeans, alfalfa and other legumes) and cool-season carbohydrates (corn, wheat, and other grains), resulting in big, healthy bucks. The benefits of enhanced nutrition are not limited to the Midwest and central Canada; they also can be seen wherever agriculture is found. So important is agriculture that there wouldn't even be whitetails in some of the best trophy country in central Canada today without it! And, there wouldn't be nearly as many big bucks in a lot of places if agriculture wasn't there to provide high-quality feed.

4. Most world records and world-record contenders have been taken in areas with relatively low deer densities.

Maybe this is just another way of saying that big deer tend to be well-fed deer. Regardless, there's no denying that areas overcrowded with whitetails seldom, if ever, produce world-record bucks. The nutrition required for producing a huge rack is simply too hard to come by in overpopulated habitat.

◆

A trophy hunter should practice shooting at moving targets, just in case.

◆

The Jordan buck from Wisconsin (1914), the Breen buck from Minnesota (1918) and the Luckey buck from New York (1939) are all products of the herd-expansion era when deer populations were low and nutritious food was abundant.

5. Many world records and world-record contenders were taken during the rut …but many others weren't.

We all know mature bucks are relatively visible and vulnerable when they're preoccupied with breeding. Thus, you would assume that hunter success on world-class bucks would be highest during this time. Interestingly, though, a fair percentage of the world's top whitetails—Jerry Polesky's Montana typical by bow and Bob Bromm's Indiana non-typical by blackpowder, for instance—have been harvested well outside the breeding period, suggesting that the rut isn't the only productive time to hunt trophy deer.

6. Most world records and world-record contenders have been taken as a result of forced movement.

Even during the rut, only rarely do you encounter a gigantic buck that moves around much in daylight. This pattern seems to hold true regardless of habitat type or the degree of hunting pressure. So, it shouldn't surprise us to learn that most successful hunter encounters with world-class

whitetails have been the result of forced movement—some intentional, others accidental. From the 1958 hunt for Bobby Triplett's North Dakota buck to Milo Hanson's 1993 rendezvous with the current world-record typical, the majority of these animals were pushed out of their hiding spots. And so, No.7 on our list shouldn't come as a surprise.

7. Many world records and world-record contenders have been shot on the run.

No deer hunter in his right mind prefers to shoot at a moving target, especially one that's moving rapidly. But, many hunters who have taken world-record whitetails had little choice—shoot at a running buck or don't shoot at all.

What's most amazing is to review the bowhunting records and see just how many of those bucks were shot on the move. For example, the three whitetails honored as Pope and Young world records in 1960 all were arrowed on the run. Frankly, it's hard to advocate flinging arrows at running deer, regardless of how "easy" the shot might seem, but there's no denying that some such opportunities have been turned into world-record trophies. What this suggests, perhaps, is that a trophy hunter should practice shooting at moving targets, just in case.

And so…

Successful trophy hunting is a game of odds. The more you can stack those odds in your favor, the better your chances. With this in mind, my suggestion to anyone wanting a world-record whitetail is simple: Look for that rare situation in which you can put the percentages to work for you. If taking a No.1 buck was a matter of life and death for me—and I'm thankful it isn't—here's what I would try and where I would try it.

First, I would head to an agricultural area known for producing top-end whitetails in recent years. My choice would be somewhere in the Midwest or central Canada. Second, I would hunt with a muzzleloader. While the top-ranked typicals and non-typicals in the Longhunter Society record book are stunningly big, they score less than the top bucks in either the B&C or P&Y rankings. Because of this and the effectiveness of modern muzzleloaders, the blackpowder records are more likely to be broken next, at least in theory.

---◆---

For those who pursue trophy bucks for the right reasons, the attraction lies at least as much in the journey as in the destination.

---◆---

Third, I would put together an energetic hunting party and employ forced movement from the beginning to the end of the hunt. Fourth, I would hunt all season if possible, not relying strictly on the rut. Fifth, as a result of considerable practice on moving targets, I would be ready, willing and able to make a killing shot on a running trophy buck if I had to. And finally, I would heed reports of possible sightings of giant bucks and, if I could validate such a sighting, I try hard to hunt there because record-breaking bucks are rare in the extreme even in the very best country.

Of course, no matter how well conceived such a strategy might be, it almost certainly is destined to failure when a world record is the target because of extraordinary long odds. But even if I came up empty, I don't know that we should call it failure. You see, for those who pursue trophy bucks for the right reasons, the attraction lies at least as much in the journey as in the destination. We can't all shoot world-record whitetails, but we all can enjoy satisfaction from the sunrises we witness, the wildlife we watch and the campfires we share. And when we look back over a lifetime of deer hunting one day, we just might find that those memories are our greatest trophies anyway.